The Political Economy
of North American Indians

The Political Economy
of North American Indians

Edited by
John H. Moore

University of Oklahoma Press : Norman and London

This book is published with the generous assistance of the Wallace C. Thompson Endowment Fund, University of Oklahoma Foundation.

Library of Congress Cataloging-in-Publication Data

Moore, John H.
    Political economy of North American Indians/ John H. Moore.
    ISBN 978-0-8061-5352-0 (paper)
        p. cm.
    1. Indians of North America—Great Plains—Economic conditions.
    2. Indians of North America—Great Plains—Politics and government.
    3. Indians of North America—Great Plains—History. 4. Economic anthropology—Great Plains. 5. Subsistence economy—Great Plains.
    6. Great Plains—Economic conditions. I. Title.
    E78.G73M66   1993   92-50719
    330.978'008997—dc20   CIP

*This book is
respectfully dedicated
to my friend and colleague
Valery Tishkov*

Contents

Figures

Tables

Preface

This volume began as a correspondence between me and Valery Tishkov, then the Deputy Director of the Institute of Ethnography in Moscow in 1986. Seeking to apply a political economic approach to the study of North American Indians, we discovered that our networks of like-minded colleagues were largely complementary, his in Canada and mine in the United States. With the quadrennial international meetings approaching, we organized a session on "Political Economy of the American Indians" for the 1988 Zagreb, Yugoslavia, meetings of the 12th International Congress of Anthropological and Ethnological Sciences.

The participants who gathered at our session could never have anticipated the momentous events which have transpired so quickly since 1988. Although we heard the usual complaints from our Soviet friends about shortages and standing in line, we did not suspect that these failures in the Soviet economy would soon cause a total restructuring of the Soviet Union. Also, as we visited the beautiful lakes of the Plitvice area, who could predict that Croatia would soon become the scene of a bloody civil war?

The scholarly papers included here are largely the ones delivered at the meetings, with some papers added and others deleted for various reasons. Originally the coeditor of this volume, Valery Tishkov had to withdraw his participation under pressure to write for Russian readers a new, post–Cold War appreciation of modern American culture. In view of the importance of his project, I have gladly agreed to be sole editor.

—JOHN H. MOORE

The Political Economy
of North American Indians

CHAPTER 1

Political Economy in Anthropology

John H. Moore

A recurring myth of capitalist democracy is that "politics" and "economics" are two different concepts which should be kept separate both in theory and in practice. Consequently, in our universities academic disciplines are presently organized with different departments for economics and political science, and most scholarly journals feel obliged to state in their names which they are—journals of economics or of politics. Even in ordinary discourse the English language nowadays requires that we consider *economics* to be exclusively concerned with "the production, distribution, and consumption of commodities," while the domain of *politics* is restricted to "political government" (Morris 1982). But it was not always so, and a little etymology of the relevant words should tell us why.

Among classic Greek and Latin philosophers, especially Aristotle, and among scholars who rediscovered the classics in feudal times, the word "economics" was only intended to describe the functioning of a household, not a nation-state. The Greek roots of *oikonomia* are *oikos*, "house," and *nomos*, "managing," and the Latin *oeconomia* is derived from *oikonomia* (*Oxford English Dictionary* 1989, 5:58–60). Only with the writing of *Leviathan* in 1651 did the word

3

come to have a broader scope, when Thomas Hobbes entitled a section of that work, "For speciall Administration, as for Oeconomy" (Hobbes 1960 [1651]:156-57).

By contrast, the scope and meaning of "politics" has changed little since the writing of Aristotle's *Politics* in the fourth century B.C. (Aristotle 1981). Ultimately the word is derived from *polis*, or "city-state," to *polites*, "citizen," to *politikos* (Latin *politicus*), "having to do with the state or its citizens." The English version of the word first appears in the sixteenth century, with the additional French meaning of "polite" or "appropriate" (*Oxford English Dictionary* 1989 12:32–34). With the development of "political science," a phrase apparently invented in the eighteenth century by David Hume, politics has been defined among scholars as "the use of power" (Hume 1875 [1748], 2:135; Ball, Farr, and Hanson 1989).

The juxtaposition of "political" with "economy" is a result of the invention of capitalism in the seventeenth and eighteenth centuries. In that period the feudal states jousted with capitalist enclaves and made alliances with them for dominance over European politics. The mercantilist scholars, as the first ideologues of capitalism, began to discuss such matters as manufacturing, trade, and profit under the rubric of "economy," and they considered government as part of the economy, functioning as "the good father of the family, to provide everything necessary for supplying the wants of the society and its members." James Steuart developed the analogy to Aristotle's family household by stating, "What oeconomy is in a family, political oeconomy is in a state" (Steuart 1767, 1:2).

As the science of political economy developed in the eighteenth and nineteenth centuries, it had at least two definitive characteristics. First of all, the scope of inquiry was unprecedented. Political economists considered as single projects such momentous events as the colonization of India, the rise of the textile industry, and the status of Egypt in the world economy. The actors of history were also of unprecedented stature, for it was countries—nation-states—which were seen as taking discrete roles in the world drama. Nowadays we are accustomed to hear news commentators discuss what "Iraq" or "Israel" really want in the Middle East, as if these nation-states were in every way comparable to persons, having motivations, histories, memories, and conspiratorial designs. But this kind of discourse is a product of the grand perspective developed by political economists in the eighteenth century.

The science of political economy can also be defined by its methods. Fundamentally, political economy assumes that if the internal economy of a nation is analyzed and if the political and economic relations among nation-states are clearly understood, then scholarly problems of lesser scope will quickly resolve themselves. For example, if one wants to understand the history of British seafaring, then look first at the distribution of resources and population among European nation-states. And if one wants to understand the American Civil War, then first understand the world market in cotton. Or, to pick a recent example from an anthropologist, to understand the development of Caribbean society and politics, first understand the manufacture and sale of sugar (Mintz 1985).

As political economy developed in the eighteenth century, one particular scholar caused a bifurcation of efforts which still persists. Although Adam Smith explained history in the same manner as his predecessors, he disagreed with the moral thrust of Steuart. In *The Wealth of Nations* Smith proceeded in an orthodox fashion in showing how nations behaved holistically, mobilizing their internal economies and competing with other nations for world trade. But Smith disagreed about whether the state *ought* to have the role of *paterfamilias*, as defined by Steuart and other mercantilists. For those scholars the phrase "political economy" implied not only the international role of the nation-state, but also the welfare aspect of emerging capitalist democracies, or in a broad sense, the "socialist" aspect. In those days, of course, the term socialist was used in its broader sense of "bureaucratic" or "organized," not in the sense of a competitive kind of society antagonistic to capitalism.

Smith's more strident ideology of capitalism, however, argued that state socialism was unnecessary and that the laws of economics were of themselves sufficient to ensure general well-being. He argued that government and bureaucracy were actually harmful to production and to competition. Discussing the difficulties of accumulating capital in England, Smith complained about the expenses of the state structure: "The sovereign, for example, with all the officers both of justice and war who serve under him, the whole army and navy, are unproductive labourers. They are the servants of the public, and are maintained by a part of the annual produce of the industry of other people" (Smith 1979 [1776]:430).

After Smith, then, there was an increasing interest in matters of marketing and a concomitant disinterest in the moral and governmental aspects of political economy. By 1836 Nassau Senior felt obliged to explain:

We believe that by confining our own and the reader's attention to the Nature, Production, and Distribution of Wealth, we shall produce a more clear, and complete, and instructive work than if we allowed ourselves to wander into the more interesting and more important, but far less definite, fields by which the comparatively narrow path of Political Economy is surrounded. The questions, To what extent and under what circumstances the possession of Wealth is, in the whole, beneficial or injurious to its possessor . . . ? What distribution of Wealth is most desirable in each different state of society? and What are the means by which any given Country can facilitate such a distribution?—all these are questions of great interest and difficulty, but no more form part of the Science of Political Economy . . . than Navigation forms part of the Science of Astronomy. (Senior 1836:2)

Although he recited a charter for redefining the discipline, Senior nonetheless preserved the term "political economy" in his own work, and several decades passed before William Jevons explicitly argued for "dropping the troublesome double-worded name of our science," and several more decades passed before the first academic units were dubbed departments of "economics" (Clark 1991:32–93).

While the Smithians were abandoning the original broad

charter implied by the phrase "political economy," other scholars wanted to salvage the term and transform it into a rallying point for various kinds of progressive political agendas. These critics, from liberal to radical, were opposed to untrammelled capitalism and wanted the state to continue to interfere with Smith's "laws" of economics, but for the benefit of the poor and working classes rather than for the capitalists or the big landowners. They were especially interested in one topic specifically downplayed by the classical political economists—the manner in which wealth was distributed among the various social classes. In England these progressive forces included the Ricardian socialists, the Utilitarians, the Fabian Socialists, and ultimately, the Marxists (Jay and Jay 1986).

Redefined in this period, political economy was both a set of scientific observations about politics, economy, and history, and a recommendation for government policy. That is, observations of the intimate relations between the state and the capitalist class were intended as an indictment of the social order, and the complement to these observations was the political praxis of such leaders as Jeremy Bentham and John Stuart Mill. Taking the same role as observer/activist was Karl Marx, who argued that the British state, like the other states of capitalist societies, was not the enemy of capitalist designs, as Adam Smith had complained, but was instead a crucially important tool for expanding and extending the power of capital. This explicit, scholarly idea, as a theory of imperialism, was carried further by Hobson and Lenin (Hobson 1938; Lenin 1960 [1917]). After Lenin, especially, the term "political economy" became suspect to the capitalist establishment, who considered it a code term for hostility to the social order. And it was assumed that anyone who even noted the existence of imperialism was not merely a scholarly observer or social critic, but quite possibly a communist.

The Marxists also added an analysis of social class to the tool kit of political economy. They tried to differentiate between political behavior which was a phenomenon of nationality or ethnicity, and behavior which was a result of class consciousness. Generally, they considered ethnic or racial consciousness to be reactionary in nature, and they argued that class consciousness was pan-national and should be encouraged among the working class.

For anthropologists especially, differentiating between class and ethnic behavior has sometimes been difficult to achieve, as the reader will see in this volume. For example, are American Indians best considered as independent tribal nations politically engaged with the forces of capitalist democracy, or are they merely farflung and culturally exotic members of the capitalist proletariat? In this volume, the reader will find arguments for both positions.

Toward the beginning of the twentieth century, then, "political economy" as a scholarly enterprise became identified with critical theory, and more and more it operated outside the mainstream of orthodox scholarship as practiced in the universities of Britain and North America. Within the mainstream of the university, there developed versions of political science and of economics that were more useful to the dominant capitalist establishment. A great part of political science became devoted to the question of how elections are won or lost—determining which sectors of the electorate were likely to vote for which of the proferred candidates, and why. An integral part of this enterprise, as an exercise in public relations or outright propaganda, was the denial that sullied "economic" interests should have any effect on the outcome of elections. Ideally, the electorate should vote for "the best man" on the basis of his personal characteristics, not on the basis of his ability to mobilize campaign contributions from wealthy contributors. The assertion by political economists that wealthy contributors have undue influence over elected officials still constitutes the greatest barrier between the ideology of capitalist democracy and the perspective of political economy. As ideology, capitalist democracy argues that the interests of all classes and sectors are equally represented in government—the "pluralist" position. Political economy assumes that there is a dominant or "ruling" class whose interests are represented in government policy in a manner all out of proportion to their total numbers, a manner which reflects their control over money and the economy.

Another aspect of political science which became important, especially after the beginning of the Cold War, was the analysis of international politics. This period saw a proliferation of nonprofit "think tanks" on international affairs, supported by donations from capitalist institutions, which supplemented the work of political scientists in academic departments. The faculty and graduates of these departments and think tanks became prominent social scientists, parading through the White House and other government agencies in various important roles (Critchlow and Hawley 1988). Many such scholars were employed by the State Department, the Department of Defense and other government agencies.

Equally useful to capitalist democracy was the kind of economics which developed after political economy had been "discredited" in the establishment. Relieved of any responsibility for explaining political processes, economics in the early twentieth century engaged in the wholehearted search for Adam Smith's economic laws, as an aid to marketing, neglecting other aspects of culture and society which Smith, Ricardo, and Marx had found equally interesting. Only after Keynes did the search for economic laws comprise any concern for the role of government in controlling banking or stimulating the economy by its own spending (Staniland 1985; Bose 1975; Sawyer 1989).

For radical scholars calling themselves political economists, being thrown out of the academy was both a curse and a blessing. It was a curse because they were denied a large audience for their views and were denied the opportunity to debate directly against those with contrary views. But it was a blessing because, like the economists and like the political scientists who remained in the academy, they could go freely in a different direction. As political economy evolved outside the academy, it developed a new vocabulary, and publishing outlets were found where books and articles could be presented without much fear of censorship (Burkitt 1984; Sherman 1987).

We should note here that during the twentieth century, some political economists of liberal persuasion, such as Schumpeter and Polanyi, remained within British and North American universities, while the more radical scholars, especially Marxists, had to find employment elsewhere (Polanyi 1968; Schumpeter 1954). This, of course, changed during the university upheavals of the 1960s, when politicized graduate students in economics, like graduate students elsewhere, began earning doctoral degrees without sacrificing their progressive political principles (Attewell 1984:7–39). There seemed to be many more such students in economics than in other social sciences, both because the discipline itself was large and because the kinds of questions posed there seemed to encourage the approach of political economy. Radical political economists began to populate economics departments significantly in the 1970s and, by weight of numbers, began to exert a noticeable influence on their discipline. They organized themselves in 1968 as the Union for Radical Political Economics, currently with about five thousand members, and the important journal *Review of Radical Political Economics* was founded in 1969. In other disciplines, radical political economists have not been so numerous or so well organized, but the "respectability" gained by those in economics has tended to carry over into other social science disciplines. In fact, the perspective of political economy seems still to be gaining in popularity among academics. There is now even a journal of the *History of Political Economy*.

As anthropology developed during the twentieth century, it revealed only pale reflections of the debates raging about political economy in other disciplines, for various reasons. In the first place, field ethnographers ordinarily had no difficulty with the proposition, controversial in other disciplines, that politics and economics were essentially the same thing, for they witnessed undifferentiated political/economic behavior every day in tribal societies. For social anthropologists, kinship became the nexus of analysis, from which all kinds of behavior could be observed—political, economic, or otherwise. The partition of economic behavior from other kinds of behavior only became an issue in the analysis of class societies, especially the "peasant" societies examined by George Dalton, Manning Nash, and others in the postwar period (Dalton 1967). Here the debate began concerning whether the liberal political economic theories of Schumpeter and Polanyi should be adapted for anthropology (the "substantivist school") or whether "economic anthropology" should be consistent with more orthodox theories currently popular in the discipline of economics, the "formalist" school. Soon the debate was compounded by the entry of several Marxist opinions, structuralist and otherwise (Scholte 1979; Gregory 1984).

More controversial in anthropology was the idea, promoted by the nineteenth century political economists, that there was a "world economy" affecting all societies everywhere, no matter how quaint or isolated they might seem to be. For different reasons, both the evolutionists and the functionalists liked to consider tribal societies to be distinct and self-contained. The evolutionists wanted societies to be discrete and independent so that they could be seriated into evolutionary schemes, without worrying about possible feedback from large, stratified nation-states into societies of more modest political scale. That is, the evolutionists wanted modern tribal societies to be at least analogous if not identical to prehistoric societies. For their part, while the structural functionalists had no objection to erasing the boundaries between economics and politics as they wrote ethnography, they were reluctant to consider the impact of colonialism and the world market on the societies they studied. Both "social" and "cultural" phenomena were seen to be theoretically unique and explicable only in terms of themselves. In this period, dominated by the ideas of Boas and Durkheim, it was apparently only the Marxist anthropologists who carried the banner of political economy and seemed to be willing to put local tribal societies within the context of the world order. The precocious and pioneering ethnography of this sort in North America was Eleanor Leacock's study of the Montagnais of Labrador. These issues continue to be discussed in the current debate over "primitive communism" (Lee 1990; Wilmsen 1989).

The original debate on the Montagnais was between Leacock and Frank Speck, who had alleged, among other things, that "the whole territory claimed by each tribe was subdivided into tracts owned from time immemorial by the same families and handed down from generation to generation in the male line." From her own fieldwork and ethnohistorical research, however, Leacock was able to show that the modern system was a product of the international fur trade, and that the transition from a preexisting communal system to a system of private ownership was still going on. Within ethnology, these two features of political economy emphasized by Leacock became the hallmarks of this approach. First, ethnographic researchers tried to show how a tribal economy fitted into the larger picture of world economy. Second, researchers emphasized the diachronic or dynamic qualities of the system. It was emphasized that each institution of a society, such as the private ownership of a trap line, was impermanent and invented for particular historical reasons. That is, institutions had a life history—they were born, they survived for a while within a set of interclass and international relationships, and then they inevitably became obsolete.

Studies such as Leacock's, however, were rare in anthropology before the 1970s, when a new generation of politically conscious anthropologists rediscovered the broader and less structured nineteenth century definition of political economy. Eschewing any necessary connection to Marxism, they began to use a redefined "political economy" to study everything under the sun. A survey of my own university library shows over two hundred recent titles embodying the term "political economy," many written by anthropologists, and ranging from orthodox Marxist to post-processual, from studies of "world thought" to analyses of airport statuary. Prominent among them are works written in the "world systems" idiom of Immanual Wallerstein, who began a school of thought by describing approximately the same imperialist events as Lenin, but using his own politically sanitized idiom instead of a Marxist vocabulary (Wallerstein 1974).

The forerunners of this trend in anthropology were those who contributed to the volume *The Political Economy of Development* (Uphoff 1972), which considered a variety of cultural topics. But the first full-blown anthropological commitment to the newly redefined phrase "political economy" appears in the volume *New Directions in Political Economy: An Approach from Anthropology*, published in 1979 from a 1974 session at the Mexico City meetings of the American Anthropological Association (Leons and Rothstein 1979). The organizers of the session, who became the volume's editors, took the broadest possible approach, including the whole political spectrum of authors, and the topical range was just as varied. The editors essentially presented a charter for exploring any topic under the rubric of "political economy," sometimes leaving the reader wondering what the enterprise had to do with political economy as defined by Steuart or Adam Smith or Marx.

In the last decade, we must note, both the phrase and the perspective have developed unevenly in the various subdisciplines and special fields of anthropology, often with unexpected results. While it might have been predicted that archeologists and economic anthropologists would be attracted to this perspective, simply from the quantitative and concrete nature of the data, it seems less predictable that this approach would soon dominate medical anthropology or become important for the study of games and sport (Roseberry 1988; Spriggs 1984; Patterson 1986; Singer 1989; Klein 1989). Why has this perspective become so recently popular? Let me suggest a few salient features other than the characteristics which endeared it to the mercantilists and the Marxists.

Insofar as anthropology itself has been holistic in the last century, it has tended to welcome theoretical approaches which were likewise holistic. One attraction of political economy is that, like theories of "culture" and "society," it encourages the idea that all aspects of human thought and behavior are interrelated. The focus of attention for the scholar is a core of events which are both political and economic, as will be demonstrated by the contributions to this volume. But the analysis does not end there. Not only is the barrier between politics and economics broken down, but all such disciplinary separations are treated with scepticism, criticized explicitly, or ignored.

Rather than beginning with restrictive definitions about what are to be the topical limits of scholarly concern, political economy maintains the freedom to explore. For example, the reader will see in this volume Tom Biolsi's exploration of the relationship between flag-raising and the size of the family farm. In the same spirit, but two hundred years earlier, Adam Smith was interested in the relationships between personal conceit and lotteries, and Marx and Engels wanted to know about the relationships among romantic love, sexual reproduction, and unemployment (Smith 1979 [1776]:210; Marx 1906 [1867]:629–33; Engels 1942 [1884]:68–74). I would suggest that, after a generation of considering such confining topics as "amoral familism in the Mediterranean" or "Arctic hysterias", the breadth of scope and the topical freedom provided by political economy seem quite refreshing to the present generation of anthropologists and other social scientists. Consequently, many scholars are addressing old topics with a new enthusiasm. In the future, one might envision such studies as "amoral familism and the decline of tourism in Sardinia," or "Arctic hysteria and the rise of snowmobile culture." Where does this present volume belong in the range of interdisciplinary scholarly freedoms encouraged by a political-economic perspective? And what scholarly themes will be represented here?

Although the contributors to this volume have unanimously cut across the customary boundaries of academic disciplines in maintaining an approach of "political economy," they have done so in different directions. In breadth, the papers range from highly specific and ethnographic to very abstract and philosophical. What they all share is an orientation toward a core of economic and political events which they consider to be focal and causal. That is, they share the opinion that most social and cultural events, most of the time, find their roots and explanations in matters of production, trade, and consequent political conflict. The contributions also illustrate another traditional idea of political economy, that government mostly represents the interests of various sectors of the dominant capitalist class—financial, agricultural, manufacturing, and trading. The papers by Littlefield, Frideres, and Castile especially embody this idea.

Another implicit, shared idea among these contributors—and it is a very profound notion—is that Native American history is best understood not as a *cultural* conflict between Indians and European invaders, but as an *economic* conflict between precapitalist or communal modes of production and capitalist modes. That is, the important fact about the invasion of North America is not so much that the invaders were European foreigners, but that they were *capitalist* foreigners. It was the capitalist mode of production which determined the form of the conflict, not religion, culture, or ethnicity. At the risk of stretching the point, let me suggest that if North America had been invaded by Chinese capitalists or African capitalists, the results would have been much the same.

Last, it must be added that, for the authors contained herein, the perspective of political economy is necessarily a critical perspective. Having adopted a premise that it is changes in economic arrangements which cause history to happen, a scholar is necessarily drawn into conflict with those who believe that history is made by great men or by great ideas. And to present one's own perspective properly, it is necessary to criticize other scholars and other perspectives, as Leacock did with Speck, and as Cox does in this volume with Harold Innis. To generalize this last point, we must note that political economists usually operate under the academic ethic that conflict is good, actually promoting education, rather than confounding it.

As editor I might have arranged these papers in many different ways, for example by historical period or geographical area. However, I have chosen to arrange them in a manner which would be enlightening to readers who open this book without knowing much about political economy. To ease such readers into a new perspective, I have begun with the least complicated pieces before offering some more challenging, even profound issues. The first article, a colorful and dramatic one, is Tom Biolsi's explanation of why the Lakotas, who have every reason to be militantly resentful of the United States of America, nonetheless raise the American flag at their major ceremonies. This puzzle finds its explanation in matters of political economy.

The next article, also elegant and straightforward, is Alice Littlefield's interpretation of Indian education as implementing the desires of an American ruling class which has changed, in the last hundred years, in its composition and ambitions. She explains changes in curriculum, school locations, and instructional style by reference to a changing United States economy. Here again, the unintelligible becomes intelligible, showing the explanatory power of the political economic perspective.

Presumably convinced of the value of our perspective, the reader is then led to an article which is easy to comprehend intellectually, but emotionally hard to believe. Greg Campbell argues that the death and disease that were typical of early reservations in the United States were not self-happening events, were not caused by the cultural dissonance of the Indians, but were the result of a cold and calculated disregard on the part of the United States government, which could find no good use for Indians in American society and decided to let them die. The moral questions raised by Campbell might be couched as follows: Clearly, if someone consciously causes the death of another person, that is murder. But what if someone indirectly causes another person to die? Or, if one comes upon a person who is dying, and refuses to help, is that murder? More to the point, if one neglects thousands of Indian people who are dying, is that genocide? Seeing the facts gathered carefully by Campbell, one must ask these disturbing questions.

In the next article, Bruce Cox presents an explicit critique of an important premise of conventional Native American history, that the "laws of supply and demand" (a product of post-Smithian "economics") adequately describe the development of the fur trade. Arguing logically and theoretically, referring to the most relevant data, he shows that they do not and that the proper explanation is to be found in the actual *interactions* between European and Indians, not merely in the stated motives of the Europeans, as reported by their historians.

Patricia Albers has also written a critical paper, but hers is longer and more ambitious. She attempts nothing less than a new synthesis for understanding all of Plains Indian history in the ethnohistorical and early historical periods. To accomplish this, she criticizes particular theories of reciprocity which have been used to explain the economic and political behavior of Plains Indians. Finding these inadequate, she substitutes a tightly reasoned but elaborate model which calls attention to geographical conditions, distribution of resources, and the consequently different economic commitments of Plains Indian societies. By this model a host of fragmented observations and theories are modified and fall into place, and this article will no doubt be pivotal for the interpretation of Plains societies and their histories for the next several decades.

Alan Klein helped inspire Albers' new synthesis, as she notes, and in his own contribution he provides an example, constrained in time and place, of the issues which he and other contributors think are important in North American Indian history. Within the context of "the trading post" he asks first why it existed at all; and since it did exist, he questions its effect on the "bourgeois" agents of capitalism, on the Indians,

and on the proletarian elements who developed around the
post. Concerned about the interactions between class and
ethnicity, he provides some surprising answers.

James Frideres's article provides an overview of the Canadian government's attitudes and policies toward Indians,
emphasizing recent events. In the classic manner of political
economy, he shows that the government and important sectors of the capitalist class have been in close lockstep devising
official policy. He points out the discrepency between the
"official line" and what was actually happening on the reserves. In the role of "applied anthropologist," he recom-
mends sensible and scientifically based programs of development for reserve areas.

Within the framework sketched by Frideres, Max Hedley in
the next article takes a longitudinal, ethnographic approach to
a specific Canadian Reserve, Walpole Island. In a brilliant analysis he shows the interplay among economic, political, familial, and ideological phenomena, and shows how the events of
political economy took the lead in determining cultural
change. He describes Walpole history not as structured and
inevitable, but as a series of dilemmas which were exacerbated, resolved, and then exacerbated again in a dialectical
manner.

The next two papers, by Sandra Faiman-Silva and me, are
largely ethnographic, like Hedley's paper. Taking a traditional
holistic approach, Faiman-Silva uncovers the interrelation-
ships among the supposedly distinct realms of employment,
land tenure, taxes, and social welfare in the Choctaw area of
southeastern Oklahoma. Here the Weyerhaeuser Company
enjoys hegemony in all areas and uses its power to maximize
profits. In my own contribution, also taken from Oklahoma, I
show the ingenuity of Indian people in creating a means of
survival for themselves within a chaotic and insecure economic situation where apparently few people in the dominant
society care whether they survive. Since the institutions of the
dominant society are not structured for their needs, Indian
people have devised their own strategy for survival, creating

networks for sharing the means of subsistence within a colorful, ritualized system of pow-wows and giveaways.

   With this much background in political economy, I feel the
reader is ready for the challenging and provocative article by
George Castile, which ends the anthology. Castile has been
notable in his career for getting to the fundamental issues of
history and ethnology and describing them in a lucid and lively
manner. Adopting a widely comparative framework, he argues
here, in contrast to other contributors, that North American
Indian policy has little to do with incorporating Indians into an
economic system, but is better understood as a public relations gambit by the federal government. By showcasing Indian
policies the government seeks to convince all the citizens of its
fundamental good will toward minorities and of its commitment to democratic principles. Castile is unconvinced.

   In sum, this anthology is intended to exhibit the methods of
political economy by reference to the study of historical interactions between Native Americans and European invaders.
The methodology illustrated here is deep and dynamic,
emphasizing contradiction and change rather than structure
and function. The tradition is critical, showing a skepticism
toward the public pronouncements of government and industry and toward the social theories, often complimentary to the
dominant society, created by mainstream academics. Peda-
gogically, this book of essays is based on the idea that dis-
agreement is good, that everyone's intellectual convictions are
worth challenging, and that all readers will benefit from reading about these debates, even if some readers cannot agree
with some of the various themes and premises.

CHAPTER 2

The Political Economy of Lakota Consciousness

Thomas Biolsi

One of the most common manifestations of Lakota tradition on contemporary South Dakota reservations is the *wacipi*[1] (dance) or pow-wow. Wacipis are celebrations involving secular singing and dancing, dinners, and rituals such as namings and giveaways. They take the form both of small community gatherings and large extravaganzas with visitors from distant places. During the summer in Lakota country there is a nearby wacipi almost every weekend.

Wacipis are traditional in the sense that they are derived from the ritual of a nineteenth-century sodality, the *omaha* society. By the early twentieth century the ritual had become secularized, and anyone was allowed to participate (Powers 1990; Wissler 1912:48–52). What was to become the wacipi, however, was from the beginning an arena of struggle between Bureau of Indian Affairs (BIA) surveillance and indigenous resistance. By the 1890s the omaha dance had become one of the manifestations of Lakota tradition that the BIA was intent on eradicating. Administrators believed that the omaha should not be banned outright as the sun dance had been. Its most objectionable features, after all, were not barbaric self-torture but disruption of Indian "industry" (farming on individual allotments) and celebration of the old ways. It should therefore be limited and regulated, and as the old people died off, it would gradually disappear. BIA police prevented young people or returned students from participating in the omaha, and the number of dances and dance halls were limited so that dancing would not interfere with industrial pursuits (National Archives, RG 75, Rosebud Agency, n.d.; Prucha 1984, 2:800–805; National Archives, RG 75, Superintendent, 1914, 1916). BIA surveillance of omaha dancing did not disappear until Commissioner John Collier issued an administrative order banning BIA interference in Native American religion and culture in 1934 (U.S. Dept. of Interior, BIA, 1934).

Given this history of colonial surveillance, it should not be surprising that the contemporary wacipi is not an unselfconscious expression of Lakota tradition. The wacipi has a "nativistic" or "reaffirmative" (Spindler and Spindler 1972:510) character in that leaders and participants self-consciously valorize the Indian way *(lakol wicoȟan)* not only as traditional but also as opposed to the *wasicun* (white man) way. The wacipi does not involve what Pierre Bourdieu (1977) calls "doxic"—tacit, unreflexive, automatic—tradition, but rather highly reflexive *traditionalism*, a traditionalism which gets much of its meaning from its symbolic opposition to assimilation among Lakota people. Like the sun dance (Medicine 1981), the wacipi constitutes a stand against assimilation for Lakota traditionalists.

It is therefore not a little interesting that Lakota people precede their wacipis with honoring the American flag. Veterans raise the flag, and as the participants stand the singers perform the Lakota flag song:

t'nkasilayapi tawapaha kin oihankeśni he najin kte lo.
Iyoȟlate kin oyate kin cana wicicaǧin kta ca lecamon welo.

The flag of the United States [literally, the grandfather's—the president's—flag] will stand forever. Beneath it the people will live on. That is why I do this [honor the flag] (adapted from Powers 1990:79).

Anthropologists, exposed as they are to the diverse local manifestations of a truly global system (capitalism), are familiar with many such apparently incongruous cultural juxtapositions (see, for example, Comaroff and Comaroff 1987). Such juxtapositions are often said to be the defining feature of social life in late capitalism, a feature which is celebrated but not understood by postmodernism (Jameson 1984). But the flag raising at the Lakota wacipi—at their most important secular celebration of Lakota tradition and resistance to assimilation—is particularly perplexing because Lakota people have such exceptionally good reasons, both historic and contemporary, to question United States commitment to their persistence as a people and to oppose the effects upon them of incorporation into the nation-state.

One dramatic cause for question is the memory of the 1890 Wounded Knee massacre. To remind the reader of the terror of that incident in which as many as three hundred Lakota people were killed by the United States Army, consider this description by an attorney for the Lakota:

It has been difficult for [the Lakota] . . . to appreciate the beauties of a civilization which can shoot down men, women, and children fleeing for their very lives, unarmed and unresisting. It is a little difficult for the [Lakota] to agree with the conclusions of the Government and the Army that the shooting by the Army was in self defense, when the bodies of women and children were found three to four miles away from the spot where the shooting began and who apparently were shot in the back while trying to flee still further. (Case n.d.)

White South Dakotans think of the Wounded Knee massacre as "history" in the popular sense of random past events about which little can be done, which have very little to do with the present and which are really best forgotten as we get on with the present. For Lakota people, however, Wounded Knee is living, unconcluded history. In 1990 the Lakota people marked the one hundredth anniversary of the massacre, and the Wounded Knee Survivors Association insists upon a formal apology from the United States government as well as compensation for the descendants of the victims, actions Congress is not presently prepared to take.

If the Lakota social memory of the brutal violence of the Wounded Knee massacre and the failure of the government to make amends for it is not enough, there is the Black Hills matter. The Black Hills were taken from the Lakota in violation of treaty provisions in 1877. As the United States Supreme Court noted, "a more ripe and rank case of dishonorable dealing will never, in all probability, be found in our history." Although the Indian Claims Commission and the Supreme Court have awarded the Great Sioux Nation a monetary settlement, it has not been accepted; many Lakota people continue to feel profoundly wronged by the United States over the Black Hills. The Black Hills Steering Committee is seeking return of federal lands in the Black Hills via legislative action, but this, too, Congress is reluctant to do at present.

And then there is the poverty—and the substance dependencies, family dysfunction, crime, violence, and other forms of misery associated with poverty—which continues to be visited upon the Lakota people. Shannon County, on Pine Ridge Reservation, and Todd County, on Rosebud Reservation, had respectively the first- and second-lowest per capita personal incomes for all counties in South Dakota in 1984 (U.S. Dept. of Commerce 1988:464). These two counties also had the first- and eighteenth-lowest per capita personal incomes for all counties in the United States in the same year (U.S. Dept. of Commerce 1988:xxvi). At this writing, the unemployment rates for Pine Ridge and Rosebud reservations have been realistically estimated at between 80 and 90 percent. In 1984 the infant mortality rate in Todd County on Rosebud Reservation was 42.9 per 1,000 live births, four times the rate for the state, and the fifth highest rate for all counties in the United States (U.S. Dept. of Commerce 1988:xxiv). Lakota people, if they had any doubts, could see the direct connections between reservation poverty and the United States government as the

Fig. 2.1. Lakota area of South Dakota and Nebraska in the vicinity of Rosebud Indian Reservation.

federal budget cuts of the 1980s trickled down to the reservations in the forms of lost jobs and reduced services—human misery.

In short, the Lakota people would appear to have little reason—by their own or any other reasonable person's accounting—to honor the flag, whether the flag represents the government or the nation. Yet they continue to raise the flag above their wacipis and other public events, even sacred ones such as the sun dance, and to proclaim ceremoniously their faith that "the people will live on" under the watchful eye of their "grandfather" in Washington.

How can we interpret this political consciousness? Any person who takes Marx's analysis of oppression seriously might be inclined to consign Lakota consciousness to Gramscian "hegemony" (Gramsci 1971:12) in which the oppressed internalize the cultural categories of the oppressors, or to the (mis)-understandings of "prepolitical" people who have not yet developed a modern political consciousness (Hobsbawm 1959:2), or to some other notion of "false consciousness." Indeed, any thinking person—aware or unaware of the ideas of Marx—would be forced to wonder about Lakota consciousness regarding the flag, the government, and their place in the nation.

The "false consciousness" hypothesis, however, would lead us in the wrong direction in understanding Lakota political consciousness. The raising of the American flag at the wacipi is not about internalizing the cultural categories of the oppressors. There are good theoretical reasons to doubt that the oppressed ever cooperate so simply in their own oppression (see, for example, Berreman 1988; Comaroff and Comaroff 1991:chapter 1; Scott 1985; Williams 1977). Honoring the American flag at the wacipi entails an indigenous subtext about *treaty rights*. Respect for the flag is connected to a legal, political, and moral claim Lakota people make to a special status in the United States, a status that many Lakota people conceptualize as based on treaties. This claim is ultimately a form of resistance to assimilation in particular and to capitalism in general because it allows the Lakota to withstand the forces of the agricultural economy which would otherwise depopulate the reservations and largely eradicate Lakota communities and the native culture and language they support.

In order to understand the significance of the special status the Lakota claim, it is necessary to examine the political economy of the reservations in the context of agriculture in the American West. Since the end of World War I agriculture in the West has been characterized by clear trends: increasing mechanization and increasing size of viable operations, and the concomitant decrease in the number of farms and in the demand for agricultural labor. These trends were originally initiated when falling agricultural prices after the World War I forced farmers and ranchers either to mechanize and produce more commodities on larger acreages or to leave agriculture altogether. Both paths were taken by different rural families. Those who left did so because they could not meet subsistence and production costs, could not make loan repayments, or could find more profitable sources for the investment of their cash and labor in enterprises other than agriculture. Those who stayed in agriculture bought and/or rented additional acreages, plowed profits into new technological inputs, and increased both productivity and absolute output. It had become necessary to expand productivity and output in this way in order to stay in business in the face of the cost-price squeeze—the increasing gap between the costs of commodities farm families had to buy (equipment, fertilizer, pesticides, fungicides, feed, clothing, etc.) and the market price they received for agricultural commodities.

Expanded productivity and output on the part of family farmers and ranchers to make ends meet only exacerbated the basic problem on the macrolevel, however, by flooding the market with increasingly larger yields of commodities for which there was increasingly insufficient demand, thus driving prices down still further. American agriculture was—and is—caught in a vicious cycle of overproduction in which the gap between supply and free market demand widens. Government agricultural programs have been able to ameliorate only partly the overproduction and cost-price squeeze problems (on the structural trend in western agriculture, see Fite 1981, 1989; Henderson and Krueger 1965; Malone and Etulain 1989: chapter 1).

These trends in agriculture are clearly visible in South Dakota. Figure 2.2 shows the increase in the size of the average farm in South Dakota from 464 acres in 1920 to 1,214 acres in 1987. The concomitant decrease in the number of farms in South Dakota from a peak of 83,303 in 1935 to 36,376 in 1987—a 43 percent reduction—is graphed in figure 2.3.

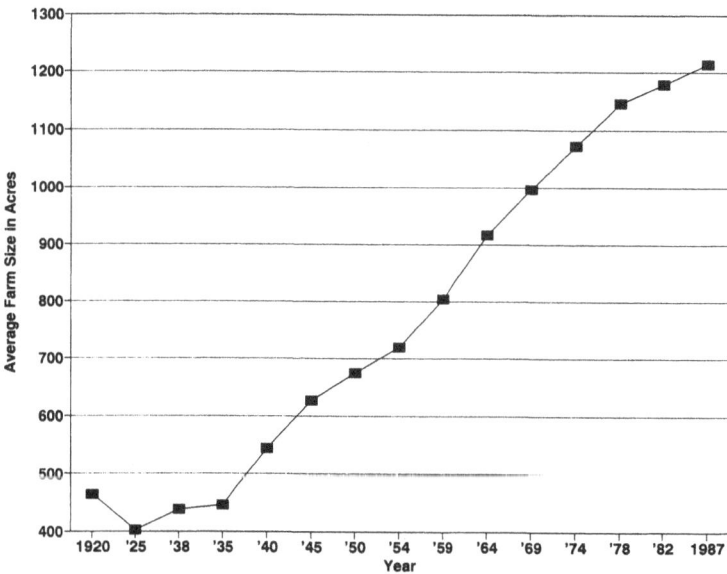

Fig. 2.2. Historical trend in the average size of South Dakota farms, 1920–87. (The data for figs. 2.2–2.7 are from U.S. Department of Commerce, *Census of Agriculture,* Geographic Area Series, various years [Washington, D.C.: Government Printing Office].)

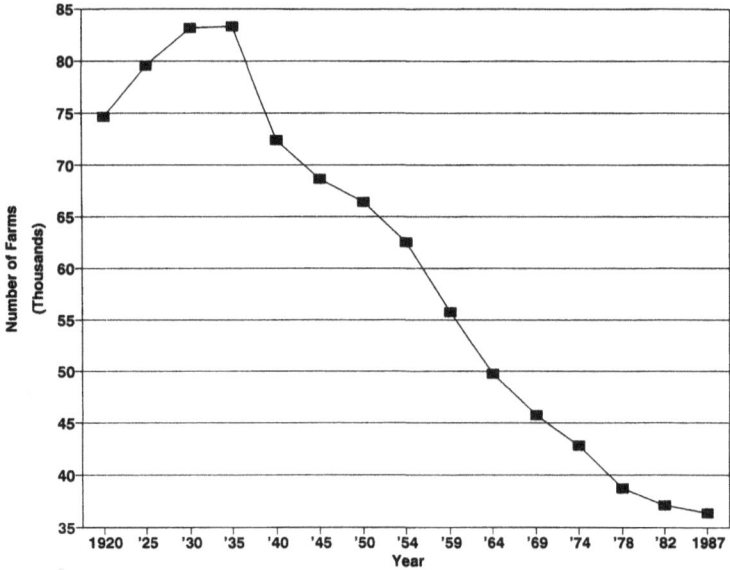

Fig. 2.3. Historical trend in the number of South Dakota farms, 1920–87.

Figure 2.4 graphs the increase in the size of the average farm in three counties chosen for analysis. Todd County, South Dakota, constitutes part of the Rosebud Reservation. Although non-Indians also live in Todd County, 77 percent of the population is Indian according to the 1980 census (Department of Commerce 1988:459). Neighboring Cherry County, Nebraska, and nearby Jones County, South Dakota, are nonreservation counties with the same general agricultural economy as Todd County—beef cattle ranching. It can be seen that both the reservation and the nonreservation counties show a clear increase in the size of the average farm. Figure 2.5 indicates that the reservation and nonreservation counties also manifest a general decrease in the number of farms.

These trends in the agricultural economy which have characterized both Indian reservations and off-reservation areas

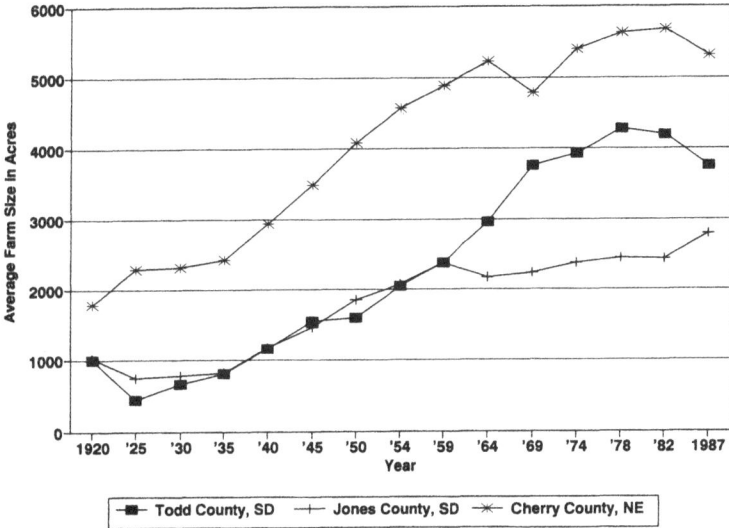

Fig. 2.4. Historical trend in the average size of farms in Todd and Jones counties, South Dakota, and Cherry County, Nebraska, 1920–87.

have a clear demographic implication: rural population loss. As can be seen from table 2.1, forty seven (71 percent) of South Dakota's counties lost population between 1960 and 1980. These are the rural counties dependent on agriculture and with no substantial metropolitan components or alternatives to agriculture for the generation of wealth. The population loss has resulted from farm consolidation, diminishing agricultural employment, and outmigration. In social terms, this means the demise of family farms and ranches and the transformation of farmers and ranchers into wage workers who leave the rural environment for work elsewhere. While this does not always involve the drama of a loan officer overseeing the auction of a tearful family's farm (it also involves grown children deciding not to remain on the farm or ranch), the effects on rural social life are extensive enough. As one drives across the countryside in South Dakota, one comes occasion-

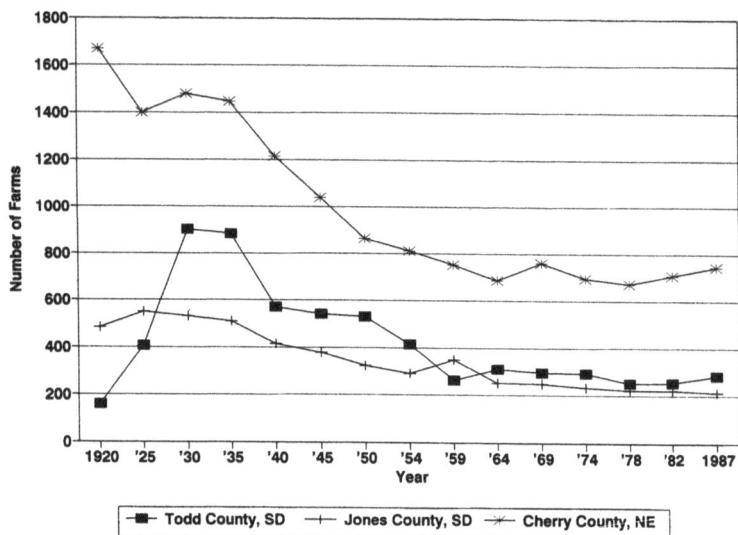

Fig. 2.5. Historical trend in the number of farms in Todd and Jones counties, South Dakota, and Cherry County, Nebraska, 1920–87.

ally upon abandoned railway lines, derelict grain elevators, empty churches, and even ghost towns—archaeological remains of a thriving family farm economy which once supported a much denser (non-Indian) population and rural community life. Of 377 rural South Dakota hamlets on the landscape in 1911, only 148 were still to be found in 1951 (Schell 1975:363).

Only 19 (29 percent) South Dakota counties gained population during the period 1960 to 1980 (the state as a whole saw a 2 percent increase from 680,514 to 690,768). These counties fall into one or more of four classes (exempting anomalous Jackson County, which gained population because of its consolidation with Washabaugh County): (1) counties with substantial metropolitan components and/or universities; (2) counties enjoying the development of the tourist industry in the Black Hills; (3) Meade County, where

Table 2.1 Population changes in South Dakota counties and Cherry County, Nebraska, 1960–1980

County	1960	1980	Loss (%)	Comments
Stanley	4,085	2,533	38	
Campbell	3,531	2,243	36	
Clark	7,134	4,894	31	
McPherson	5,821	4,027	31	
Miner	5,398	3,739	31	
Sanborn	4,641	3,213	31	
Jones	2,066	1,463	29	
Harding	2,371	1,700	28	
Jerauld	4,048	2,929	28	
Kingsbury	9,227	6,679	28	
Hand	6,712	4,948	26	
Hanson	4,584	3,415	25	
Potter	4,926	3,674	25	
Faulk	4,397	3,327	24	
Moody	8,810	6,692	24	
Sully	2,607	1,990	24	
Aurora	4,749	3,628	23	
Day	10,516	8,133	22	
Deuel	6,782	5,289	22	
McCook	8,268	6,444	22	
Fall River	10,688	8,439	21	
Perkins	5,977	4,700	21	
Spink	11,706	9,201	21	
Hyde	2,602	2,069	20	

Table 2.1 (Continued)

County	1960	1980	Loss (%)	Comments
Marshall	6,663	5,404	19	
Douglas	5,113	4,184	18	
Gregory	7,399	6,015	18	
Charles Mix	11,785	9,680	17	
Roberts	13,190	10,911	17	
Tripp	8,761	7,268	17	
Turner	11,159	9,255	17	
Brule	6,319	5,245	16	
Hamlin	6,303	5,261	16	
Mellette	2,664	2,249	16	
Edmunds	6,079	5,159	15	
Haakon	3,303	2,794	15	
Hutchinson	11,085	9,350	15	
Lyman	4,428	3,864	13	
Walworth	8,097	7,011	13	
Bon Homme	9,229	8,059	12	
Beadle	21,682	19,195	11	
Corson	5,798	5,196	10	
Grant	9,913	9,013	9	
Lake	11,764	10,724	9	
Ziebach	2,495	2,308	7	
Butte	8,592	8,372	2	
Bennett	3,053	3,044	<1	

Table 2.1 (Continued)

County	1960	1980	Gain (%)	Comments
Shannon	6,000	11,323	88	Includes part of Pine Ridge Reservation
Jackson	1,985	3,437	73	Gain accounted for by consolidation with former Washabaugh County
Meade	12,044	20,717	72	Includes city of Sturgis and Ellsworth Air Force Base; in Black Hills tourist district
Todd	4,661	7,328	57	Includes part of Rosebud Reservation
Clay	10,810	13,689	26	Includes University of South Dakota
Minnehaha	86,575	109,435	26	Includes city of Sioux Falls
Custer	4,906	6,000	22	In Black Hills tourist district
Brookings	20,046	24,332	21	Includes city of Brookings and South Dakota State University
Pennington	58,195	70,361	21	Includes city of Rapid City
Buffalo	1,447	1,795	16	Includes part of Crow Creek Indian Reservation
Lincoln	12,371	13,942	13	Includes outskirts of city of Sioux Falls
Hughes	12,725	14,220	11	Includes city of Pierre (the state capital)
Brown	34,106	36,962	8	Includes city of Aberdeen and Northern State University
Yankton	17,551	18,952	8	Includes city of Yankton
Lawrence	17,075	18,339	7	In Black Hills tourist district
Union	10,197	10,938	7	Includes outskirts of city of Sioux City, Iowa
Davison	16,681	17,820	6	Includes city of Mitchell
Codington	20,220	20,885	3	Includes city of Watertown
Dewey	5,257	5,366	2	Includes Cheyenne River Reservation

Sources: Department of Commerce, *Characteristics of the Population* (Washington: Government Printing Office, 1970, 1980).

Ellsworth Air Force Base is located; and (4) Indian reservations. The explanation for the population increases in the first
three classes is clear enough. Metropolitan areas, university
towns, and military and tourist districts generate more jobs,
have larger local government budgets, can provide more public sector services, and are able to support denser populations
than districts with only an agricultural base. But what about
Indian reservations? How are they able to support growing
populations?

Two Indian reservations, in fact, are right at the top of the list
of population growth. Shannon County, part of the Pine Ridge
Reservation, had the highest rate of population growth in the
state—a remarkable 88 percent. And Todd County, part of
Rosebud Reservation, had the third highest growth rate in the
state (exempting anomalous Jackson County), after Meade
County with Ellsworth Air Force Base. Figure 2.6 compares

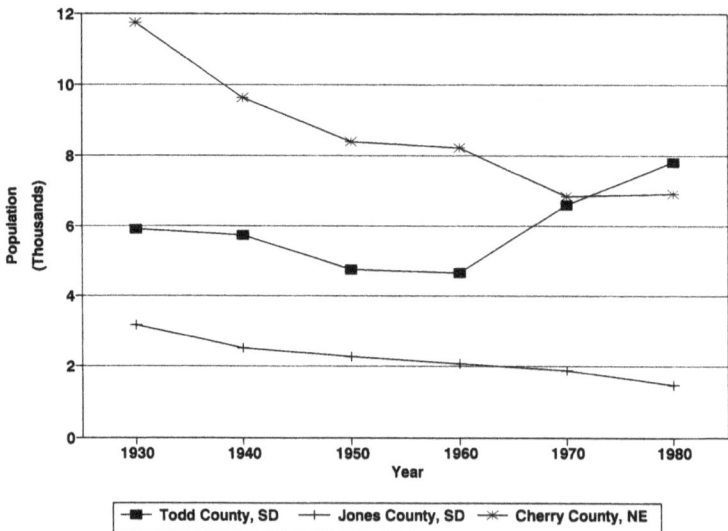

Fig. 2.6. Population changes in Todd and Jones counties, South Dakota,
and Cherry County, Nebraska, 1930–80.

the population curves of Todd County and neighboring Jones County and Cherry County. Figure 2.7 compares the population density curves for these three counties. The political-economic significance of rising population on an Indian reservation as compared to rural nonreservation counties is not the Indian birthrate (although the rate on some South Dakota reservations is about twice the rate for the state as a whole [Dept. of Commerce 1988]). The significance rather has to do with how a rural county such as Todd is able to support a rising population/density when the agricultural economy supports decreasing populations/densities in neighboring counties. The answer has to do with what the Lakota people call treaty rights.

Indian reservations, in comparison to non-Indian rural counties, receive higher inflows of federal funds. This is evident in table 2.2. Todd County, a reservation county, receives

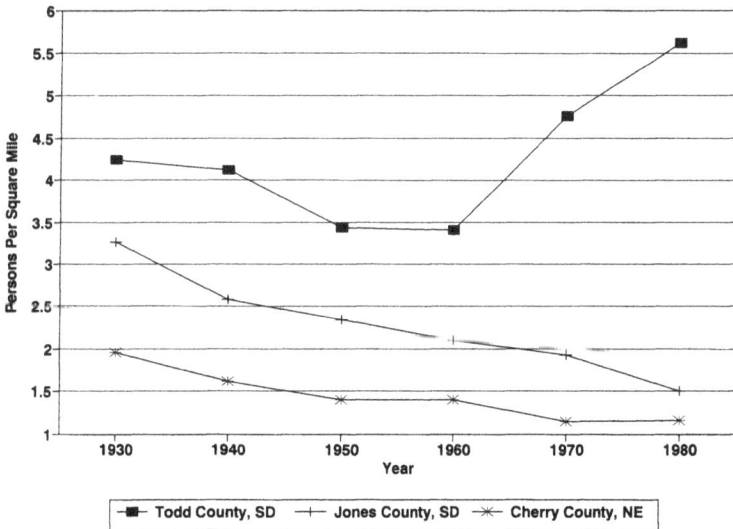

Fig. 2.7. Historical trend in population density in Todd and Jones counties, South Dakota, and Cherry County, Nebraska, 1930–80.

Table 2.2 Government and livelihood in three rural counties

	Per Capita Federal Funds and Grants 1986	Local Government Jobs 1982*	Federal Jobs 1984	Per Capita Property Tax 1981–82	Per Capita Money Income 1985	Total Federal Funds and Grants 1986 ($ million)	Total Agricultural Sales 1987 ($ million)
Todd County, S. Dak. (Rosebud Reservation)	8,359	418	263	57	4,250	56.8	21.976
Jones County, S. Dak.	5,197	50	19	741	6,689	7.8	17.764
Cherry County, Nebr.	1,922	342	67	602	4,931	13.1	87.194

*Includes county employees (predominantly in public schools) but not tribal government employees.

Sources: Department of Commerce, *County and City Data Book* (Washington: Government Printing Office, 1988); Department of Commerce, *Census of Agriculture,* 1987, Geographic Area Series (Washington: Government Printing Office, 1989).

significantly more federal funds and grants than do neighboring Jones and Cherry counties. This money includes the generic kinds of transfer payments such as social security (surplus commodities, food stamps, and AFDC are not calculated as federal expenditures, since they are administered by the state) and federal programs (for example, HUD and grants for education), for which all areas in the country are potentially eligible. It also includes special federal spending for Indian reservations. The latter would include the Bureau of Indian Affairs budget, the Indian Health Service budget, and special funding for Indian education. Together, the generic federal funding (reservations qualify for more because of their low income levels) and the special Indian funding allow the higher populations/densities on Indian reservations. These federal funds provide government services—police protection, fire protection, highway construction and maintenance, water and sewer service, education, housing, health care delivery, and social services—above the level which local agricultural production would be able to support if taxes on it had to fund services. These funds also create most of the jobs available on the reservation—many more jobs than agriculture can provide. Reservation economies are artificial economies.[2]

This is decidedly not to say that Indian people live better than non-Indians. The pauperization of the reservations has been described above. Although it is much greater than that for non-Indian counties, the level of federal funding is woefully insufficient to generate jobs to employ more than an fraction of the Indian labor force or to bring Indian income up to a level comparable to that of non-Indians. There is no question that this level of federal funding can underwrite the Indian population only because Indian people accept a much lower standard of living and because they share meager resources in kin and friendship networks (see Albers 1982; Jorgensen 1971, 1972:116–20, 1990; Mekeel 1936; Moore, this volume; Hedley, this volume).

But there is also no question that this federal funding allows Lakota communities to survive on the reservations and to resist the forces of agricultural capitalism and rural population loss that act on rural nonreservation counties and that have liquidated so many non-Indian farms, ranches, and communities, literally making them disappear from the landscape. In Todd County federal funding provides twice the amount of money that agriculture does. This funding gives the Lakota people, their communities, and the cultural and linguistic matrix of these communities, some insulation from the forces of agricultural capitalism. The implications for the ethnic survival of the Lakota—especially as compared to the crisis faced by white rural communities and the family farm way of life—are obvious. Because of federal funding, Lakota reservations constitute "homelands" in Frederick Hoxie's (1979) terminology, or "sustained enclaves" in George Pierre Castile's (1974).

Anthropologists need to recognize two implications of the political economy of the reservation for Indian political consciousness. First, we should not expect reservation Indian people to see themselves as having much in common with other disempowered groups in the United States (see Deloria 1985). Lakota people conceive of their special legal status, and the associated federal funding and services, as treaty rights, as benefits they receive as members of a particular tribe (or *nation*) because of specific tribal lands ceded to the United States through specific signed agreements.[3] Most of the special legal status of and special federal funding for Lakota people is not, in a technical legal sense, based on treaties, but rather on other federal legislation. But this legislation is clearly based on Lakota people in particular and Indian people in general being perceived as a special case in which justice requires considerations not made for other disempowered people in the United States. Lakota people would stand to lose much if they were perceived by the American voters and/or the powerful politicians who make policy as no different—from a policy point of view—than African or Hispanic Americans, merely poor "people of color," a "minority group." It is no surprise that the political consciousness of Lakota people entails appeals to treaties signed by the Lakota and the United States, not to the constitutional rights of minorities or to universal civil rights.

The other implication of the political economy of the reservation for Lakota consciousness concerns how the federal government is perceived. Because the flows of federal funds are so critical to the survival of Lakota communities, we would not expect Lakota people to have an unambiguous conceptualization of the federal government as an oppressor, no matter how oppressive it is. There is certainly recognition among Lakota people that the BIA and other federal agencies involve domination, but there is simultaneously a recognition that the federal government is necessary—paradoxically—for the physical, cultural, and linguistic survival of the Lakota. Even during the occupation of Wounded Knee in 1973, there was no direct or serious plan for severing completely relationships between the Lakota and the United States government. Lakota people may want the federal government off their backs, but they also recognize that a special relationship with the federal government—conceptualized by them as a treaty relationship—serves both their short-term and their long-term interests (see Biolsi 1992).[4]

Even though Lakota people conceive of their special legal status and special federal funding as treaty rights, they are keenly aware that in the real world there are no *guarantees*. Federal Indian law is made by Congress, implemented by the executive branch, and tested in the courts. Treaty rights thus ultimately depend upon the discretion of all three branches of the federal government. No one is more aware of this than Indian people who have lived on reservations and have seen the threat of termination in the 1950s (when, interestingly, the Lakota flag song was composed) and the budget cuts of the 1980s. Therefore, it is not surprising that Lakota people would hoist the flag over their wacipis when they celebrate the Lakota way and the persistence of the Lakota people. By this act they tacitly express their faith, their demand, and their hope, that the "grandfather" in Washington, and Congress, and the courts, will humanely and honorably abide by the spirit of the treaties, as those treaties are interpreted by the Lakota. Nothing less than the survival of the Lakota as a people hangs in the balance.

In Ole E. Rölvaag's *Giants in the Earth,* a novel about 1870s settlers on a public domain only recently cleared of Indians in Dakota Territory, a Norwegian family discovers an Indian grave on their homestead. The discovery of the grave reminds both the novel's characters and the reader that another people and another way of life had not long ago been swept aside by the broom of history. "Do you suppose they'll ever come back?" a child asks his mother regarding the Dakota Indians. "Yes, maybe—if we stay here long enough," his mother replies (Rölvaag 1927:40). Neither the characters nor Rölvaag

Fig. 2.8. Carter, South Dakota, 1913. (Photograph, *Gregory,* S. Dak., *Times-Advocate*)

Fig. 2.9. Carter, South Dakota, 1988. (Photograph, Thomas Biolsi)

could have foreseen the persistence and growth of Dakota and Lakota communities on the same landscape where rural white communities would eventually disappear. Just east of Rosebud Reservation sits the little town of Carter on U.S. Highway 18. Carter was once a thriving border town. "The future of Carter is assured," a booster wrote in 1913 (*Gregory Times-Advocate* 1984:59). Now Carter is a ghost town—the empty buildings of the Home Cafe and the Carter State Bank and the vault of the Farmers State Bank are all that are left on Main Street. Like the Dakota Indian burial found by Rölvaag's characters, these are the archaeological remains of a way of life—family farming, in this case—being swept aside by the march of capitalism upon the landscape. Lakota political consciousness, and their claim to treaty rights, is about resisting this immense historical force. Lakota resistance has prevailed as of this writing.

Acknowledgments

I would like to thank Diane Ciekawy and David Nugent for reading earlier versions of this paper. I would also like to thank Mark Bordeaux, John Boyd, Rose Cordier, Cheryl Crazy Bull, Margaret Douville, Betty Emery, and Frank Lapoint, for kindly providing information. Finally I thank the Red Leaf Singers and the Band Hand family for taking me to wacipis.

CHAPTER 3

Learning to Labor

Native American Education in the United States, 1880–1930

Alice Littlefield

Between 1880 and 1930 the United States Bureau of Indian Affairs maintained a large system of on- and off-reservation boarding schools for the education of indigenous children. Descriptions of this system written by historians, ethnographers, and educators have focused on the role of the schools in the attempted assimilation of Native American children. From its inception the boarding school system aroused considerable controversy. The schools were assailed for attempting too much, for not achieving enough, and, especially in recent years, for their destructive impact on indigenous cultures and indigenous children.

In this article[1] I argue that "proletarianization" better characterizes the efforts of the federal Indian schools than assimilation. To the extent that assimilation was accomplished, it consisted very largely of incorporating some Native Americans into the lower strata of the working class. Placed in the context of other government policies toward Native Americans and the general economic history of the period, the practices of the boarding schools were quite successful in facilitating the entry of previously independent farmers, hunters, and gatherers into the wage labor force. They did not succeed, however, in incorporating Native Americans into the larger society on a basis of equality with Euro-Americans.

Scholarly studies of the federal Indian schools have tended to focus on changes in policy emanating from particular presidents, interior secretaries, Indian affairs commissioners, or reformers, and to explain the failures and accomplishments of the system in terms of the imprint left by such influential policy makers. In this paper, I take the position that a broader view is necessary, that although the impact of some individuals, such as Col. Richard Henry Pratt (founder of the Carlisle School) or Commissioner Thomas Jefferson Morgan, was indeed great, their ability to implement their views depended on favorable politico-economic conditions. I will argue that the twists and turns in Indian education policy were ultimately conditioned by the changing character of the rural economy in the United States during the period under discussion, and that if we look beyond the high-sounding rhetoric of policy makers and study the specific practices of the schools, the impression emerges that changing labor needs dictated by the larger economy were often decisive in decisions to expand or retrench particular programs.

During the period under consideration, the labor needs of the expanding American economy often seemed insatiable. Between the Civil War and 1900 the frontier regions rapidly filled with Euro-American settlers, the railroads penetrated the most remote regions, and the shift from subsistence to commercial agriculture accelerated throughout the continent. Industry grew apace, as did the size of industrial enterprises. By the turn of the century monopoly capitalism was well established, and with the Spanish-American War in 1898 the United States made its entry onto the stage of global imperialism.

Between 1880 and 1920 the demand for cheap labor in the United States economy was met largely through importing European, Asian, and Mexican immigrants. The utilization of the labor of the indigenous peoples was quantitatively less significant and has not been as thoroughly documented. Nonetheless, existing historical and ethnographic studies suggest that, in certain times and places, indigenous labor played a key role in America's economic expansion,[2] and that federal policies during this period, including educational policy, were important in facilitating the utilization of Native American labor by Euro-American employers.

As in other developing capitalist nations, all precapitalist economic relations in the United States came under attack and were either destroyed or modified to meet the needs of capital. With regard to the indigenous peoples, their communal economies were undermined by measures designed to transform their land and labor into commodities, through the twin policies of allotment and education. In reading the statements of policy makers of the period, one is struck by the frequency with which allotment and education were linked together as cornerstones of federal Indian policy.

Numerous studies have attested to the effects of the allotment programs in separating the indigenes from their means of production. The resulting land losses are well known and need not be detailed here. But how did education fit into the overall process of proletarianization?

Before the expansion of the federal boarding school system in the 1880s, much of the education of indigenous children was provided by missionary organizations through facilities located on or near reservations, an arrangement which received extensive federal financial support in the period just after the Civil War. The transition to direct federal provision of education came about for several reasons, including problems with Protestant-Catholic rivalry (Prucha 1981; R. Keller 1983). I suggest, however, that the missionaries were simply considered too inefficient for the task of transforming indigenous peoples into employable workers—especially those missionaries who focused on spiritual matters and biblical study in native languages. Among those who had little respect for missionary efforts, and who lobbied for direct government provision of education, was Col. Richard Henry Pratt.

Perhaps more than anyone, Pratt played a key role in launching the off-reservation boarding schools. Founder of the Carlisle School (1879), Pratt was a military man who believed strongly in the capacity of indigenous peoples to master all of the skills and knowledge of which Euro-Americans were capable. He believed that, like European immigrants, they could be assimilated in one generation. Pratt's writings repeatedly emphasized the goals of assimilation and "Americanization." To accomplish these, he argued, indigenous youth must leave their families and reservations and be educated in close association with Euro-Americans (Pratt 1964).

Toward this end, Pratt devised the "outing system." Carlisle students were placed with Pennsylvania farm families during the summer months, the boys to learn farm work and the girls to learn domestic skills. After three years at Carlisle, students were sometimes placed with families throughout the year, continuing their studies in local public schools. Pratt saw this as the ideal way for Indian youth to become fully integrated into the dominant society and enabled to compete successfully with Euro-American youth. He insisted that his students be treated as family members, and the outing system he devised probably duplicated the conditions experienced by many non-Indian hired hands and domestic servants on northeastern farms in the 1880s (Pratt 1964; Trennert 1983).

Although Pratt's rhetoric and his lobbying activities continually emphasized complete assimilation, the practices of the Carlisle School focused on training in the manual trades, trades chosen for their utility in the rural economy of the day. Boys were trained in agriculture, carpentry, smithing, harness- and shoemaking, printing, tailoring, and baking; girls in cooking, sewing, and laundry. Throughout his writings, Pratt repeatedly emphasized the importance of work and industry in the transformation of Indians into acceptable citizens, a theme echoed by other policy makers of the day. He continually cited the outing system as the most successful aspect of the Carlisle curriculum, and the manual trades played a significant part in every display organized to present Carlisle's accomplishments to the public (Pratt 1964).

Pratt and other reformers of the period had a Jeffersonian view of American society as based on the independent farmer and artisan as the pillars of freedom and democracy. Pratt had begun his own career as a tinsmith and, through service in the Civil War and on the frontier, had risen to the rank of colonel, demonstrating in his own life the opportunities open to ordinary persons of ability (Hoxie 1984: 54–55).

By the time Carlisle opened its doors, however, American society was already changing. In industry and in agriculture, enterprises were increasing in scale, and the independent artisan was giving way to the factory worker repetitiously performing a small part of the total production process. Increasingly, masses of cheap labor were needed to feed economic expansion. Grain cultivation in the Great Plains was already becoming highly commercialized and increasingly mechanized. Adoption of horse-drawn machinery had become common, and the labor needs of agriculture were shifting away from the permanent hired hand to the use of large numbers of seasonal workers (Barger and Landsberg 1942; McWilliams 1942). Farther west, railroad expansion facilitated the rapid growth of commercial livestock production and, somewhat later, the introduction of specialized crops such as cotton, citrus, and sugar beets.

As Hoxie (1984:43–48) has pointed out, the railroads were among the most powerful business interests lobbying to break up the reservations and turn the "surplus" lands over to settlers. By 1880 the capital stock of railroads amounted to $5.4 billion. Economically and politically, railroad capital was stronger than either industrial or finance capital (J. Keller 1983:170). The rail companies were often able to negotiate rights of way through treaty lands but then found that profitable operation required vastly expanded production in the areas through which the routes passed. Owners were instrumental in opening up the Great Sioux Reservation, the Blackfeet and Crow lands of Montana, Indian Territory, and other areas (Hoxie 1984: Miner 1976).

These land cessions, combined with allotment policies, greatly facilitated the growth of commercial agriculture throughout the plains and Far West and also provided greater opportunities for mining operations. All of these activities, like the building of the roads themselves, required an abundant supply of cheap labor.

Before indigenous peoples could be drawn into rural wage labor, however, several obstacles had to be overcome. They had to be separated from their means of production, and during the period under consideration this was largely accomplished through the allotment policy. Rations and annuities, which allowed Indians to survive without working, or at least without working for Euro-Americans, had to be phased out. Even so, a surprising number of Indians preferred to eke out a living by combining varied subsistence activities with the income from leasing their allotments, working for wages only when forced to do so. Education, then, was necessary to teach American Indians English and disciplined work habits. It was reasoned that the boarding schools could accomplish this better than day schools, by separating the children from the example set by their parents. The boarding schools also had another function: by exposing children to a new material standard of living, schools created new desires and motivated youth to work for the cash necessary to acquire the material possessions common among Euro-Americans. The off-reservation boarding schools, in combination with the outing system, could presumably accomplish these ends most efficiently.

In the United States Congress, support for the boarding school system came most consistently from northeastern Republicans. Western politicians were more likely to question the wisdom of spending money on peoples with whom they had so recently engaged in hostilities. Henry Teller, senator from Colorado, was initially inclined to such a view. When appointed secretary of interior in 1882, however, he quickly became a supporter of the off-reservation boarding schools and the outing system. During his tenure from 1882 to 1885, enrollments of Native American students increased at both Carlisle and Hampton Institute, and six new off-reservation schools were founded: Fort Stevenson, Dakota; Genoa, Nebraska; Fort Yuma, Arizona; Haskell Institute, Kansas; Fort Hall, Idaho; and Chilocco Training School, in Indian Territory (Hoxie, 1984:58).

With the 1884 election of Grover Cleveland, the first Democratic president since the Civil War, expansion of the Indian school system slowed, but the off-reservation system enjoyed renewed support under Commissioner Thomas Jefferson Morgan, appointed in 1889. Morgan was a professional educator with a deep belief in the value of public education for promoting citizenship and "Americanizing" all races. During his four years as commissioner, a dozen off-reservation schools were opened (1890: Santa Fe, New Mexico; Fort Mojave, Arizona; Carson, Nevada; 1891: Phoenix, Arizona; Pierre, South Dakota; 1892: Fort Lewis, Colorado; Fort Shaw, Montana; 1893: Perris, California; Flandreau, South Dakota; Pipestone, Minnesota; Mt. Pleasant, Michigan; Tomah, Wisconsin. Trennert 1988:218). Morgan worked to make primary instruction in reservation day schools universal and compulsory, with boarding schools providing the higher grades and vocational training (although in many areas the boarding schools continued to take students with no previous schooling).

Typically, boarding school students spent only half the day in the classroom, with the other half devoted to manual training or work assignments presumed to have educational value. Morgan also ordered that no language but English be allowed in any of the BIA schools (Kvasnicka and Viola 1979:193–203; Hoxie 1984:64–67; Trennert 1988:9–11). He supported the outing system and hoped that the industrial schools would encourage indigenous youth not to return to the reservations. This position directly contradicts the notion that BIA educational policy was aimed at training Indians for independent farming on their allotments or reservations. In 1892 Morgan wrote that "We must either fight Indians, feed them, or else educate them. To fight them is cruel, to feed them is wasteful, while to educate them is humane, economic, and Christian" (Kvasnicka and Viola, 1979:199). Morgan also issued regulations providing that any Indian who "habitually spends his time in idleness and loafing" should be deemed a vagrant and guilty of a misdemeanor (Kvasnicka and Viola 1979:199–200).

By 1895 the government was spending $2 million annually to educate 18,000 indigenous students in 200 institutions (Hoxie 1984:189–90). Although Western congressmen sometimes opposed expenditures for Indian education, business leaders in the communities where the schools were located were usually supportive. The schools injected large amounts of federal dollars into the local economies through their payrolls, purchase of supplies, and building contracts. In the case of the Phoenix School, local businessmen, eager to have the school established, contributed $3,000 toward the purchase of the land. Phoenix was dominated by a group of land speculators who envisioned a great commercial future for the Salt River Valley. Development of citrus cultivation had already begun. An Indian school promised to encourage real estate development, and students from the school would provide cheap labor for the adjacent orchards through the outing system (Trennert 1988:20–27). Local entrepreneurs were similarly supportive of the Mt. Pleasant Indian School, contributing $3,400 toward the purchase of land for the school (Bureau of Indian Affairs 1934).

In the western schools the outing system often became little more than a means of providing child labor to area employers. Trennert's study of the Phoenix School indicates that by 1900 the school was placing about two hundred students in area homes, many of them girls employed as domestic servants. Boys were placed as farm workers and construction laborers. Throughout the period, the demand for student labor exceeded the supply. All of these placements were presumed to be educational, although they were often poorly supervised, and in most cases the students received no academic instruction once they left the school to work. In some cases youths were recruited from reservations and sent directly to placements without spending any time in school. The outing system operated on similar lines at the Sherman Institute, in California, where students did seasonal work on ranches and railroads, and at the Albuquerque School, in New Mexico (Trennert 1983).

With the turn of the century, federal policy makers began to reject the rhetoric of rapid assimilation and to advocate more gradual approaches. Increasingly, doubts were expressed about American Indians' ability to benefit from academic training. Ironically, in spite of talk about gradualism, the process of incorporating indigenes into the wage labor force accelerated, and the schools became even more subordinate to this process.

This shift in policy accompanied important shifts in the United States political economy. The depression of the mid–1890s marked a decline in the dominance of railroad capital and an increase in the importance of industrial and finance capital. Increasingly, American capital looked abroad for expanding markets and fields of investment. With the Spanish-American War, the United States took its position as a major imperial power and, in the period between 1900 and 1920, intervened on an unprecedented scale in the internal affairs of other nations.

Once the United States found itself in control of the Philippines, Puerto Rico, and other regions populated by racially and culturally diverse peoples, a resurgence of racist ideology occurred. Social scientists and policy makers began to revive an old theme: the darker races were incapable of handling their own affairs and needed the white man to do it for them. Correspondingly, "inferior" peoples were seen as capable in most instances only of menial and unskilled work. Such work, however, would be good for them, establishing habits of industry and helping them to advance in a gradual manner (Hoxie 1984:115–45).

Francis E. Leupp, commissioner of Indian Affairs from 1905 to 1909, epitomized this approach. Under his administration the emphasis shifted from the off-reservation boarding schools to the reservation day schools, and these were encouraged to focus on practical instruction. From 1905 to 1910, boarding school attendance declined 10 percent and day school attendance increased 47 percent. In 1909, on Leupp's recommendation, Congress closed four of the boarding schools (Hoxie 1984: 203). The day schools were not only cheaper to operate; in Leupp's opinion an elementary education was sufficient for the conditions faced by indigenous children after leaving school. Leupp and his successors also encouraged public school education for Native American children where possible, although the bureau made no effort to insure that the states provided them with equal educational opportunity (Hoxie 1984:209).

During the same era progressive educators were calling for a revamping of rural education in general, in order to enhance farm productivity. President Theodore Roosevelt's Country Life Commission, formed in 1907, recommended courses in agriculture, industrial arts, and domestic science in all rural schools and pushed for school consolidation to make these possible (Danbom 1979:44–45). Similar moves toward tax-supported vocational education had taken place even earlier in the nation's cities, where it was advocated by business leaders as more appropriate for working class youth than an academic course of study. By 1917 the federal government moved to provide financial support for local vocational education through the Smith-Hughes Act (Hogan 1985; Gonzalez 1982).

In 1910, Leupp expressed his views on Indian affairs in his book, *The Indian and His Problem*. He had this to say about education:

Of the thirty or forty thousand Indian children of school age in the United States, probably at least three-fourths will settle down in that part of the West which we still style the frontier. Most of these will try to draw a living out of the soil; a less—though, let us hope, an ever increasing—part will enter the general labor market as lumbermen, ditchers, miners, railroad hands or what not. In simple terms, the great mass of Indians have yet to go through the era, common to the history of all races, when they must be mere hewers of wood and drawers of water. Now if any one can show me what advantage will come to this large body of manual workers from being able to reel off the names of the mountains of Asia . . . I shall be deeply grateful. To my notion, the ordinary Indian boy is better equipped for his life struggle on a frontier ranch when he can read the local newspaper, can write a short letter . . . and knows enough of figures to discover whether the storekeeper is cheating him. (1910:45–46)

Under Leupp's administration, the outing system was considerably expanded. He placed great emphasis on getting Native Americans to acquire the habit of working. He took the greatest pride in having launched an employment bureau to recruit laborers from reservations to work for farms and industries. Beginning in the Southwest in 1905, the Bureau placed five thousand tribesmen in its first year. The program spread to the northern plains in 1907, to the Imperial Valley of California in 1908, and to Wisconsin in 1909. The employment service specialized in migrant labor (Leupp 1910:151–72; Hoxie 1984:201–202).

The necessity for Indians to work is one of the most common themes in policy statements of the period. To be sure, some educators may have assumed that their graduates would work for themselves as independent farmers or artisans. Nonetheless, the Indian education program was repeatedly defended to the public in terms of its ability to teach Indians to work for others.

The history of the Mt. Pleasant (Michigan) Indian School suggests also that something more than the creation of independent farmers was envisioned by those who advocated the off-reservation boarding schools. In Michigan the allotment of Chippewa and Ottawa lands was begun in the 1850s as a result of treaty provisions. By the 1890s many Native Americans had already lost their allotments through sale or fraud (Rubenstein, 1974) and had become dependent on wage labor in lumber camps and on the farms of settlers. The 1910 census reported 7,519 Indians in Michigan, but only 253 of these were farmers, while 627 were farm laborers. Hundreds of others were employed in nonagricultural occupations such as lumbering. Of 150 students who graduated from the Mt. Pleasant School between 1915 and 1922, only 24 were reported to be farmers (Chase 1922:154–55). Yet the Mt. Pleasant School offered essentially the same curriculum as other off-reservation schools, emphasizing agriculture, carpentry, and smithing for the boys, and domestic skills for the girls.

Under Leupp and his successors, Robert Valentine (1909–1912) and Cato Sells (1913–1921), the pace of allotment was vastly accelerated, and several changes in law and regulations were made to facilitate the leasing and sales of allotments to non-Indians. The national goals of efficiency and economic development were presumed to take precedence over protecting the Indians' welfare (Hoxie 1984:173).

One of Leupp's plans which sheds light on the interactions between government policy and business expansion was a scheme involving sugar beet companies. Sugar beet cultivation had been encouraged by the high tariff enacted on imported sugar in 1897. In the next ten years sugar beet cultivation in the United States increased tenfold to over 370,000 acres (Schwartz 1945:102). Sugar beets required abundant hand labor for planting, blocking, thinning, and harvesting. Leupp arranged twenty-year leases for the sugar companies on Indian lands at the Fort Belknap, Uintah, and Wind River reservations, in exchange for their pledging to employ Indian labor. Leupp then recruited the labor through the employment bureau and the schools (Hoxie 1984:168).

Sugar beet production appears to have been a branch of agriculture in which indigenous labor played a particularly important role. The Albuquerque Indian School sent students to work in the beet fields of Colorado (Trennert 1983:283; U.S. Dept. of Interior, *Report of the Commissioner* 1921 and 1923), and Pueblos from New Mexico were still being used as seasonal labor in the Colorado beet fields when Carey McWilliams published his well-known study of migrant farm labor, *Ill*

Fares the Land, in 1942 (109–29). Students from the Genoa Indian School worked in Nebraska sugar beet fields (Trennert 1983), and Mt. Pleasant students were similarly employed in the Michigan beet fields (personal communication, former students). In 1924, 220 Indian boys were recruited by the BIA for employment by a sugar beet company in Garden City, Kansas (U.S. Dept. of Interior, *Report of the Commissioner* 1925).

Unlike some of the earlier commissioners, Cato Sells opposed the leasing of Indian allotments to whites and encouraged Congress to fund loans to Indians for irrigation, livestock and other improvements that would allow them to utilize their own lands. In spite of a promising beginning, this program fell prey to the drought of 1919 and the agricultural depression of the early 1920s. Many small farmers, Native Americans as well as others, were simply unable to survive the crisis. At the end of Sells' administration in 1921, only 762,000 acres of Indian land were farmed by Indians, while 4.5 million were leased by non-Indians (Kvasnicka and Viola 1979:243–50).

The shortage of manual labor in rural America reached its peak during World War I. American farmers were exhorted to produce more than ever before and were offered guaranteed price supports for the first time (Danbom 1979:102–03). The Indian vocational schools were ordered to increase their agricultural production as well. At the Phoenix School academic studies were disrupted as students were mobilized to contribute to the war effort (Trennert 1988:161–63).

One consequence of wartime labor shortages was to accelerate mechanization in United States agriculture and to initiate a radical improvement in productivity that led within a few years to a decline in the demand for farm labor. By 1921 the country entered into an extended crisis of agricultural overproduction from which it did not recover until World War II (Shideler 1957; Danbom 1979). In 1920 and 1921 farm prices tumbled, falling to one-third of their previous levels.

Bumper crops in the fall of 1921 intensified the crisis. Industry also experienced a postwar depression, with four million unemployed by the end of 1920 (Shideler 1957:46–51).

In the 1920s farm acreage, the number of farms, and farm population all dropped (Shideler 1957). As a percentage of the labor force, those working in agriculture declined from 27 percent to 21 percent during the decade, while output per worker increased by 41 percent (Barger and Landsberg 1942:253; McWilliams 1942:322). Although industry recovered and enjoyed renewed prosperity until the crash of 1929, agriculture continued to languish, with farm bankruptcies peaking in 1926 (Shideler 1957:195).

The crisis of 1920–1921 and renewed problems of unemployment marked the beginnings of another shift in the national political economy. Faced with a labor surplus, the government responded with legislation curtailing immigration and child labor. With high productivity and cheap food prices achieved, Department of Agriculture policy shifted from trying to keep people on the land to encouraging the inefficient and marginal to leave. By 1930 farming had been industrialized to the point that those without capital faced a marginal existence at best (Danbom 1979:136–42). After 1920 the hourly earnings of farm workers and factory workers increasingly diverged (Schwartz 1945:13). As industry grew and agriculture stagnated, rural youth, including indigenous youth, were attracted to the cities where the jobs were.

Problems of low wages and irregular employment among both rural and urban Indians came under investigation in the late 1920s. Educators became increasingly aware that the vocational training in agriculture and domestic science offered by the boarding schools was obsolete. But school administrators had few alternatives. As the century progressed, Indian education suffered increasingly from underfunding. Boarding schools could only make ends meet by using student labor to grow their own food and perform most of the cooking, cleaning, and other menial tasks necessary to keep the schools going. These activities had a questionable relationship to the goals of vocational training. All too often, students were kept busy at relatively unskilled tasks with minimal value in the job market (Trennert 1988; Meriam 1928).

The 1920s were marked by growing criticism of the old assimilationist policies. During this period John Collier emerged as one of the most vocal critics of the schools' failure to achieve stated goals. In the fall of 1926 Collier and Wisconsin Congressman James A. Frear made an extensive tour of the western reservations. Upon completion of the tour they issued a stinging denunciation of the boarding schools for providing overcrowded and unhealthful facilities and for destroying the Indians' heritage (Trennert 1988:173–81).

In response to a rising tide of criticism, Interior Secretary Hubert Work commissioned an investigation of Indian affairs by the Brookings Institution. The results, published in 1928, became known as the Meriam Report, after Lewis Meriam, director of the survey staff. The report made extensive criticisms of the federal school system, with the boarding schools especially coming under attack. The stringent budgets of the Harding and Coolidge administrations had reduced the schools to penury. Diets were poor, and the schools were overcrowded by 40 percent. Tuberculosis and other diseases were common. Discipline was harsh, and the training provided was seriously deficient in meeting the educational needs of the times (Meriam 1928; Szasz 1974).

Although the Hoover administration made budget cuts in many areas, an effort was made to implement the reforms suggested by the Meriam Report. On-reservation day schools were given greater emphasis, off-reservation boarding schools were restricted to secondary education, and some of the schools, such as the one at Mt. Pleasant, were closed. In others, grades were added and increased emphasis placed on academic subjects, with less time devoted to manual training and monotonous work assignments. Salaries and staff qualifications improved. By 1933 appropriations for Indian education, health, and welfare were double what they had been in 1928 (Kvasnicka and Viola 1979:263–70).

After 1930, federal policy increasingly emphasized transferring responsibility for the education of indigenous peoples to the local public schools. The federal school system had been successful in helping to incorporate thousands of indigenous youth into the rural wage labor force, but an expanding rural proletariat was no longer needed. Through the 1930s the supply of farm labor far exceeded the demand, and the plight of farm workers became a subject of national concern. In view of these developments, it is not surprising that federal Indian policy during the New Deal era shifted toward the revival of tribal economies, polities, and cultures that the BIA had earlier tried to destroy.

In sketching this picture of the federal Indian school system as subservient to the needs of an expanding capitalist economy, I have said nothing about the reactions to these policies by the indigenous peoples themselves. The social arrangements of capitalist society are not simply a reflection of ruling class needs, but the result of struggles among contending interests and classes. Although the history of the making of the indigenous working class in the United States is, in large part, a history yet to be written, it is clear that the boarding school came to play an important part in the indigenous peoples' own strategies to survive in an industrial capitalist society.

In the 1800s, federal efforts to educate indigenous children often met with parental resistance. By the 1920s the boarding schools were besieged with more applicants than they could handle. Many Native Americans had come to see education in the vocational boarding schools, with all its limitations, as an opportunity for their children to learn marketable skills, an opportunity owed to them by a government which had promised so much and delivered so little.

It is not surprising, then, that every wave of boarding school closings met, and continues to meet, resistance from students and their parents (see McBeth 1984). The opposition to the school closings which occurred under the Reagan administration, and to the BIA proposal to turn bureau schools over to the states, is a recent expression of this phenomenon. This opposition, and the century-long struggle of indigenous peoples to regain control over their own education, is another part of the story, and one demanding greater attention in future research.

CHAPTER 4

Health Patterns and Economic Underdevelopment on the Northern Cheyenne Reservation, 1910–1920

Gregory R. Campbell

> The policy of forced assimilation, which has been conducted by the United States for many decades, is nothing less than cultural, spiritual and psychological forms of genocide.
> —Ivanov, *Genocide* (1985)

The Soviet scholar Ivanov summarizes what most Indian people and many American scholars have known for a long time. While this statement succinctly encapsulates American Indian policy objectives since its inception, there is a fourth factor which Ivanov should add to his list of genocidal practices—ill health.

Over the last four decades there has been an increasing interest in the impact of European colonization on American Indian demography (Boyd 1985; Cook 1935, 1940, 1945, 1955, 1972, 1973a, 1973b, 1976a, 1976b; Cook and Borah 1969, 1971, 1974, 1979; Denevan 1976; Dobyns 1966, 1976, 1983, 1984; Jacobs 1974; Ramenofsky 1982, 1987; Reff 1985, 1990; Trimble 1985; Thornton 1987). What has emerged from this scholarship is a standardized formula for American Indian population change. The most accepted historical trajectory of postcontact American Indian demographic history is severe population collapse to a nadir, followed by a subsequent demographic recovery, especially after the surviving tribes were placed on reservations. The general processes of demographic change are well known. Most scholars agree that the introduction of European contagions was the primary cause of the population collapse, with genocidal warfare, geographic removal, and the destruction of aboriginal lifeways as important contributory causes (Thornton 1987:42–133). While few would deny the general validity of this historical formula, the majority of scholarly debate has centered around two related issues: the extent of population decline during the prereservation period, and the establishment of precontact tribal population sizes (Dobyns 1966, 1976, 1983; Jacobs 1974; Ramenofsky 1987; Thornton 1987; Thornton and Thornton 1981; Ubelaker 1976). By their nature, these past works have remained largely descriptive, failing to link American Indian population change to the specific relationships between mortality, fertility, and morbidity. This situation is particularly true for the postreservation period (Johansson and Preston 1978; Kunitz 1981).

In fact, it has been assumed by most scholars that once American Indians were placed on reservations, their health improved because of exposure to Western medicine. Ironically, they have used population growth as empirical evidence to indicate an improvement in health status during the reservation period (Dobyns 1976:42–45; Thornton 1987:172–74). Such an assumption obscures the historical reality of reservation life, in that health levels were intimately linked to the reservation political economy and that ill health must be conceptualized as a societal event with ideological, political, and socioeconomic dimensions.

In this article, I will examine the continued deterioration and persistence of ill health among the Northern Cheyenne Indians of Montana during the early reservation period from 1910 to 1920. It is argued that the persistence of ill health and the resultant population changes were intimately linked to a process of economic underdevelopment as part of the United

States government's policy of forced assimilation on the Northern Cheyenne reservation. In order to make the relationship between health patterns and economic underdevelopment explicit, it is necessary to outline a material theory of disease causality.

A Materialist Approach to Health

As an axiom, any critical discussion of health must be understood in relation to political economy. That is, as Kelman pointed out, health is socially defined and rooted in the proposition that individuals, as members of a society, "... are the basis of both the forces of production ... and the relations of production ... in any society, and that therefore, appropriate human organismic condition (i.e., health) can only be understood in the concrete context of the particular mode of production and the dialectical relationship between the productive forces and relations" (Kelman 1976:630).

Therefore, to fully comprehend health patterns in any society, a critical examination of the contending forces in and out of the health arena becomes essential (Baer, Singer, and Johnson 1981). Changes in health status must be analyzed within concrete historical and social conditions (Navarro 1976; Singer 1986:128). As Turshen (1989:24–26) has reiterated in *The Politics of Public Health*, the causes of disease and debility are revealed less by their biological and physical manifestation in a population than by a population's development within the context of social history.

Such a perspective demands a different notion of disease causality. Changing health patterns are more than biological or clinical manifestations. Ill health is not exclusively environmental or biological but social, coming from inherently oppressive social relationships (Doyal 1979; Elling 1981; Navarro 1976, 1979; Singer 1986:129; Singer 1989; Stark 1977).

Under conditions of colonialism and exploitation these inherent relationships become even more apparent. In an analysis of medical colonialism in Tanzania, Turshen (1984:10–11) has referred to the historical origins of such diseases as the "unnatural history of disease." Any critical examination of disease processes necessarily leads to new conclusions about the nature and development of ill health. Thus the theoretical position presented here argues that the major cause of disease and death among the Northern Cheyenne was not solely biological, but rather a direct result of the political and economic control held by the Indian Office.

Under full governmental control, the Bureau of Indian Affairs launched an assimilation program designed to force Indian people out of a state of "savagery" and into "civilization" (Campbell 1989:2). The imposed reservation infrastructure produced rapid changes in Northern Cheyenne settlement pattern, social organization, political-economic structure, diet, and ideology (Campbell 1989:2). These changes divorced Northern Cheyenne people not only from their primary means of subsistence, but, through an active program of cultural oppression, denied them access to critical resources necessary for good health and medical care (Lyng 1990:119–61). The result was continuing ill health.

Reservation Underdevelopment

Direct Indian Bureau control of the Northern Cheyenne began with the establishment of the Tongue River Reservation on 16 November 1884 (U.S. Dept. of Interior, *Annual Report* 1885:322) (figure 4.1). In accordance with prevailing Indian Office policies, Agent Robert L. Upshaw, the first BIA appointee, attempted to move the Northern Cheyenne toward self-sufficiency through the implementation of agriculture and a wage-labor economy. These two economic programs were part of the Indian Office's overall mission of the forced assimilation toward "civilization." This program of forced social evolution, raising American Indian societies from a state of "savagery" to one of "civilization," was to be accomplished by

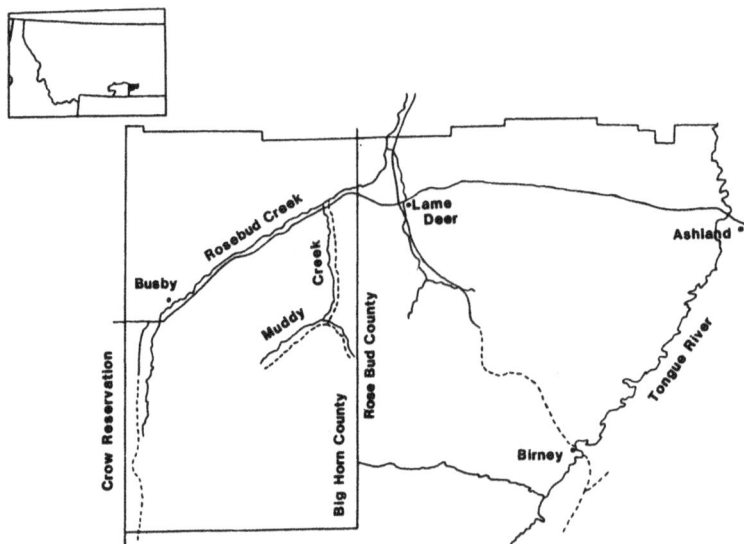

Fig. 4.1. Northern Cheyenne reservation and reservation communities, circa 1900. The reservation was in two Montana counties, Big Horn and Rosebud, and shared its western boundary with the Crow Reservation.

the introduction of agriculture, education, ownership of private property, a wage economy, and Christianity (Prucha 1984, 1:594–97).

Throughout the early reservation period, from 1886 to 1903, attempts at establishing a sustained agricultural base and a wage economy failed dismally. Neither developmental program made any appreciable impact on the reservation economy or, more importantly, on Northern Cheyenne subsistence (U.S. Dept. of Interior, *Annual Report* 1886, 1895, 1897). With no viable or stable economic base, the Northern Cheyenne became increasingly dependent on government-issued rations for their survival (figure 4.2). From the United States government perspective, rations were a necessary economic burden. Indian agents and Washington bureaucrats

Northern Cheyenne Subsistence, 1888-1901

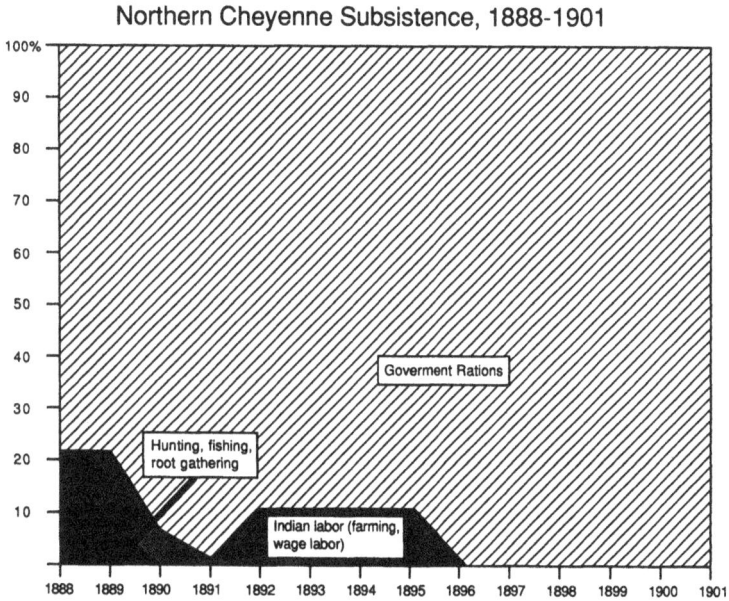

Fig. 4.2. Northern Cheyenne subsistence, 1888–1901.

alike realized that the economic policies were a failure, especially among the reservations located in the northern plains.
Instead of reformulating a new policy, the Indian Office instituted the ration system as a corollary to the reservation political economy. Indians such as the Northern Cheyenne had to
be fed for their survival, but rations were used also as an in-
ducement to comply with the bureau's assimilation policies.
Northern Cheyenne who resisted farming, education and mis-
sionization of their children, or earning a wage through individual labor were starved into compliance (U.S. Dept. of
Interior, *Annual Report* 1890; T. Weist 1977:123).

Political and economic conditions on the reservation
became more oppressive after 1900. Following an Indian
Office directive of 1903 the Northern Cheyenne agent began

to withdraw rations based on the estimated amount of labor productivity of Northern Cheyenne men. The policy was designed to coerce the Cheyenne toward self-sufficiency at an accelerated pace by forcibly stimulating Northern Cheyenne men to direct their labor input into the reservation agricultural and wage-labor economic sector. Both economic arenas continued to fail but were perpetuated artificially by input from the Bureau of Indian Affairs.

Under prevailing conditions the Northern Cheyenne faced severe malnutrition. They existed on what was called "short rations." Short rations amounted to approximately twelve ounces of beef and four ounces of flour per individual, issued every two weeks. According to one observer, the short ration issue "rarely lasted from one ration day to the next and was barely adequate to sustain life" (Svingen 1982:131; T. Weist 1977:114).

The Northern Cheyenne were caught in a continuous cycle of dependency. The more an individual worked, the more the Indian agent would slash his ration issue—a situation which led to further economic suffering and malnutrition. This vicious cycle of coerced labor and malnutrition was observed by naturalist-historian George Bird Grinnell in 1904 during one of his many visits to the Tongue River Reservation to collect ethnographic information. Grinnell wrote in protest to the commissioner of Indian Affairs:

In accordance with policy ... the rations of the Northern Cheyenne Indians have been so reduced that able bodied men and their families no longer receive subsistence. Money has been set aside to pay for work done by these people, whereby they may earn wages to pay for food. ... The sum allotted is wholly insufficient to purchase subsistence. ... [W]hen they have no work, they are in a starving condition, living on their horses, and under temptation to kill ... the cattle of White ranchers. (National Archives, RG 75, 1905)

Faced with an unstable labor base to supplement the continuous decline in ration issues, forced to eat an important means of production and wealth (horses), the Northern Cheyenne resorted to poaching white-owned cattle that roamed freely within the reservation boundaries. Poaching eventually led to sporadic violent confrontations, leaving a number of dead on both sides. The Northern Cheyenne agent responded by stationing military troops near the agency (Svingen 1982).

In response to the failure of economic progress and, to a lesser extent, to the hostilities between the Northern Cheyenne and local whites, the BIA sent Inspector McLaughlin in 1898 to report on the reservation conditions. McLaughlin's report resulted in a number of important political and economic changes for the Northern Cheyenne. Politically, he resolved the hostility between the Cheyenne and local whites by removing whites from the reservation and moving Cheyenne settlers, who earlier had built permanent cabins on the east side of the Tongue River, to the west side of the river. In addition, the United States government extended the eastern boundary of the reservation to the Tongue River.

On the surface, the resolution seemed equitable for both parties, especially since local white ranching interests were calling for the dissolution of the reservation. Once again, the Northern Cheyenne lost legal title to valuable lands and were not compensated for their losses. Whites received approximately $142,945.00 for their loss of land and property. The Northern Cheyenne for their loses received $25.00 per family head for their land and improvements. Illegal white squatters on the reservation received more compensation than did the Cheyenne, who received their payment for the inconvenience of the move (Svingen 1982:222).

Economically, McLaughlin's recommendations called for the BIA to abandon the development of agriculture and institute a cattle raising program, a recommendation the bureau eventually would implement on a number of northern plains reservations, including Tongue River. The decision to introduce cattle raising was based less on rational economic planning than on racist ideology. Because many northern Plains Indians were equestrian pastoralists before their confinement to reservations, Indian agents and bureau officials assumed

that they would have a "natural predisposition" to cattle raising as an economic pursuit (Svingen 1982:216).

In 1903 the Northern Cheyenne received 1,000 cows and
40 bulls which were issued to 430 family heads as private
property. Within two years the herd doubled by natural
increase. By 1912 the herd had increased to 10,000 head, and
Northern Cheyenne stock began bringing top prices at the
Chicago cattle exchange (R. Anderson 1951:186; T. Weist
1977:161).

Paralleling the nominal success of stock raising, a more stable, but temporary, labor market for Northern Cheyenne men
was created through extensive governmental projects. The
government used Northern Cheyenne labor to build reservation branding corrals, to improve roads and bridges, to haul
freight, and to construct a 6.8–mile irrigation project near
where the present-day village of Birney now stands (Svingen
1981:18; T. Weist 1977:164). The "Birney Ditch" was completed in 1910 and irrigated approximately 600 acres at a cost
of $266.00 per acre. (U.S. Senate, Survey 1932:12845). Be-

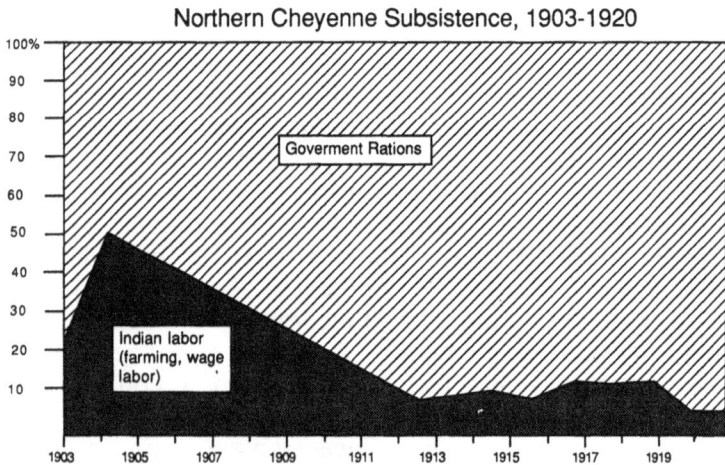

Fig. 4.3. Northern Cheyenne subsistence, 1903–20.

tween 1910 and 1915 only 24 families farmed 480 acres (G. Anderson 1951:183, U.S. Senate, Survey 1932:12845). In other words, during that period each family farmed an average of twenty acres of irrigated land at a phenomenal cost of $5,320.00 per year. The low agricultural returns reported by the Indian agents for this period indicate that costs far out-weighed agricultural and nutritional benefits.

Pointing to the nominal success at stock raising, coupled with the "progress" of the "Birney Ditch" agricultural project, the BIA accelerated the reduction of rations among the Northern Cheyenne. Again, the argument presented by bureau officials was that the action would promote further economic self-reliance. Instead, the Northern Cheyenne were forced to spend their earned capital in making up for the deficiencies in their rations. In reality, the policy ensured that the Northern Cheyenne would remain economically dependent and chronically malnourished.

This malnourished state was described by Iron Teeth, an elderly Northern Cheyenne woman, around 1916: "I am given very little food. Each month our Indian policemen brings me one quart of green coffee, one quart of sugar, a few pounds of flour and a small quantity of baking powder.... To keep myself from starving, I do yet some work" (Limbaugh 1973:24–25).

Iron Teeth's statement is testimony not only to the malnourished state of the Northern Cheyenne in general, but also to the differential impact that federal reservation policies had on women, the elderly, and, most likely, the very young. The labor sector of the bureau's assimilation policies was directed exclusively toward Northern Cheyenne men, perceiving the remainder of Northern Cheyenne society as unproductive and a burden to economic progress. With limited economic resources available, malnourishment and ill health was widespread, cross-cutting age and sex.

The Bureau of Indian Affairs recognized the magnitude of ill health that existed on all reservations; nevertheless, the bureau's policies and appropriations had little impact on health. The principal reason for failure rested in the contradiction between the continuing process of underdevelopment imposed upon American Indians and the attempts at raising them out of their state of "savagery" to "civilization" through assimilation. What bureau officials, reservation agents, and reservation physicians failed to recognize was that it was official political and economic policies that created and perpetuated ill health.

In 1914 a new United States administration came into office and instituted major changes in reservation Indian policy. John A. Buntin, the newly appointed Northern Cheyenne superintendent, believed in the development of dry farming instead of irrigation agriculture. He therefore discontinued the employment of ditch riders to maintain the "Birney Ditch" canals, allowing the irrigation project to fall into disrepair. By 1918 the project fell into complete disuse (T. Weist 1977:164). The total cost of the "Birney Ditch" was $160,000.00, including a debt of $73,109.62 for which the Bureau of Indian Affairs held the Northern Cheyenne financially responsible (G. Anderson 1951:184).

The new commissioner of Indian Affairs, Cato Sells, argued that the northern Plains Indian's cattle raising program was a limited success. Sells directed all agents to confiscate individually owned cattle and form tribal herds. The philosophy behind the policy was not to institute a collective labor enterprise for each tribe. Instead, Sells firmly believed greater herd growth and profit could be realized under Indian Bureau management. Logically, the greater the growth in both economic sectors meant the faster Indians would progress toward self-sufficiency and "civilization."

Following Commissioner Sells' directive, Superintendent Buntin ordered the Northern Cheyenne to relinquish their cattle to form tribal herds. The Northern Cheyenne resisted giving up their cattle, and they had good cultural, legal, and economic reasons for their open refusal. Aboriginally, the Northern Cheyenne owned horses as private property. Horses served as a source of social prestige and wealth. In similar fashion, individually owned cattle on the reservation became not only an integral component of their means of subsistence, but a source of prestige. Responding to Northern Cheyenne defiance, Superintendent Buntin threatened force and lengthy jail terms for anyone who refused to comply with the order (T. Weist 1977:172).

Between 1912 and 1920 the herd decreased by 42 percent under the Indian Office's charge (U.S. Senate, Survey 1932:12846). The failure of the tribal herd experiment prompted the BIA to withdraw the policy. An attempt was made in 1924 to return the surviving cattle back to their former owners. Some Northern Cheyenne men were issued a few head, but most received nothing because their cattle had perished under bureau control. The decade of mismanagement virtually crippled Northern Cheyenne efforts at cattle raising for at least two decades. Not until after World War II would cattle raising recover from these losses.

To compensate for their own fiscal mismanagement, the Indian Bureau held the Northern Cheyenne tribe responsible. The tribe was charged $130,000 for debts incurred while the cattle were under bureau care (G. Anderson 1951:187; U.S. Senate, Survey 1932:12846). By 1924 the Northern Cheyenne people owed the Indian Bureau $203,109.62 for failed economic development projects.

In an attempt to recover these expenses, a policy was implemented to tap the only economically viable resource remaining within the reservation boundaries—the land. As the bureau-controlled cattle industry eroded, the Northern Cheyenne superintendent began to lease reservation grazing lands to whites residing off-reservation. The leasing program represented the first major intrusion of private capital investment on the reservation.

To accelerate the program, the superintendent ordered the systematic slaughter of Northern Cheyenne horse herds. The policy was predicated on three economic factors. First, the superintendent saw no economic value in maintaining horse herds. Indian ponies were too small to serve as plow horses, and he was unaware of their intrinsic social value in Northern Cheyenne political and kin relations. Second, the slaughter of Indian ponies would serve as a protein substitute for the expensive beef ration, saving the agency the cost of beef, transportation, and slaughtering (T. Weist 1977:173, 188). Last, the dramatic decline in the horse herd, in conjunction with the collapse of the tribal cattle herd, released valuable grazing land for lease and profit. The horse slaughtering program continued until 1929, when the herd was virtually destroyed (T. Weist 1977:188).

Superintendent Buntin entered into long-term leases on large reservation land tracts. For example, C. M. Tainter, a lessee from New York, fenced off 90,000 acres in the southwest corner of the reservation for the annual sum of $31,250 (U.S. Dept. of Interior, *Annual Report* 1919:42). None of this capital, either directly or indirectly, entered into Cheyenne hands. All of the leasing profits were used to pay off the Northern Cheyenne debt (created by the Indian Bureau) and maintain agency daily operations. The end result of the leasing policy was the further alienation of the Northern Cheyenne from their land base, economic resources, and remaining source of income. The tribe was pushed into ever-increasing debt and dependency, a situation portrayed graphically in figure 4.3.

Economic dependency and malnourishment continued far beyond the 1920s and has become a part of contemporary Northern Cheyenne reservation life. The policy of supplying rations according to tribal annual income guaranteed that the Northern Cheyenne would remain in a cycle of poverty, malnourishment, dependency, and oppression. The Indian Bureau, as Boggs pointed out, "used Cheyenne resources to support its own oppressive bureaucracy, while under its management the Cheyenne people were going hungry and dying of tuberculosis and other diseases" (1984:217).

Malnutrition, Morbidity, and Mortality

The relationship between malnutrition and susceptibility to various diseases is very complex, but it is generally recognized that malnourishment has a synergistic effect on most diseases. Malnutrition increases an individual's susceptibility to, and the severity of, infection through immune system dysfunction (Hamilton, Popkin, and Spicer 1984:17). Impaired immunocompetence increases susceptibility to respiratory, dermal, intestinal, or other systemic infections. As early as 1903 Dr. Ellis P. Townsend reported on the "diseases of poverty" that were prevalent among the Northern Cheyenne: "The prominent diseases on this reservation are those of throat and lungs, eyes, skin diseases, and scrofulous enlargements of glands. . . . [E]xopthalmic goitre is predominant in both sexes. Tape worm and other worms [are] very frequent" (National Archives, RG 75, 1903).

Just as in contemporary underdeveloped countries, these infectious and parasitic diseases are directly associated with the unsanitary, malnourished, and culturally oppressive environment under which the Northern Cheyenne were forced to live. In large part these conditions were created and engendered by the BIA's assimilation mission.

Throughout the early reservation period the Northern Cheyenne continued to be plagued by many of the acute infectious diseases that they experienced aboriginally through contact with Euro-Americans. Diseases such as whooping cough, smallpox, and influenza remained prevalent during the early reservation period. Although acute infectious diseases afflicted the Northern Cheyenne, the frequency and severity of these diseases declined over time. While one might assume, as other scholars have, that the decline in frequency of some diseases was a reflection of the success of Western medicine, in reality the decline was a result of a more dynamic process.

Experiencing new political and economic conditions, the Northern Cheyenne were undergoing an epidemiological transition from more acute infectious diseases to more chronic infections in response to their changing political and economic conditions. This transition is most apparent in the appearance of trachoma, and especially tuberculosis, as the leading causes of debility and death after 1910.

Trachoma was first noted by an agency physician on the reservation in 1901, but the disease did not become a perceived health risk by the Indian Bureau for the Native American population at large until after 1910. The bureau's concern was in response to a number of surveys, conducted on reservations nationwide, indicating that the disease was of epidemic proportions, afflicting not only the young and old, but productive adults as well. The concern was not for the Indian people stricken with the disease, but that trachoma inhibited the "civilization" process.

On the Tongue River Reservation, Dr. C. H. Dewey, a special physician assigned to assess the health status of the Northern Cheyenne, noted the debilitating effects of trachoma: "The condition of the eyes on this reservation is far from satisfactory. The percentage of trachoma is nearly double that given by the public health service. The sequelae of the disease have been severe, pannus and corneal opacities are quite common and many are blind in one or both eyes" (National Archives, RG 75, 1914).

In 1893 the period prevalence rate for trachoma among the Northern Cheyenne was 31.84 per 1,000. Although this rate is relatively high, the disease reached epidemic proportions after the collapse of the reservation economy in 1911 (Pringle 1958:49). Over the next decade trachoma became endemic. The prevalence rates summarized in figure 4.4 attest to the continued severity of the disease.

Parallel to the dramatic increase in the incidence of trachoma, the morbidity of tuberculosis rose to epidemic proportions. In 1910 the agency physician estimated that at least 20 percent of the Northern Cheyenne population was infected with tuberculosis (National Archives, RG 75, Narrative Report 1910). Similar to trachoma, tuberculosis was perceived as a

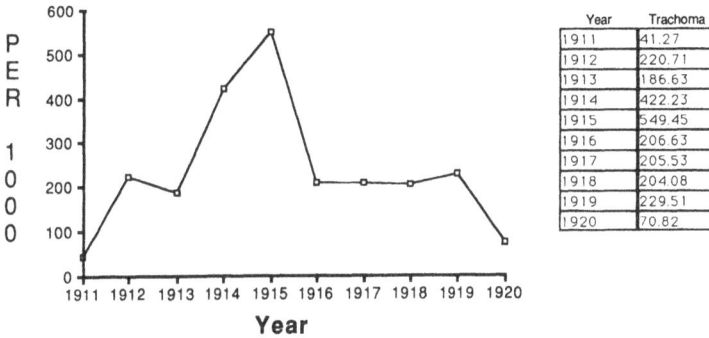

Year	Trachoma
1911	41.27
1912	220.71
1913	186.63
1914	422.23
1915	549.45
1916	206.63
1917	205.53
1918	204.08
1919	229.51
1920	70.82

Fig. 4.4. Prevalence rates for trachoma among the Northern Cheyenne, 1911–20.

health risk and treated not out of any altruism for the Cheyenne people, but because the disease inhibited economic progress and created a dependent, unproductive population.

The tuberculosis period prevalence rates presented in figure 4.5 illustrate the impact tuberculosis had on Northern Cheyenne morbidity. Unlike trachoma, which usually maimed its victims, tuberculosis was a significant cause of mortality. The epidemiological crisis is aptly illustrated in figure 4.6, which present the cause-specific death rates for tuberculosis from 1911 to 1920. In fact, the situation became so acute that by 1915, 50 percent of all deaths were caused by tuberculosis (National Archives, RG 75, Narrative Report 1916).

The high morbidity and mortality of Northern Cheyenne tuberculosis, particularly after 1914, paralleled the campaign by Superintendent Buntin to have every Northern Cheyenne family build and maintain a permanent residence. Again, the rationale behind the policy was that tipis represented a state of "savagery," whereas permanent dwellings fit the agrarian ideal of "civilization." Because of their mobility, tipis offered the Northern Cheyenne the advantage of moving when the surrounding area became unsanitary or of congregating around new economic resources that were unevenly distributed on

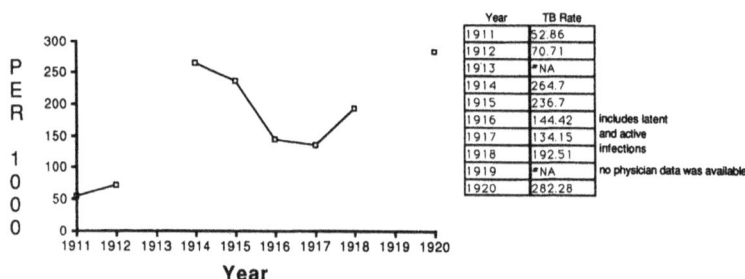

Year	TB Rate
1911	52.86
1912	70.71
1913	*NA
1914	264.7
1915	236.7
1916	144.42
1917	134.15
1918	192.51
1919	*NA
1920	282.28

includes latent and active infections

*no physician data was available

Fig. 4.5. Prevalence rates for tuberculosis among the Northern Cheyenne, 1911–20.

Year	Death Rate
1911	11.58
1912	16.42
1913	*NA
1914	23.92
1915	21.29
1916	18.56
1917	24.64
1918	24.48
1919	22.59
1920	10.62

Fig. 4.6. Cause-specific death rates from tuberculosis among the Northern Cheyenne, 1911–20.

the reservation. Either by accident or design, the superintendent failed to recognize the benefits of tipi living. Following Indian Office blueprints, each Northern Cheyenne family was strongly encouraged to build cabins. These structures were often small, crowded, and poorly designed for eastern Montana weather conditions. The cabins led to a crowded, unsanitary, disease-promoting environment. These deplorable conditions did not go unnoticed by eastern delegations who surveyed reservation living conditions.

In response to the eastern liberals' outcries about the poor health conditions on all reservations, the United States government was forced into action. Private and governmental surveys conducted between 1911 and 1914 made it clear that Indian health problems far outpaced services. One national survey, for example, noted that the death rate for Indians was 42.8 percent higher than the national average. Of 42,000 Indians examined, 16 percent had advanced cases of trachoma and 17 percent, or 6,800 Indians out of a 40,000 survey population, had clinical cases of tuberculosis (*Congressional Record* 1912). President Taft, in a message to Congress, responded to the growing political pressure and the crisis in Indian health. He recommended $253,350 to be appropriated for health care and stated that "as guardians of the welfare of the Indians, it is our immediate duty to give the race a fair chance far an unmaimed birth, a healthy childhood, and a physically efficient maturity" (*Congressional Record* 1912).

Responding to his plea, Congress appropriated only $90,000 to solve the nationwide Indian health crisis. While it is not possible to assess accurately how much of the appropriation reached the Tongue River Agency, between 1916 and 1918 the BIA launched a service-wide program in response to three of the American Indians' greatest health problems— tuberculosis, trachoma, and infant mortality (National Archives, RG 75, Narrative Report 1916). With regard to infant mortality, the bureau launched the "Save the Babies" campaign. The program was inaugurated on the Northern Cheyenne reservation that same year (National Archives, RG 75, Narrative Report 1916), and three field nurses traveled throughout the reservation to educate women with children on "proper" child care (National Archives, RG 75, Narrative Report 1917). From all indications, the program operated under the assumption that the infant mortality problem was due to cultural ignorance and incompetence of Cheyenne mothers, rather than malnutrition, unsanitary living conditions, and cultural oppression.

Between 1914 and 1920 the reported death rate for Northern Cheyenne children less than three years of age averaged 16.21 per 1,000. Infant mortality rates remained high into the 1930s, when it was reported by state epidemiologists that the Northern Cheyenne infant mortality rate was three times the prevailing rate for white Montanans (U.S. Senate, Survey 1932:12843).

During this period, a number of special state and federal government health teams visited the Northern Cheyenne to evaluate the persistence of tuberculosis. As part of one health team, Dr. H. J. Warner, the state medical director of District 2, recognized the social nature of tuberculosis on the reservation. Warner reported that "a reduction of the tuberculosis rate can be anticipated only when their economic status is such as to provide adequate food, clothing, and shelter" (Montana State Board of Health 1932:7–8). That is, only by eliminating the social origins of the infection could the biological aspects of the disease be controlled. It seems his recommendations fell on deaf ears, because to recognize the social origins of Northern Cheyenne disease would bring into focus the Indian Bureau's policies of forced assimilation as the cause of ill health.

While the Indian Bureau and Northern Cheyenne Agency physician struggled to cure these chronic afflictions, the Northern Cheyenne fell victim to the Spanish influenza epidemic of 1918–1919. Once again, the Indian Bureau's policies prompted the epidemic. Since the late 1890s the bureau had actively suppressed American Indian religious ceremonies and indigenous health practices. Methods of suppression ranged from threat of force to economic inducements in the form of agency-sponsored tribal fairs in lieu of ceremonies such as the sun dance. It was during one of these fairs that the infection was transmitted to the Northern Cheyenne by a visiting Sioux from the Standing Rock Reservation (National Archives, RG 75, Special Memorandum, 1919). The tragic impact of the epidemic was described by Belle Highwalking: "One time a great sickness came to us. We called it 'yellow sickness.' Many people died from it. So many people died that at the cemetery there were seven wagons at once waiting to bury people. . . . It was terrible" (T. Weist 1979:18).

During the 1918 Spanish influenza epidemic the agency physician contracted the virus and resigned on November 21, 1918, leaving the Northern Cheyenne without a physician to treat influenza patients. It would be two years before another permanent agency physician arrived on the Northern Cheyenne reservation (National Archives, RG 75, Report on Tongue River Agency 1920). The lack of medical care was nothing new at the Tongue River Agency. During the decade under discussion, there was no physician for five out of ten years on the reservation. This lack of medical care was compounded by confirmed reports of medical incompetency, difficulty in delivering health care because of climate and topography, lack of confidence in the physicians, and resistance among the Northern Cheyenne (National Archives, RG 75, Narrative Report 1915, 1916, 1919, 1920).

Throughout the decade, agency physicians and field matrons continued to target tuberculosis and trachoma for eradication, despite the appearance of other infectious diseases (National Archives, RG 75, Narrative Report 1920). Dr. J. R. Collard, while treating trachoma on the reservation, noting the relationship between the persistence of these two diseases and the impoverished conditions on the reservation, reported that:

although it might not be considered within my province to report on tuberculosis, so much of it was manifest in my visits at the Indian homes that I would feel remiss in my duties did I not mention the matter. This comes about by under-nourishment, poor sanitation and lack of knowledge as to its contagion. I feel that trachoma and tuberculosis on this reservation have not been given the attention they deserve during the past. (National Archives, RG 75, Medical Report 1925)

The high incidence of disease among the Northern Cheyenne was a direct consequence of their political and economic condition. Health care delivery, appropriations, and agency medical personnel were all directly linked to reservation policies of forced cultural and economic change. To adequately address the poor health of reservation residents meant a radical shift in policy mandates—it was a price that neither Washington bureaucrats nor Indian Office personnel living on the reservation were willing to pay.

Just as health was linked to the evolving underdevelopment of the Tongue River Reservation, so, too, was Northern Cheyenne population change. The deterioration of their health is directly reflected in the Northern Cheyenne's demographic change.

Demographic Structures

According to Coale (1957), a population's vital rates can be estimated from changes in the age-sex structure of a population. The changing age-sex structures reflects the Northern Cheyennes disease experience. The 1910 population pyramid for example, represented in figure 4.7, correlates with the appearance of tuberculosis in epidemic proportions. Tuberculosis mortality rates tend to be high at the 0 to 4 age cohort, but decline at the ages 5 through 9. In the older cohorts mortality rates increase, peaking in the 15 to 24 age group, especially among females. The mortality then declines until about age 45, where mortality is greater for males than females (Sutherland 1977:185). The 1910 age-sex structure conforms to the general mortality pattern of tuberculosis.

By 1915 the age-sex structure shows an expansion in the 0 to 4 age cohort, but the remainder of the population cohorts are very uneven. In some age cohorts there is a marked constriction, possibly indicating differential mortality between age and sex cohorts (figure 4.8). As figure 4.9 indicates, this trend continued up to 1920.

The diseases that the Northern Cheyenne experienced not only affected their age-sex structure, but also the patterns of their birth and death rates. The population data reveals the demographic impact that ill health and economic underde-

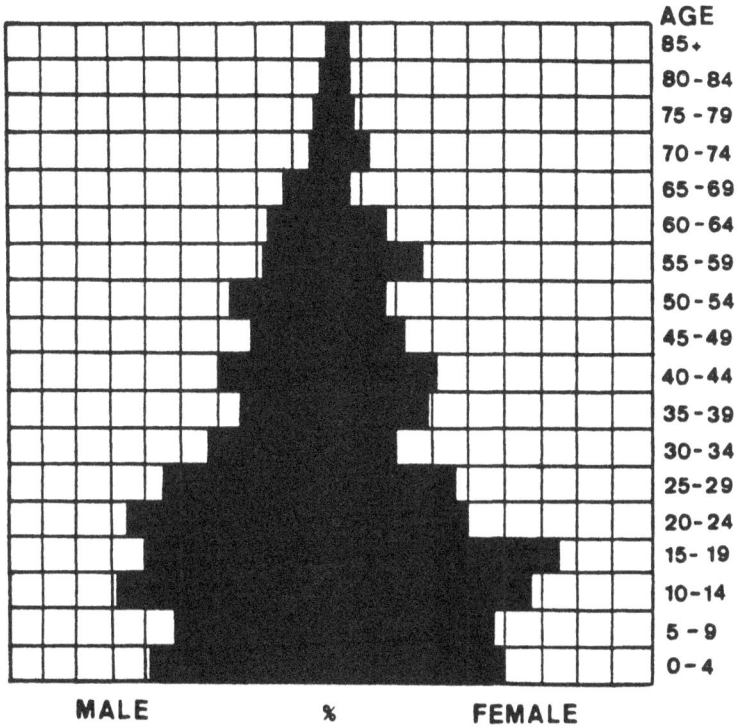

Fig. 4.7. Northern Cheyenne age-sex structure, 1910.

velopment had on the Northern Cheyenne (figure 4.10). In 1914 for example, the crude death rate (CDR) was 42.92 per 1,000. By 1920 the CDR rose to 47.14 per 1,000. As the data indicates, with the exception of 1916 and 1917, deaths exceeded births during this decade.

Compounding the mortality from tuberculosis was the 1918–1919 influenza epidemic. Although this was not the only appearance of acute infectious diseases on the reservation for this period, it certainly had the most impact on morbidity and mortality. During those years, the CDR increased

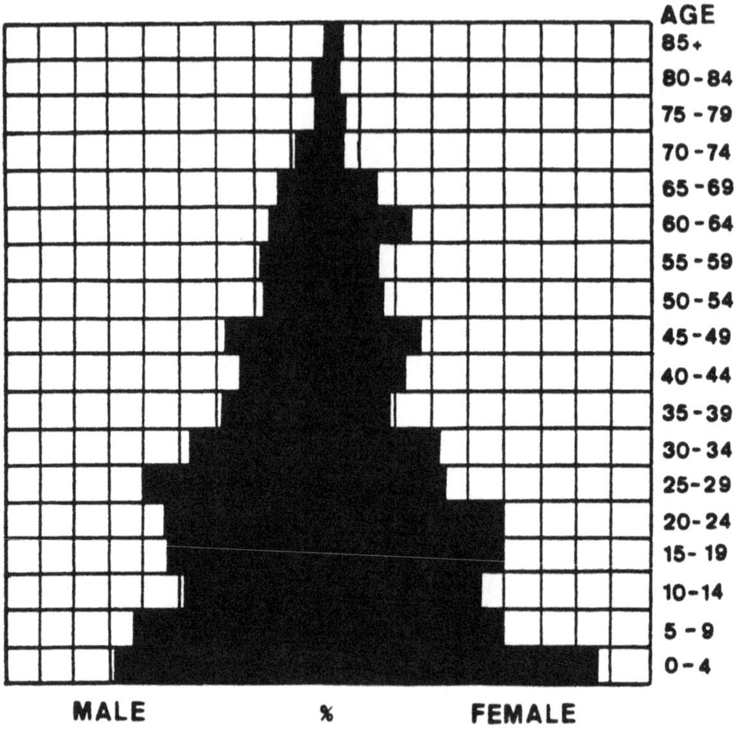

Fig. 4.8. Northern Cheyenne age-sex structure, 1915. (Nine females did not report their ages and were not included in the calculations.)

from 44.49 per 1,000 in 1917 (just before the epidemic) to 81.21 per 1,000 in 1919 (during the height of the epidemic). Concomitant with the sudden rise in mortality from influenza, the crude fertility rate dropped to 26.53 in 1918 and did not reach the pre-epidemic level until after 1920.

There is a correlation between the rate of population growth, the increase in ill health, and the reservation political economy. Demographic data collected for this decade, especially after 1911, suggest that the Northern Cheyenne population initially experienced a temporary rise in fertility and a

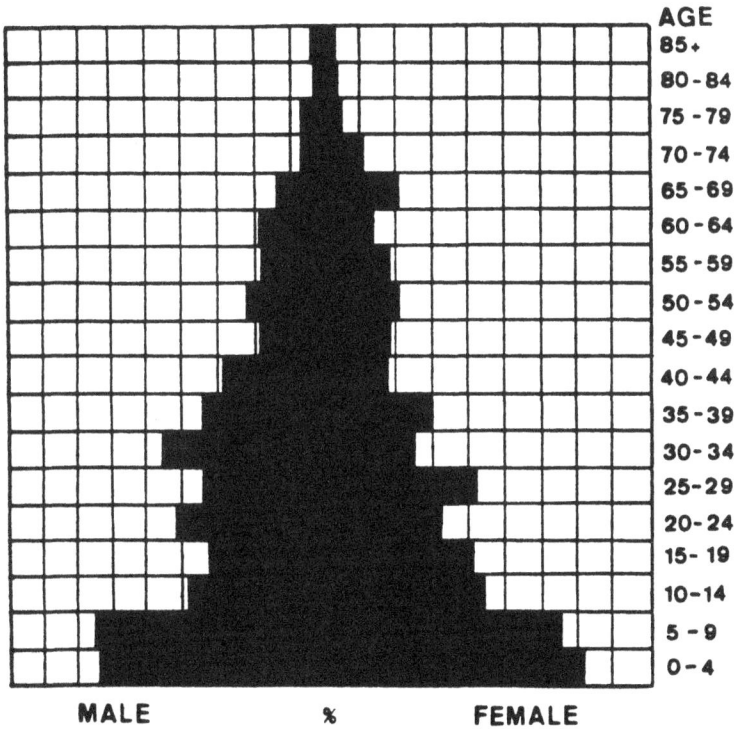

Fig. 4.9. Northern Cheyenne age-sex structure, 1920.

decrease in deaths. This increase was offset by the dramatic rise in tuberculosis deaths, beginning in 1914. Thus for this period the Northern Cheyenne population increased by only 1.9 percent.

Northern Cheyenne population growth under conditions of oppression, malnutrition, and economic underdevelopment has many parallels to the circumstances of indigenous peoples and developing nation-states today. One only needs to examine the demographic histories of various tribal societies to find striking similarities (Early and Peters 1990; Howell 1979; Hugh-Jones 1977; Romaniuk 1974; Stannard 1989;

Gregory R. Campbell

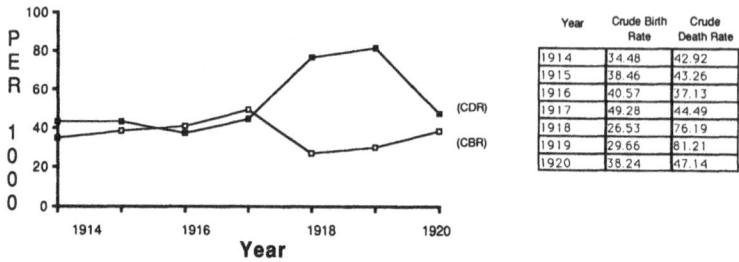

Year	Crude Birth Rate	Crude Death Rate
1914	34.48	42.92
1915	38.46	43.26
1916	40.57	37.13
1917	49.28	44.49
1918	26.53	76.19
1919	29.66	81.21
1920	38.24	47.14

Fig. 4.10. Crude rates of birth and death for the Northern Cheyenne, 1914–20.

Thornton 1987; Young 1988). Moreover, a survey of developing countries would reveal similar patterns (Grant 1989; Turshen 1984, 1990; Valentey 1977:155–64). To comprehend these parallels and similarities, we need only to approach these population histories with respect to political economy. Patterns of population change and, for that matter, health levels are linked with economic laws within a given social formation (Valentey 1977:15). All of these societies, despite their particular histories, faced similar demographic and health dilemmas as a direct result of their colonial experiences.

Summary and Conclusions

Northern Cheyenne ill health and subsequent demographic changes are the product of the underdeveloped conditions on the reservation. The Northern Cheyenne were denied the necessities of life—that is, adequate food, clothing, shelter—and experienced extreme cultural oppression. Deprived of material and social necessities, the Northern Cheyenne experienced a marked deterioration in their health status and began a demographic cycle of periodic disruption by severe mortality and rectification through a rise in fertility rates (Seccombe 1983:34). As the late Steven Polgar stated, "the greatest demographic influence of colonialism, albeit one that is not easy to recognize, derives from the imposition of Western economic dominance" (1971:4–5).

For the Northern Cheyenne, the Bureau of Indian Affairs's policy of economic self-sufficiency through assimilation created the material and social conditions for the creation and perpetuation of ill health. Yet, the destruction of Northern Cheyenne lifeways created social conditions which had consequences beyond their failing health: "By destroying the old ways and not providing acceptable alternatives, Europeans left the native in a dilemma. The native manners of coping with health problems remained unchanged while conditions, specifically, diet, and cleanliness changed around them" (Rice 1977:15).

With the imposed Western medical care system linked to Indian Office assimilation policies and the indigenous medical system actively suppressed, not only did Northern Cheyenne health practices erode, but their ideological system was partially eradicated as well. Northern Cheyenne doctors were arrested for treating patients, conducting ceremonies, and receiving gifts for their services.

What emerged from the suppression of the indigenous medical system and the marginal acceptance of the other, was the continuation of Northern Cheyenne sickness and death. Their epidemiological experience is not reflected in the demographics for this period. In general, the Northern Cheyenne population continued to increase, masking the connection between the domains of politics and economics with the continued degradation of Northern Cheyenne health.

Acknowledgments

An earlier version of this paper was delivered at the 12th International Congress of Anthropological and Ethnological Sciences, Zagreb, Yugoslavia. A number of the symposium participants provided critical commentary. I would like to thank Dr. Valery Tishkov, Dr. Immanuel Marx, and

Dr. David Aberle for their observations and criticism. Their suggestions clarified many points and are incorporated into the paper. A special debt of gratitude is owed to Dr. John H. Moore, for his constant criticism and encouragement. Finally, portions of this research were supported by an American Institute of Culture Research Grant sponsored by the American Indian Studies Center, University of California, Los Angeles, and a University Research Grant from the University of Montana.

CHAPTER 5

Natives and the Development of Mercantile Capitalism

A New Look at "Opposition" in the Eighteenth-Century Fur Trade

Bruce Alden Cox

Most studies of the North American fur trade emphasize the effects of mercantile capitalism on the Natives who became involved with it. This essay takes things the other way round, as it deals with the role played by the Native fur producers in the competition between the various European fur-trade interests. Canadian historians, in particular, have long been fascinated by the rivalries between European powers, especially France and Britain, played out in the far-flung fur trading posts of the Canadian subarctic. Nevertheless, these scholars have long failed to write convincingly, probably because they seldom have taken full account of the role of the native fur producers. This paper will look again at early scholars of the Canadian fur trade, particularly Harold Adams Innis and his critics. I will argue that this scholarship treats the Natives only as customers to be attracted from one chain of shops to another, never as active agents in their own right. Much of this critique and reanalysis will focus on Innis's classic study, *The Fur Trade in Canada,* subtitled *An Introduction to Canadian Economic History,* which was first published in 1930.

Harold Innis helped create the discipline of political economy in Canada, transforming the way Canadians think about

their history and identity. In examining his work I have come to
understand why Anthony wanted merely to bury Caesar, not to
praise him. How can we dare to carp at giants who have gone
before us? Nevertheless, the living should be served, and
founding fathers may sometimes get it wrong. In that spirit,
the historian William Eccles called for a thorough reassessment of Innis' work on the fur trade. Eccles's "Belated Review"
of *The Fur Trade in Canada* raises more issues than can be
addressed here. Prominent among them, however, is Innis's
view on the consequences of competition during the eighteenth-century fur trade. We will soon consider such consequences of competition; let me note at once, however, that
this essay is not just about Innis and his detractors. It is also
about the rival traders' customers, the Native fur producers of
the western Great Lakes and Hudson's Bay regions. In this
connection, historians have made untenable assumptions
about the Native fur producers.

Let us explore the assumptions behind the debate about the
effects of competition on fur production. Consider first what
Innis termed "the competition of cheaper goods" which "enabled Great Britain to prevail" in the fur trade (1970:391). Innis
seems to assume here that price differences would have been
decisive, that the principle of supply and demand governed
the fur trade. Rich (1960) and Ray and Freeman (1978:tables
22, 23) have produced copious evidence to counter this
assumption. We need not belabor this point here, except to
observe that if the principle of supply and demand applies,
then it should have been reflected in the trade figures: one
side or the other should get the best of it—unless there was
no difference in price or quality between French and English
suppliers (a claim nearly unknown in Canadian historical
writing).

This essay is primarily a study of the effect of competition
on fur exports, but it also will serve to test whether the principle
of supply and demand applied in the trade. Let us now turn to
the main question, however, the effect of competition, starting
with a contemporary observer.

"Opposition destroys trade, creates vice, and renders people crafty, ruins good morals and almost totally abolishes every human sentiment in both Christian and Indian." So believed W. F. Wentzel, writing in the early 1800s (Masson 1960 [1890]:1:96). Wentzel, a trader for the Montreal-based Northwest Company, set down a view adopted by nearly all scholars since his time: "opposition destroys trade." Perhaps this view held true at the time it was written, but there is no evidence to support it for the first half of the eighteenth century. Nevertheless, the view persists in much historical writing on the early fur trade. A recent commentator maintained, for example, that "had the Seven Years' War not intervened, the Hudson's Bay Company might well have been driven to the wall by the Canadians." He goes on to say, "In the eighteenth century down to the Conquest the British share in the fur trade was in steady decline." (Eccles 1979:434)

A generation or more ago Murray Lawson (1943:33) maintained that his figures from English customs entries showed "declining English (fur) exports from the colonies" during most of the eighteenth century, evidently due to French competition. In the same connection, Krech comments on what he feels was an "intense" English-French trade rivalry, with Bay Company prices "sensitive to French competition": "English-French competition was most intense in the mid–18th century when Indians traded often high-value furs for lightweight French goods and lower-value furs for durable bulky HBC goods only once every two years.... In addition, English-French competition increased gift giving and Indians received more by simply appearing at posts" (1980:641).

Although Krech stops short of claiming that this "intense" rivalry was ruinous to either party, he does claim that the fur producers "exploited" it (1980:641). Finally, even Innis (1970 [1930]:138) detected "a decline in supply of the better furs" during 1738–48 as a "result of French competition."

Did "opposition" destroy trade? This paper tries to answer that question by carefully marshalling the data available. Unfortunately, no new trade figures are available to us, nor are there likely to be any. All the more reason, then, to make careful, critical use of what we have in the way of early trade figures. And a critical reading of these data is crucial to our enterprise. We know, for example, the Montrealers seemed to increase their efforts in the western fur trade from the Treaty of Utrecht in 1713, and especially from the 1730s on (Allaire 1984; Finnegan 1980; Massicotte 1930:47). But what effect had these increased efforts by the Montrealers on the Bay Company's fur exports? Did the Bay's share of Canadian beaver exports decline until the Seven Years War began (in 1753), as Innis's critics believed? Could this decline, if it occurred, be laid at the door of the Montreal traders? And finally, what of the Native fur producers?

Certainly the outcome of competition between firms for customers depends on decisions taken by customers as well as firms. What were the intentions of the "customers" of the fur posts? Eccles argues, "All things being equal, the Indian preferred to trade with the French. They appear to have traded with the English mainly to preserve that [trading] option"[1] (1979:425n). Did the Indians judiciously weigh their options with each nation of traders? If competition were a matter of "winner-take-all," and if the Natives tended to throw their trade to one party rather than the other, this would show up as a tendency for one party to gradually gain the lion's share of Canadian beaver exports. This is the early fur trade as a zero-sum game, and most scholarly opinion has seen it in exactly those terms. But is this view accurate?

To answer this question, we need some indication of the early trade figures. The Montrealers' fur returns, for example, are found in another work by Innis, which reports beaver exports out of Quebec from 1701 until 1755 (Innis 1929:149–52 in Lawson 1943:136). Returns are scattered early on, but they are 68 percent complete (or twenty six years of thirty eight) for 1717–1755. Admittedly, beaver export figures cannot tell the whole story. They cannot, for example, account for furs smuggled past the excise officers, to say nothing of the buckskins, bearskins, martens, and so on, always a major part of the Montreal fur pack (Adair 1947). Despite their limitations, Innis's figures should give a fair gauge of French production.[2]

For an estimate of beaver exported on the Hudson's Bay Company's ships, I draw on the work of Ray and Freeman (1978:170–74), who record the number of beaver pelts collected at the Hudson's Bay forts into the 1760s (some tallies were also checked against post accounts in the HBC archives). Summing the post's returns with the Montrealers' figures gives a yearly grand total of beaver pelts exported from Canada for each of the twenty six years Innis tallied from the Quebec archives (the HBC's fiscal year ended in August, so totals for, say, 1731–1732 are entered here under 1732).

These figures are plotted on the graph of figure 5.1. From this we see that the fur trade, in this period at least, was far from being a zero-sum game, and neither party was gaining a permanent advantage over the other. On the contrary, we see in figure 5.1 that if the French managed to hold their own, so also did the English.

How can we understand the relationship shown in figure

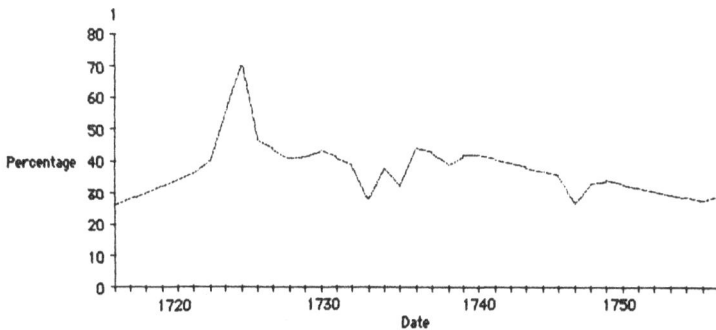

Source: Lawton (1943:136) and   Ray & Freeman (1977: Table 18)

Fig. 5.1. The Hudson's Bay Company's share of beaver exports from Canada, 1717–55. (Sources: Lawson 1943:136 and Ray and Freeman 1977:Table 18)

5.1? First, this is what we should expect to find if we are correct about Indians wishing to preserve their options. Thus, if
one party succeeded in urging the producers on to greater
efforts, the other party might benefit as well from the increase
in production. If, on the other hand, one set of posts suffered
from bad hunting weather, so likely would the other. Thus, an
unusually severe winter or an early thaw might affect the trade
of many posts, and hence the aggregate figures (Ball 1984).
So also might game cycles and epidemics of various sorts,
human and animal (Elton 1942; Kormondy 1969:96). Finally,
we cannot discount the disruption likely worked by hostilities
during the 1750s and before. Eccles remarks in this connection that during the 1700s "fur posts became a chain of garri-
soned military forts where furs had to be traded" (1979:423).
Surely the Hudson's Bay posts, and their fur producers, could
not long remain unaffected at midcentury by wars and rumors
of war. All these factors would be likely to affect both French
and English traders in the same general way, and this probably accounts for the relationship shown in figure 5.1.

Bad weather, game cycles, epidemics, and raids—these are
admittedly paltry sorts of explanations. In fact, they are worthy
of mention here only because they are likely to be dashed
aside by the grand sweep of historical generalization involving "the downfall of New France," "England with her more
efficient industrial development," and so on (Innis 1970
[1930]:391). In the great historical sweeps pictured by traditional historians, however, the Indians are given a very small
role to play. At times, to be sure, "the cultural traits of the Indians were important factors" (Innis 1970:143). We are also
reassured to learn that "the saying that the only good Indians
were dead Indians never applied to the fur trade" (Innis
1970:144).

Consider, however, the real situation. Often, as for the Plains
Cree, visits to the trading posts were fitted into a *preexisting*
network of Native trading alliances; in these networks no one
(or everyone) was a "middleman," and an eagle feather might
be as highly prized as a trade musket (Cox 1984; Milloy 1988).

All this is a far cry from Innis' view of fickle Indian customers, bargain shopping in one chain of stores or another. Their true role was much more active than that reflected in recent scholarship (e.g., Ray 1974, 1980; Milloy 1988; Judd and Ray 1980). Thus, the results shown by figure 5.1 make perfect sense if we try to see them from the point of view of the fur producers, although they may seem anomalous from the perspective which historians generally adopt. This is no small matter, and I do not wish it glossed over. We have worked through a test of Innis' assumptions, and found that they are not borne out by the figures he himself collected. I said when I began that we were here to bury Caesar, and so we have done, although I hope with fitting honor.

Acknowledgments

Many have been helpful. My thanks are due to the Hudson's Bay Company, for permission to cite materials in their archives, to Gregory Finnegan, Arthur J. Ray, and Donald Freeman, who kindly allowed me access to their fur trade statistics. Several colleagues offered advice, including Don Whyte, Bob Surtees, and S. F. Wise. Ken Innes, Wendy Watkins, and Tony Kiar helped with the statistical analyses. Funds for this study were kindly provided by Carleton's Dean of Social Sciences and the Social Science and Humanities Research Council of Canada.

CHAPTER 6

Symbiosis, Merger, and War

Contrasting Forms of Intertribal Relationship Among Historic Plains Indians

Patricia C. Albers

In contrast to the nineteenth century, when the study of politics, economy, and society were combined and integrated, a tendency in modern scholarship has been to disaggregate these elemental dimensions of the human experience and treat them as distinct realms. One necessary consequence of this has been the growth of fragmented interpretive frameworks that divorce history from nature and ethnicity from population and that, in the process, often obscure the fundamental connections that tie peoples of differing cultural backgrounds together (Albers and James 1991). Nowhere has this been more evident than in the history of ethnographic studies of intertribal relations among Plains Indians.[1]

For many years the only kind of intertribal relationship to receive serious attention in Plains Indian ethnography was warfare. Warfare was to the plains what the potlatch was to the Northwest Coast: an all-consuming theme, a configuration in Ruth Benedict's (1932) sense, that unified and gave meaning to all aspects of Plains Indian culture (Voget 1964). Although warfare received exhaustive coverage, it was evaluated in terms of its role in exclusive tribal groups. Most ethnographies contained detailed accounts of how tribal members fought in battle, prepared for combat, and rewarded the warrior, and some (Mishkin 1940; Hoebel 1960) offered elaborate descriptions of how warfare supported Native American status systems and how it united a tribe's loosely consolidated bands. Generally speaking, there was little discussion of the nature of the historical relations between those who fought.

In contrast to warfare, which was regarded as the dominant mode of intertribal relationship, peaceful contacts among Plains Indians were depicted as adventitious, taking place outside an institutionalized sphere of relationship. For the most part, intertribal trade and marriage were not taken into account in descriptions and analyses of Plains Indian culture. This sort of disregard, whether intentional or unwitting, fostered a highly fragmented view of social formations in the native Plains, one in which the supposedly cohesive and harmonious structure of the tribe was opposed to the divisive and antagonistic organization of the intertribal sector (Hoebel 1960).

Not until 1950, when Joseph Jablow's classic monograph on Cheyenne trade was published, did a study devote full attention to intertribal contacts in an arena other than warfare. This was a ground-breaking work not only because it linked Cheyenne destinies to their trading relationships with neighboring peoples, but also because it contextualized these relationships in an historically evolving regional landscape. Since Jablow's pioneering monograph, numerous writings have appeared on the historic intertribal relations of Plains Indians. Most of these studies (Schmitt 1950; Ewers 1954, 1969, 1975; Lange 1957; Pope 1966; Kenner 1969; Dempsey 1972; Wood 1972, 1973; Ray 1974; Giannettino 1977; Klein 1977; Loscheider 1977; Sharrock 1977; K. Weist 1977; Fromhold 1981; Springer 1981; Biolsi 1984; Thistle 1986; Hanson 1987; Judy 1987; Schilz 1988; Milloy 1988; McCullough 1990) focus on trade and military alliances, but some (Bowers 1965; Bruner 1961; Bittle 1971; Albers 1974; Sharrock 1974; Taylor 1977; Weist 1977; Wood and Downer 1977; Hanson 1986, 1987; Albers and Kay 1987; Moore 1988) have documented intertribal relations in the areas of kinship, residency, and territorial use. These studies, along with evidence from other regions of North America,[2] indicate that even though American Indian populations maintained distinct ethnic identities and even differentiated cultural patterns, they did so while embedded in geographically far-ranging and ethnically mixed social formations. Whether constituted in war or peace, the intertribal ties that linked various Indian populations were not haphazard. They were institutionalized, and they created social formations in which relations between different tribes and relations internal to each group were mutually interdependent (Elmendorf 1971:354).

Most of the work that has been done on intertribal relations among historic Plains Indians has been descriptive and particularistic, however. It has described which populations were linked to each other, how they were related, and some of the conditions under which relations were established at particular moments in history. Where interpretive analysis has been undertaken, much of it has drawn heavily on alliance and exchange theory.[3] Here intertribal relationships are understood primarily in terms of the character of their exchanges in raiding, trading, and ceremonious giving. The problem with this is that intertribal relationships among historic American Indians were not simply the sum of their alliances and underlying exchange transactions. Although raiding and other forms of self-interested seizure prevailed in settings of war, it was not uncommon for enemies to trade and exchange gifts. Since different kinds of reciprocity coexisted and appeared across a variety of different types of relationship, exchange was not a definitive criterion. That contradictory forms of exchange existed between different tribes at the same moment in time is well documented, but the paradox has never been adequately explained because the very terms of most exchange-alliance models are tautological. In a framework where raiding begets war and war begets raiding, there is no entry point in an analysis beyond the isomorphic terms of the exchange.

When intertribal relations are reduced to a set of exchange

transactions, it is easy to isolate them and analyze them apart from both the historical and material conditions in which they were constituted. In so doing, the dynamic processes that changed these relations over time and that integrated them into regionally based social formations are obscured. This paper represents a beginning attempt to develop an interpretive framework for understanding some of the dynamics underlying intertribal relationships among Plains Indian populations during the historic period (circa 1670–1870). Drawing on an historical materialist methodology, its purpose is to show how the intertribal ties of Plains Indians were based on a fundamental interdependence in the appropriation of labor, land, and resources and to further demonstrate how this appropriation was organized through alliance making and exchanges within local social formations.

Toward a Political Economy of Intertribal Relations

Among the historic Plains Indians local populations were integrated in a series of distinct but overlapping regional social formations where geographically contiguous ethnic groups accommodated themselves to each other's presence in varied ways. At their most fundamental level, these formations organized the mode of production, and they did so not only at the level of a division of labor but also in relation to the distribution of products that resulted from this labor. As a means of appropriating as well as distributing labor and resources, these formations were constituted in and constitutive of the social relations of production.

Heuristically, the relations of production which organized ethnically diverse groups in a series of regionally integrated social formations can be represented by a tripartite division of contrasting forms of interdependence. On one end were relations based on war where groups divided and competed with one another over access to land, labor, and other resources. At the opposite end were relationships of merger where groups joined together and cooperated in the use of a shared resource base. Towards the middle were relationships built on symbiosis. Here groups were separated, but they maintained interdependence through a specialized division of labor and/ or functionally differentiated positions in a wider circulation of commodities. Each of these forms of interdependence stipulated different ways groups jointly appropriated resources and organized their populations in relation to them.

The social relations which linked tribes together were based primarily on ties of kinship and sodality. On the plains, as in other areas of North America (Goldman 1941; Hickerson 1960; Walker 1967; Elmendorf 1971; Burch and Correll 1972; Albers and Kay 1987), relationships did not exist on a random basis among anonymous social parties; they were always embedded in some kind of social nexus. Kinship was one of the constituting idioms through which multiple tribal groups were connected in wider, regional social formations (Bruner 1961; Albers 1974; Sharrock 1974; Albers and Kay 1987; Moore 1988). Following Eric Wolf, kinship is viewed "as a way of committing social labor to the transformation of nature through appeals to filiation and marriage and to consanguinity and affinity" (1982:91). In the band as well as lineage-type organizations of Plains Indians, kinship mobilized and committed people of varying ethnic backgrounds to a common, opposed, or differentiated labor of transforming natural resources into socially useful products. Given its ubiquitous character, kinship was an ideal medium through which to recruit labor across diverse language and cultural groupings.[4]

Another important kind of social tie that played an increasingly important role among the historic Plains Indians was based on friendship and fictive kinship. Membership in many ritual and military sodalities involved formal patterns of adoption which were modeled after a sibling or parent-child relationship. Although having no biological basis, ties of sodality were often as compelling in their reciprocal obligations as those based on kinship. Depending on how they were formulated, they could activate social labor in the deployment of resources within and across ethnic group boundaries (Bowers 1950, 1965; Bruner 1961; Oliver 1962; Eggan 1966; Klein 1977; Maxwell 1979; Hanson 1987).

Whatever their defining social character, intertribal relationships were multistranded. They embodied diverse domains of activity from the economic and political to the social and ceremonial (K. Weist 1977:35). Since these different domains were collapsed, so to speak, within a single structural thread, all were responsive simultaneously to the effects of material forces operating at a given point in time (Wolf 1982:91-92). Although anthropologists commonly separate these domains, such that trade is singled out and handled apart from marriage, this tends to obscure the dominant character of the interdependence that linked any two groups together. When populations stood in a symbiotic relationship, for example, intermarriage and fictive kinship established the chain of social connections through which an interdependence was realized in the production and exchange of specialized goods.

Even though interactions including those based on trade did take place in the absence of some preestablished relationship, these were what Weist (K. Weist 1977:35) calls "encounters." Many historic Plains tribes engaged in brief and episodic forms of contact. They met at trade fairs, on the battlefield, or in treaty councils where they engaged in isolated exchanges. These intermittent exchanges, however, were not the stuff of which well-established relationships were built. No matter how an intertribal relationship was constituted, it involved three things: 1) a developed pattern of interdependence, in which 2) labor and resources were recruited through formalized social ties, and in which 3) exchange was carried on in a continuous, though not always consistent, fashion.

Among historic Plains Indian populations, each of the three types of exchange (generalized, balanced, negative), described in Marshall Sahlins's (1972:185–223) model of reciprocity, emerged under relationships based on war (competition), merger (cooperation), and symbiosis (complementarity). When a particular type of exchange (such as negative reciprocity) took place in a relationship based on symbiosis, its origins and effects were different than under a state of war. In intertribal settings (and intratribal as well), it is argued that both the formal properties of social relations and the ways in which social labor were activated through exchange varied according to the kinds of productive interdependence that linked two or more parties together.

Even though the character of intertribal relationships and their underlying exchanges were strongly associated with and responsive to existing material forces, they were not passive. The terms of relationship between two groups had an important impact on the way in which a contiguous natural environment was utilized. Over time, a given pattern of relationship could bring about environmental change, stimulate a shift in the kinds of exchanges through which labor and resources were circulated, and in the end, promote a transformation in the character of the relationship itself. In the remaining portions of this paper, I describe the material conditions of contrasting and changing forms of interdependence among Plains tribes, and I also discuss some of the terms of alliance and exchange through which this interdependence was realized and transformed.

Symbiosis, Trading, and Complementarity

Throughout much of the historic era, Plains Indians were linked to one or more of their neighbors through some kind of symbiotic bond. In symbiotic relationships the interdependence of local groups rested on their functionally differentiated positions in production and/or distribution. The nature of these relationships and the trade that accompanied them were affected profoundly by European markets and their commodities. These markets not only influenced the character of interdependence through the types of commodities coming from commercial centers but also through the kinds of surplus products that native groups appropriated for this trade. The patterns of appropriation which evolved in symbiotic relationships were historically as well as geographically varied, but in all instances they connected Plains Indians in a complex and ever-changing network of interdependency.

The Historical Conditions of Symbiosis. The earliest and most basic kind of specialization revolved around the production of foodstuffs. The contrastive features of the plains, open prairie and sheltered riverine environments, fostered a division of labor in food production (Wedel 1941). Sedentary villagers living in the river valleys produced a surplus of corn and other agricultural products to trade for the meats and hides of the prairie-dwelling nomads. This kind of symbiosis dominated relations between the region's horticulturalists and their nomadic neighbors in prehistoric and protohistoric times (Jablow 1951:39–44; Ewers 1954; Holder 1970:105–16; Wood 1973; Hanson 1987:39). Specialization in the production and exchange of food was the oldest and most stable kind of symbiosis in the region. It continued after the arrival of Europeans, and it persisted even after reservations were formed (Ewers 1968:22). By and large the food traffic was locally integrated, involving direct exchanges between adjacent sedentary and nomadic producers (Ewers 1969:21).

Superimposed on an interdependence in food production was a much more complex and far-ranging trade in durable goods that also had prehistoric antecedents. A wide variety of items entered this traffic, and they were transmitted to areas far removed from their places of origin. Until the beginning of the eighteenth century most of the durable goods circulating in the region were native in origin. Stones, shells, feathers, and medicinal herbs were among many different items that were locally produced and distributed through trade networks blanketing the plains and surrounding areas (Wood 1972, 1973).

The appearance of European commodities, especially horses and guns, had a major impact on the character of symbiotic relationships. After horses and guns were introduced through native trade networks, they became primary instruments in warfare and production. By revolutionizing subsistence and military techniques, the horse and gun introduced a new dimension into intertribal relations. If tribes did not have these objects, they stood little chance of surviving in the face of those who did (Jablow 1951; Newcomb 1950; Secoy 1953; Klein 1977; Hanson 1987). Since access to the horse and gun were critical to every group's survival, their very presence locked groups into an inextricable web of interdependency.[5]

The magnified interdependence of Plains tribes resulted not only from pressures exerted by guns and horses but also from the markets which secured access to these commodities. In order for Plains tribes to obtain and restock their supplies of horses, guns, and other European trade commodities, they had to meet the demands of the European trade. Whether this commerce operated under the mercantile capitalism of the British, French, and Americans, or under the feudal encomienda of the Spanish, it had two immediate sorts of consequences. On the one hand, native economic activity was focused on the production of goods (slaves, furs, hides) demanded in Europeans markets. And on the other hand, these items were produced in excess of what native groups needed for their own use or for simple exchanges with their neighbors. The specialized and surplus production of goods for mercantile markets set into motion a chain of effects which had far-reaching repercussions on native political economies (Jablow 1950).

For a wide variety of reasons described elsewhere (Jablow 1951; Ray 1974; Klein 1977; Milloy 1988), most tribes on the plains and surrounding areas were unable to maintain their dependence on European markets in an autonomous way. They were forced to involve others, directly or indirectly, in the process of appropriating specialized surpluses. This was done through a number of different strategies. In one option, groups continued to produce for the market directly, but to do so, they had to migrate to more favorable locations, either displacing or merging with peoples in their path. In another alternative, groups moved from the role of producer to that of middleman. Here, groups extracted surplus by expanding the range of their symbiotic ties with hinterland populations.

Whichever strategy was used, enough surplus had to be extracted for groups to meet their own commodity needs, those of their neighbors, and the added profits of European traders. When more and more tribes became dependent on the market and its commodities, the whole pattern of specialization in the production and distribution of durable goods was altered.

The kinds of specialized roles that Plains Indians assumed under the domination of European markets varied. Groups who lived on the southwestern perimeters of the plains specialized in supplying horses to the region. Those who occupied lands on its northeastern borders were major suppliers of guns and other European trade goods. Around 1750 the frontiers of the horse and gun traffic overlapped, and a new indigenously controlled trade network was spawned in the midsections of the plains. Here, groups like the Cheyenne and Crow functioned entirely as middlemen, intercepting the flow of horses against guns. It was through these middlemen connections that the entire plains became integrated into a regional trade system (Jablow 1950; Ewers 1954; Wood 1973; Malouf and Findley 1986).

In this system, groups with essentially identical subsistence economies were placed in a symbiotic relationship. Among foragers, complementary ties existed in the horse and gun trade as in the relations between Cheyenne and Kiowa (Jablow 1950:58–61), and they were present in the exchange of furs against guns as in the eighteenth century links between Cree and Blackfeet (Ray 1974:59–60; Milloy 1988:5–20). In addition, the bonds between foragers and horticulturalists were intensified by the presence of symbiotic ties in areas other than food production. In fact, among the upper Missouri villagers the traffic in European goods came to occupy a dominant position, overriding a much older interdependence in food staples (Klein 1977:433).

During historic times there were intense pressures on tribes to specialize in the production of commodities for trade. Although single populations can successfully alternate between hunting and farming when they are producing for their own needs, it is doubtful whether such alternation is feasible when production is geared towards the accumulation of specialized surpluses destined for outside markets. The transition of the Cheyenne from semisedentary horticulturalists to full-scale equestrian, buffalo-hunting nomads is an excellent example of a case where specialization maximized their position in the horse-gun traffic west of the Missouri (Jablow 1950; Moore 1988), and the separation of the Crow from the Hidatsa is probably a case in point as well (Wood and Downer 1977). When populations enter into surplus production, even if only for purposes of provisioning their neighbors, they must meet the demand or forfeit a controlling place in its distribution. When indigenous populations began producing for a market as well, the necessity of specialization was magnified, not only because higher levels of surplus had to be generated, but also because competition was increased among groups with identical procurement strategies (Hanson 1987:39).

By the end of the eighteenth century, a distinctive pattern of Plains regional integration had evolved, joining horse and gun suppliers. It was a pattern associated with social formations built on a series of competitive trade networks with dyadic (chain-like) properties that ran a parallel southwest to northeast course over the entire length of the plains. The geographic routes covered by the trade chains remained fairly stable, although the tribes who composed them often changed. Given the distances covered by these chains, not all tribes situated in the same route were in contact with each other. It was only adjacent tribes who maintained symbiotic relationships. Associations among distantly removed tribes were "encounters," and they were arranged through intermediaries. But even though all of the tribes in the same trade chain were not in contact, they were nonetheless interdependent (Jablow 1950; Ewers 1954, 1969; Wood 1972; Giannettino 1977; Klein 1977; Hanson 1987; Milloy 1988).

There is no question that the historic trade system that

embedded Plains Indians in a complex web of interdependence rested largely on indigenous forms of procurement and exchange. It is also clear that this system was capable of amassing large and stable surpluses (Klein 1977:431; Hanson 1987:51). Yet, for a number of different reasons elaborated upon by Arthur Ray (1974:63–70), Euro-American traders were not able to realize enough profit through the use of native trade connections. In order to increase their profit margins, traders began to bypass the middlemen and extract surplus directly from producers in hinterland areas. When this happened in the early nineteenth century, the symbiotic relationships connecting many tribes began to break down, and other forms of relationship dominated.

The Dynamics of Balanced Exchange. No matter what kinds of symbiotic ties connected Plains tribes, their specialized products were exchanged, at least theoretically, in a balanced fashion. There were two patterns of exchange, identified by Jablow (1950:46) as "ceremonial" and "individual." The ceremonial pattern, also known as the "calumet ceremony" or "trading on the pipe," was a highly ritualized and collectively negotiated exchange (Bowers 1950:329–31; Weltfish 1965:211–12; Fletcher and La Flesche 1972, 2:378–88; Springer 1981). Although ceremonial exchanges were conducted in a liberal fashion and were often phrased as "gift giving" rather than trading, it is clear from the accounts of Tabeau (Abel 1939:158) and Mackenzie (Masson 1961:391) that a trade was not concluded until both parties received what they considered a satisfactory return on goods given. In contrast to the ceremonial trade, which was accompanied by speeches, feasts, and dancing, the individual trade was less ritualized and was conducted in a one-to-one manner. This trade usually followed the more ceremonious exchanges, although by the mid-nineteenth century it often took place in the absence of ritual presentations. Of the two exchange patterns, the individual trade was probably more akin to barter. Nonetheless, both involved quid pro quo transactions in which an immediate and more or less equivalent return was expected for goods given (Jablow 1950:46–48; Klein 1977: 119–33).

Closely associated with the ceremonial trade pattern, and in some instances identified with it, was an exchange strategy that was putatively more altruistic in nature. Often called "suing for peace" or "pony smoking," this tactic involved elaborate gift giving for which there was no immediate expectation of return. Reciprocity was anticipated, no doubt, but the time and amount of return were left unspecified. This clearly contrasts with the ceremonial trade, where despite the existence of liberal giving, reciprocity of some sort was demanded at the time of exchange (Klein 1977:233–37). Ritual smoking and its accompanying gift presentations took place in a number of different contexts. When tribes occupied an advantageous position vis à vis the European trade, smoking was a tactic for increasing the range of their symbiotic relationships with groups who were either strangers or erstwhile enemies (Klein 1977:236; K. Weist 1977:42–45; Springer 1981).

Smoking was even used among tribes who were long-standing trade partners. In an area like the plains, where there was considerable competition among tribes in securing favorable places in the horse and gun traffic, there was no assurance that tribes who traded one year would be in a position to trade the next. The interdependency of two tribes had to be continuously reaffirmed at each and every trade encounter (Klein 1977:235). Finally, smoking was a way in which tribes could acquire needed goods when they had nothing to give in return. Not uncommonly, groups in need would call upon well-established trade partners for assistance, or they would forge connections with new partners who had a better and/or more reliable supply of commodities (Klein 1977:233–37).

Notwithstanding its obvious sociopolitical overtones, giving had important economic implications which cannot be ignored. One consequence of giving was that it increased the elasticity of a symbiotic bond. As Marshall Sahlins (1972:220–

23) argues, relations based on balanced exchange are fragile. They are vulnerable to disruption because, even under the best of circumstances, it is difficult to maintain an exact equivalency in the value and/or amount of goods under exchange. This was especially true in historic Plains tribes, where there were considerable fluctuations among tribes in the nature and volume of goods which they could make available for trade. Under unstable conditions it was not always possible for tribes to achieve an even balance in their short-term trading encounters. But, if in the long run tribes were to continue their trading and the wider symbiotic relationships in which this trade was embedded, the potential brittleness of balanced exchange had to be compensated for. One way this could be done, according to Sahlins (1972:304–11), was by allowing for delays in reciprocation. Since gift giving implied delayed returns, it permitted groups to more flexibly adjust their exchanges to temporary imbalances in the wider distribution and flow of commodities.

Gift giving also has another important effect: it can rapidly increase the total volume of goods in circulation. Because of its asymmetrical structure, giving can drive up the amount of goods needed to complete an exchange cycle in a way that balanced reciprocity cannot. In Sahlins's (1972:304–11) argument, giving is a much more diplomatic strategy through which to shift not only the volume but also the exchange rates of goods in circulation. The elaborate ceremonial giving which accompanied "trading on the pipe" and "smoking" may have been one of the means by which Plains Indians increased the level of surplus production needed for the European trade (Bowers 1965:47–50; Klein 1977:233–37; Hanson 1987:51). Gift giving, however, acted only as a stimulus—motivating one party to increase its surplus production to match the over-generosity of the other. The real force behind the expansion was the market and its commodities. That the calumet ceremonies and pony smokes may have been routes through which surplus was increased is not only implied in the Plains material, but it is also suggested by the history of the Great Lakes' feast of the dead, which followed a spiraling inflationary path after European contact (Hickerson 1960).

Even though tribes in symbiotic relations were related to each other through varying social ties, and although they affirmed their solidarity through gift presentations and trade, they were not above raiding one another. The coexistence of giving and trading with an exchange strategy based on theft appears, at first glance, as a paradox. But under closer scrutiny, it becomes obvious that acts of antagonism and goodwill are not always mutually exclusive. As a matter of fact, despite their different appearances, these acts perform similar functions in complementary alliances.

Raiding was another means of expanding the elasticity of a complementary bond. Under complementarity, raiding was not a negation of trade but an alternative to it. Like giving, raiding was a mechanism for resolving short-term imbalances in the distribution of goods. Among Plains Indians horses were the primary objects of raids, but women and children, foodstuffs, and other items were also fair game. Stealing horses was an endemic feature of relations not only among nomads but also among horticulturalists, and looting the food caches of the horticulturalists was a periodic activity of the nomads. Whenever tribes required goods for which they had nothing to give in return, it was not uncommon for them to seize what they needed. Although enemy tribes were the prime target of raid activity, trade partners were not immune (Jablow 1950:51–60; Holder 1970:116–17; Klein 1977:214–23).

A question obviously emerges: How could groups who relied on each other engage in antagonistic acts without jeopardizing their interdependency? The answer lies, in part, in the nature of their complementary ties. In most instances, raiding among groups in symbiotic relations was restrained. Jablow (1950:51–56) argues that the Cheyenne could not steal from the upper Missouri horticulturalists with impunity, if they expected them to take horses in exchange for European commodities. Since the Cheyenne were not well placed vis à vis the British and French trade, they could ill afford to alienate those groups who were their sole supply of guns and other valued trade goods. It was only tribes like the Teton, who had two separate trade sources, that could afford to raid the horticulturalists with abandon and then continue to trade with them when necessary. Thus, the positioning of tribes in relation to European trade centers was a critical factor in defining the character of their complementary bonds. It was also important in determining how far such ties could be stretched without being destroyed.

Raiding also played a significant role in the production of surplus, especially in horses. Stealing horses was as much an act of production as it was an exchange transaction (Klein 1977:214–15). Horses occupied a dual position in native economies, not only as instruments of hunting and defense, but also as commodities that could be exchanged for other goods (Albers and James 1986:92; McCullough 1990). Since horses were stolen at their source, they could be accumulated by theft everywhere without radically disrupting the trade of other goods. In fact, horses were the only items which could be appropriated through a mode of reciprocity that was indefinitely imbalanced. Yet the economic "causes" of horse theft have been debated at length in the literature. For years it was assumed that since raiding took place among tribes who were well supplied with horses, the motivation to raid could not be based on economic necessity. Instead, the explanation had to be located in the status and prestige systems of Plains tribes. This argument, as advanced by Frank Secoy (1953: 86–95), overlooks one critical fact—that horses were important commodities in commercial markets, not only to supply traders and later caravans of settlers crossing the plains but also to outfit military troops (Albers and James 1985, 1991; McCullough 1990). As Jablow (1950:58–69) correctly surmises, the accelerating demand for horses in nineteenth-century markets was a sufficient stimulus for the continued existence, indeed the expansion, of the entire raiding complex. Thus, even though Plains tribes may have had sufficient horses to meet their own requirements, they did not have enough to supply the market as well.

The presence of a market with insatiable needs and ever-changing commodity demands cannot be dismissed in any analysis of the historic Plains tribes. Plains Indians were under severe pressure to secure trade goods and the products that bought these in European markets. Such pressure must have strained symbiotic relationships to their limits, and without some sort of built-in elasticity, as provided by giving and raiding, balanced reciprocity might not have persisted as a viable form of intertribal exchange. The very flexibility of their exchange transactions allowed Plains Indians to maintain a long-term interdependence, despite momentary imbalances in the flow of goods, and it also permitted them to sustain fairly even-handed alliances while expanding the volume of surplus in production.

Complementary Patterns of Alliance Making. Although specializations in production and distribution were the corner-stone of symbiotic relations among historic Plains Indians, it can be argued that this sort of functional differentiation was not sufficient to keep groups dependent on each other. If symbiotic relationships were to be viable over extended periods of time, social and political mechanisms had to be devised that could simultaneously join and separate populations with economically specialized roles. One way this can be done is through restricted or complementary forms of alliance making that, as Peter Ekeh (1974:49–56) persuasively argues, create structures in which parties are integrated but separated at the same time.

Throughout the historic era populations in symbiotic relationships exchanged their specialized products through established social channels created either by marriage or fictive adoption (Jablow 1950:49; Bruner 1961:201; Wood 1972: 162–63; Sharrock 1974:105-11; Springer 1981; Albers and Kay 1987). Regrettably, detailed descriptions on the character of marriages between groups in symbiotic relationships are not forthcoming in the literature, although John Moore (1988:

263) reports that among the Cheyenne marriages took place primarily between the leading families of different bands. If these marriages had any relation to those between Indians and white fur traders, it is likely that the unions were arranged by fathers and cemented by gift presentations committing both parties to a long-term cycle of reciprocal obligation (Van Kirk 1980:35–39; K. Weist 1983:44; Moore 1988:186). And just as the calumet ceremony was used in adoptions of white traders (Anderson 1984:3), so was it also associated with interethnic alliances built on marriage (Van Kirk 1980:37).

There is much better information, however, on adoption practices. When the Hidatsa traded with outsiders, for example, they adopted prominent members of foreign groups as "sons." Once adopted, the father and son became the leaders of their respective groups whenever a trading encounter was arranged (Bowers 1965:47–50). Father-son adoption and its associated calumet ceremony was a major channel through which Plains Indians mobilized labor to produce wealth for trade, and at least among the Hidatsa, these adoptions also provided one of the avenues through which men achieved positions of leadership in their villages (Hanson 1987:40, 51). Father-son adoptions were common occurrences, and those Hidatsa who initiated and maintained them with many different bands and villages were highly esteemed (Bowers 1965:91). Similar forms of adoption have been reported for the Pawnee (Weltfish 1965:211–12), the Mandan (Bowers 1950:329–31; Bruner 1961:201), and the Omaha (Fletcher and La Flesche 1972, 2:378–79). As opposed to "sibling" adoption and other cooperative forms of alliance making, which are described below, father-son adoptions placed the parties in symmetrically defined social roles. It can be argued that this symmetry contributed to the elasticity of trading partnerships as well because it created an enduring structural bond that made short-term indebtedness possible. When nomadic "sons" traded with village "fathers," for example, they could appeal to the social tie between them to make allowances in the time and amount of their reciprocation.[6]

Another interesting aspect of father-son adoption, as described by Bowers (1965:211), was its association with a distinct concept of property rights. The exchange in ritual adoptions involved a complete alienation of property, where the original owners relinquished all of their rights to the sacred objects being transferred. If a similar concept of property governed trade partnerships under a "father-son" model, which it probably did, then the nature of people's mutual rights in labor and resources were specified by the particular kind of social alliance between them.

Although the complementary alliances of Plains Indians were elastic, they were not able to withstand major disruptions in the production and/or circulation of goods. When the foundation upon which groups formed a complementary tie—symbiosis—was destroyed, not even a highly flexible pattern of reciprocity was able to tolerate the change. The overall nature of the alliance became altered. In the absence of symbiosis, relations between Plains tribes shifted to the opposite ends of the structural continuum where they were transformed into either merger and cooperation, or war and competition.

Merger, Sharing, and Cooperation

Until very recently merger has been the least understood type of intertribal relationship. Available data indicate that merger, like war, developed in the absence of specialization. But instead of groups fighting over access to land and trade routes, they joined together and protected their mutual interests against outside intrusion.

In two instances of merger, small tribes became incorporated into the body politic of larger ones: the Kiowa-Apache and Sarcee maintained their ethnic distinctiveness while intermarrying and living in tandem with the Kiowa and Blackfeet respectively (Jenness 1932; Brant 1949, 1953; Bittle 1971). The case of the Assiniboin and Cree, on the other hand, represents a widely based and fully integrated pattern of fusion.

Large segments of these populations were so intermingled in residence and so mixed through marriage that it became nearly impossible to tell them apart. In fact, by the mid-nineteenth century, economic, social, and political differences appear to have been obliterated among certain segments of these two tribes. Once this happened, ethnicity had little significance in local settlement organization (Sharrock 1974; Albers and Kay 1987).

Similarly, the merger of the Hidatsa and Mandan during the same period involved a widespread institutional integration of the two populations (Bowers 1950, 1965; Hanson 1986, 1987). The Teton and Cheyenne illustrate another merger pattern, in which integration was more narrowly based, encompassing only certain bands. These two populations joined together in large-scale military excursions, they collaborated in communal buffalo hunts, and they attended each other's sun dances. Ethnic mixing took place under the aegis of each tribal group—so that the merged bands became identified either with the Cheyenne or the Teton (Moore 1988). The presence of Atsina in Arapaho camps (Flannery 1953, 1:124–25) and the movement of some Nez Percé into Crow territory (Marquis 1974:89, 97–98) probably followed a similar pattern. And unlike the Cree-Assiniboin situation, hybridized and politically distinct populations did not emerge.

The Historical Conditions of Merger. Merger is recognizable as a distinct relationship only in situations where members of separate tribes functioned, for all intents and purposes, as one political-economic unit. Otherwise, it took on characteristics that were not very different from those associated with symbiosis. A use of common territory, unified alliances against shared enemies, mutual collaboration in ceremony, intermarriage, and coresidency were found under merger as well as symbiosis. But the fact that merger evolved under conditions of economic parallelism rather than differentiation had an important impact on patterns of interdependence, exchange, and alliance.

Conditions for merger were most apparent among Plains

Indians in the years after 1820, when Euro-American traders began bypassing native middlemen and locating themselves at the various crossroads of the plains. Now that traders appropriated their goods directly from native producers, most tribes had direct access to one or more trading posts. Except for some tribes in the far southern plains, the majority were able to secure guns and other trade commodities independently of their neighbors. The horse was the only item which remained in the hands of native middlemen, and this product was acquired increasingly through theft rather than trade (Ewers 1969; Albers and James 1985:92). Once the interdependence created by the traffic in horses and guns was undermined, symbiosis was no longer a major type of intertribal relationship among the Plains Indians.

Although native populations no longer relied on one another for access to trade commodities, they still depended on one or more of their neighbors in advancing and protecting land-use rights. The whole production process underlying the traffic in buffalo hide and meat provisions placed severe pressures on the bison territories of Plains Indian populations (Ray 1974; Milloy 1988). The amount of territory needed by populations to sustain their own needs was probably very different from that required when groups were producing for a market. By the early nineteenth century, the growing competition over buffalo, coupled with the animals' wide-ranging habits and dwindling numbers, may have conditioned the Plains tribes to form the loosely structured intertribal coalitions that became so common after 1820. Most of these coalitions took on the appearance of clustered network formations built around segments of different tribes who banded together and jointly protected access to territory as well as trading posts (Sharrock 1974; Ewers 1975; K. Weist 1977; Albers and Kay 1987; Moore 1988).

As Sharrock (1974:117–19) argues, these coalitions were organized segmentally, with local groups forming large political economic units and subdividing into smaller ones as circumstances warranted. Within each coalition, the prevailing relationships were built on shared rather than symbiotic interests (Albers and Kay 1987). This created a situation where large blocks of territory were covered by peoples whose conditions of alliance were based on identical rather than differentiated economic pursuits.

The question then becomes: If both merger and war existed in the absence of specialization, what determined whether two groups fused or fought? One of the primary contributing factors appears to have been demographic. When European traders penetrated farther on the plains, they spread diseases that ravaged native populations. Since many epidemic outbreaks followed closely the paths of the traders, it is often difficult to separate economic from demographic effects. As John Taylor's (1977) and Michael Trimble's (1986) data clearly demonstrate, intertribal realignments frequently occurred in the aftermath of an epidemic. In some instances, epidemics appear to have accelerated ongoing change in intertribal relations. Thus, in the case of the Assiniboin and Cree, merger tendencies were evident well before the 1837–1838 smallpox epidemic wiped out large numbers of Assiniboin. But it was not until the years after the epidemic that large segments of these two populations become fully merged (Sharrock 1974; Albers and Kay 1987). The situation of the Arikara in the 1772–1790 epidemics illustrates another effect. After the Arikara's population declined, they were unable to defend themselves against the growing encroachments of their neighboring trade partners, the Teton, and they were forced to seek refuge among neighboring horticultural tribes. Had the Arikara not experienced such a large and sudden loss in population, it is probable that they would have thwarted Teton advances and maintained their hold over a strategic position in the Missouri River trade. In this case, the epidemic clearly spawned Arikara migrations and eventual merger with the Hidatsa and the Mandan (Taylor 1977).

Dynamics of Generalized Exchange. Under merger, reciprocity was based on principles of sharing and pooling. This is especially evident in the area of land-use, where there was little sense of territorial exclusiveness among groups in a merger relationship. Tribes freely traveled, hunted, and lived within each other's nominally designated areas of occupation (Sharrock 1974:111–15; Albers and Kay 1987). When segments of two tribes shared in the use of territories, joining together in subsistence pursuits, it logically followed that responsibility for protecting territorial prerogatives was collectively assumed. On the nineteenth century plains, tribes who regularly shared land-holdings also formed military alliances for defensive as well as offensive purposes (Sharrock 1974; Ewers 1975; Albers and Kay 1987:54).

It is clear that tribes in symbiotic relationships also used each other's territories. By and large, territorial intermingling was not as open as it was under merger. Excursions into the territories of trade partners appear to have been formally arranged. This is clearly evident in the case of the seventeenth-century Dakota, who extended land-use rights to their Chippewa neighbors in exchange for access to European trade goods (Hickerson 1971:65–67), and also when the Assiniboin gave the Crow permission to hunt in their territory (Denig 1961:89–90). In addition, trade partners tended to use each other's lands on a more occasional and short-term basis. Usually there was no intent to remain an another's lands unless, of course, relations were shifting towards the merger end of the continuum, or its opposite, war.

Sharing was reflected not only in the common use and protection of a common territory and in joint collaboration in subsistence and ceremonies, but it was also apparent in patterns of residency and settlement. Residential intermingling on the scale reported for the Assiniboin and Cree, Mandan and Hidatsa, as well as Cheyenne and Teton was clearly a merger phenomenon. Yet, in lesser degrees, coresidency is also associated with symbiosis. Evidence from the upper Missouri region indicates that individuals from foraging groups lived in the horticultural villages as friends and relatives and that some of them became fully assimilated to a horticultural way of life (Bowers 1965:218). Nomadic groups, including extended families and bands, often stayed in the horticultural villages, but their sojourns were brief, rarely extending beyond a few months. Only in rare instances, as in the movement of Yankton into Ponca villages (Howard 1960:257), did nomadic groups permanently establish themselves among the villagers. But when this happened, groups were beyond the bonds of symbiosis and into the realm of merger, especially when moving nomads adopted the patterns of village life.

When people from different tribes became parties in a merger relationship, they were invited to live with each other and to share domestic space during the duration of stays at each other's camp or village (Bowers 1965:212, 217–18). By contrast, in a symbiotic relationship, people generally encamped in places apart from the residential areas of their kindred hosts (Bowers 1965:49). The message underlying these two patterns of spatial use is clear. Whereas the first conveys a sense of cooperation and even the possibility of a shared use of labor and resources, the second communicates social distance where groups are in proximity but do not have joint rights to recruit each other's services and property freely.[7]

Giving and other forms of generalized reciprocity took place under merger as well as symbiosis; however, it can be argued that the intent of this exchange was different. In symbiosis, generalized reciprocity was a strategy to adjust exchange rates in the movement of goods between geographically separate and economically differentiated populations. A joint control over labor and resources was not its aim. By contrast, under merger, giving, sharing, and pooling were mechanisms for ensuring cooperation over a mutually held territory and settlement space.

It is not always easy to separate relationships of merger from those of symbiosis because the pooling of labor and resources is associated typically with the actions of people who hold the same ethnic background, but among historic Plains Indians, a shared tribal origin did not always confer a sense of common ownership, interest, or purpose. Some of the material on the nineteenth-century Teton, especially those who resided along the Platte River, indicate that bands living near trading posts acted as middlemen to hinterland groups who were the primary producers of hides (Hyde 1937:43–54; Mekeel 1943:188–89). During the same period Cheyenne bands who maintained close relationships with Euro-American traders were identified with peace and trade, while others who fought on the tribe's territorial frontiers were linked with war and hunting. It is probable that the kind of interdependence sustaining relations between the differentiated bands of the same tribe was more akin to symbiosis than merger (Moore 1974, 1988). Thus, even though the nomadic bands of the Teton and Cheyenne were unified under a general pattern of merger, some of them began to develop internal differentiations as a result of emerging specializations in production and trade. When internal variations of this order become widespread within a single tribal body, they can eventually lead to ethnic differentiation. And this is probably what happened in the division between the Crow and Hidatsa (Wood and Downer 1977).

In the historic Plains, the fluctuating character of resource opportunities often made it difficult for groups in merger to maintain continuity and stability in their shared settlements and territories. Just as mechanisms had to exist to allow groups to come together, so means had to be present to permit them to divide and rework their alliances on a circumstantial basis. Material on the Cree and Assiniboin (Sharrock 1974) and the Crow and their allies (K. Weist 1977) demonstrates that there was competition, even raiding, among ethnically different bands who stood in a relationship of merger. Yet it also suggests that local-level conflict was often buffered by a dense web of real and fictive kinship ties.

Even when local groups shared the same tribal backgrounds and were related through dense and ramifying kinship ties, conditions sometimes evolved whereby a jointly held territory could no longer accommodate them no matter how they readjusted their internal alliances and settlement patterns. Segmentation and war were sometimes the result, as

was the case of the Assiniboin and their former Dakota relatives (Ray 1974:23–44). Schisms within Pawnee and Cheyenne ranks produced bitter antagonisms which, under the
right set of circumstances, might have erupted into war (Hyde
1951; Moore 1974). Thus, just as it was a contradiction under
symbiosis, so raiding and other forms of negative reciprocity
were paradoxical under merger. The existence of these paradoxes, however, provided the seeds of transformation. If they
had not existed, Plains Indians could hardly have changed
their relationships as rapidly and flexibly as they did in historic
times.

Cooperative Patterns of Alliance Making. Just as specialization in the production and exchange of goods is not sufficient to maintain a symbiotic relationship, so parallelism in
economic functions does not provide sufficient grounds for
merger. Identical economic positions can just as easily result
in the diametrically opposed relationship of war. In contrast to
symbiosis, where the problem of alliance is to integrate and
separate groups at the same time, the strategy under merger
is to create a social nexus that is conducive to the easy flow of
people across group boundaries. Patterns of alliance and
exchange need to be based on the kinds of altruistic and
open-ended strategies associated with cooperative alliance
making.

Once again, Bowers's (1965:211–12) study of the Hidatsa
provides insights into this process when he discusses how
"taking in friends" was conducted. This pattern, which was
based on a sibling model, was associated with the transfer of
rights in a sodality without original ownership being relinquished. The Hidatsa commonly adopted friends, "brothers"
or "sisters," who then became joint owners of a sodality and
its ritual paraphernalia. Thus, when the Hidatsa borrowed the
grass dance from Dakota at Devil's Lake, they "purchased"
the rights to the ritual from their adopted Dakota brothers, and
later, through the same process, they "sold" the same rights
to their brethren among the Crow (Bowers 1965:91–92).
These friendship relations became permanent, and those who

became party to them were invited frequently to participate in each other's ceremonies. Adoptions of this order created linkages based on a concept of pooling in which people cooperated by virtue of the fact that they held joint rights to a sacred and/or secular resource. This stands in marked contrast to the pattern in father-son adoptions where proprietary rights were relinquished and held separately by the two parties.[8]

In its basic contours, the *hunka*, an adoption ceremony among the Lakota, drew on similar principles, and it was used in historic times to cement relations with other tribes. Hunka adoptions linked people in either a parent-child or sibling relationship, but the character of their reciprocal obligations was different. In the latter case, friendships were formed between people of the same age and sex who were committed to a lifelong pattern of sharing and cooperation (Hassrick 1964:257–59; J. Walker, 1980:206–07, 218–19).

The widespread pattern of "sibling" adoption explains, in part, how certain military and religious sodalities diffused so rapidly in the Plains, and how individuals in one tribe could recruit the labor of friends in other tribes to support a variety of different activities. In the mid-nineteenth century, the multiethnic collaboration reported for subsistence, military, and ceremonial ventures clearly rested on notions of joint participatory rights among friends qua kin who were members of the same sodalities. Although the core people who came together in the large summer encampments for buffalo hunts and sun dances were closely related, others did not have close kinship connections. In these gatherings highly formalized governing structures comprised leadership councils and soldier sodalities, which were empowered with broad lines of authority to ensure the welfare of the entire encampment and to curb the segmentary tendencies of participating groups. Members of the same sodalities organized war parties, coordinated communal buffalo hunts, monitored ceremonial collaboration, regulated redistribution, and policed the encampments (Klein 1977:299–324).

By cutting across lines of consanguinity and affinity, the soldier sodalities held an important role in monitoring the activities of the large, multigroup gatherings (Oliver 1962:52–57). By and large, the recruitment and organization of this kind of labor has been described within single tribal settings. But if Bowers's (1965:91–92; 211–212) data on the Hidatsa can be generalized, then it becomes clear that recruitment also occurred across ethnic boundaries. Indeed, I would hypothesize that the convergence of the Plains nomads' kinship systems along generational lines, as described by Fred Eggan (1966) and more recently by Joseph Maxwell (1979), was an extension of the formation of "sibling" relationships in military sodalities and under other situations promoting joint collaboration across tribal boundaries.

When segments of such tribes as the Assiniboin and Cree (Sharrock 1974) or the Hidatsa and Mandan (Bowers 1965; Hanson 1987) merged, the institutional structures linking the various populations became virtually indistinguishable along ethnic lines. In addition, ties of consanguinity and affinity became more tightly knit and ramifying. Data (Bowers 1965: 69) on the Hidatsa-Mandan merger indicates that one of every three Hidatsa marriages was with the Mandan, and that these apparently took on a variety of forms, including the less formalized patterns of elopement and those arranged by women on behalf of their sons and daughters. The existence of more flexible and less indebting marriage patterns, coupled with the growth of cognatic systems of kinship reckoning, produced expansive and overlapping kinship connections between the two horticultural tribes. Indeed, as Bowers (1965:74) reports, the integration had become so fundamental that Hidatsa murderers could no longer find refuge in Mandan households.

Cooperative alliance making creates cohesive structures that integrate people through joint proprietary rights and role repetition. This stands in opposition to complementarity, which joins people through role separation and the mutual alienation of property. Historically, both patterns existed within

tribes as well as between them. The prevalence of one or the
other depended largely on the historically changing conditions that united or differentiated populations along productive lines.

War, Raiding, and Competition

In the absence of specialization and symbiotic relationships
with their neighbors, Plains Indians not only merged but
fought as well. War was a condition of total competition, and
raiding was its principle exchange strategy. In the context of
war, raiding entailed horse-stealing and more. It involved skir-
mishes over territorial prerogatives and access to trade routes,
the theft of horses and food provisions, and the abduction of
women and children.

The Historical Conditions of War. As W. W. Newcomb, Jr.
(1950), points out, Plains Indian warfare was not a game; it
was a serious business in which groups fought to preserve or
secure favorable positions in the areas in which they lived. In
historic times the advantage of an occupational area was
determined not simply by its environmental features and its
adequacy for use-value production, but also by its location in
relation to trade routes and its productivity in relation to the
appropriation of commodities destined for and coming from
Euro-American markets.

Much of eighteenth-century warfare involved tribes jockeying for advantageous positions in trade routes. On the eastern
peripheries of the plains, where the British and French were
establishing competitive lines of trade, each European power
engaged dependent tribes to advance its own commercial
interests. Over time, tribes dependent on the commodities of
one European source stood in opposition to those under the
influence of another. Groups that occupied specialized positions in a single trade chain had a better chance of maintaining control over a route if they kept the peace along its path.
The traders recognized this, and they were instrumental not

only in forging alliances among tribes dependent on their own goods but also in fomenting war against the tribal emissaries of their rivals (Jablow 1950). Competition between tribes in opposing trade chains was a major source of warfare in the late eighteenth century. The chain that connected the Dakota and Arikara, for example, stood in competition with the one that linked Chippewa/Cree and Mandan. It is likely that endemic warfare between tribes in each of these chains not only forced the Cheyenne to leave their villages on the Cheyenne River (Moore 1988:132) but also compelled the Hidatsa to abandon their settlements near Devil's Lake (Wood 1986:30–31).

When traders began to bypass native middlemen at the end of the eighteenth century, they upset the distributive positions of tribes in the areas they entered. In order to advance their respective places within the region's altered trade, tribes in symbiotic relationships often turned against each other. The enmities that developed between the Assiniboin and Mandan in the early nineteenth century were a classic example of this, as was the shift from symbiosis to war between the Cree and the Blackfeet (Milloy 1988:31–40, 59–68). As the geographic positioning of traders shifted, many tribes with identical subsistence economies became vulnerable to change. This was because their symbiotic relations were based primarily on the specialized positions each occupied in the traffic of European trade goods. The relations between some of the horticulturalists and their nomadic neighbors, though not completely invulnerable, appear to have been able to more readily withstand disruptions in commodity circulation. As long as the horticulturalists continued their specialized production of agricultural foodstuffs, they were able to sustain symbiotic ties with the nomads. But when they reduced their agricultural production and began to procure hides and horses on a wide scale, they placed themselves in a position of competition with their nomadic neighbors. The Skidi Pawnee were a classic example. For a number of different reasons, the Skidi were forced to transform their economic system and assume a supplier role in the hide and horse traffic. This transformation pitted them against surrounding nomads, some of whom had been their complementary trade partners in earlier times (Hyde 1951:111–222).

Since the characteristics of market-oriented production were not constant over time, they had differing effects on the size and kinds of territories that Plains Indian populations needed to sustain their position vis à vis the European trade. When market demands changed, as they did in the Canadian prairies, from furs to meat provisions, and then to hides, tribes were compelled to seek more favorable locations to accommodate the shifts. In the process, they sometimes competed and fought with neighbors who held desirable territories. The southwesterly movements of some of the Chippewa and Assiniboin in the seventeenth century and their growing antagonism with the Dakota were clearly a response to their specialized and shifting roles in the appropriation of fur-bearing animals for trade (Hickerson 1972; Ray 1974; Peers 1987; Milloy 1988). But renewed Chippewa and Assiniboin migrations in the eighteenth and nineteenth centuries, along with hostilities towards the Blackfeet, Atsina, and Crow, were related to movement into territories that sustained a dependence on the surplus production of buffalo hides and meat provisions (Ray 1974:195–216). Indeed, throughout the Plains area warfare increasingly became a fight over access to buffalo-hunting and horse-grazing territories that would sustain an intense and specialized production for nineteenth-century markets (Jablow 1950; Kenner 1969; Ray 1974; Milloy 1988; Moore 1988; Albers and James 1991).

Importantly, the conditions that precipitated warfare in historic Plains Indians were geographically and historically varied. Whatever its specific causes, war took place in situations where tribes stood in identical and potentially competing positions with each other, and it emerged not only at the point of production but also in lines of trade. When either of these changed, as they frequently did, the terms of relationship between neighboring tribes were transformed as well.

The Dynamics of Negative Reciprocity. One reason that anthropologists have viewed Plains Indian warfare as a game-like endeavor has been their failure to distinguish between hostility under relationships of war and that based on symbiosis. The distinction between the two is critical, and it is best seen by examining differences in the Blackfeet's changing relations with the western Cree. In the nineteenth century the contact between these two tribes was predicated on war, and it involved bitter and uninterrupted confrontations over access to horses and the rich bison hunting grounds of Montana and southern Saskatchewan (Milloy 1988:103–18). By contrast, the eighteenth-century relationships between these two tribes, although involving intermittent raid activity, were symbiotic in nature. For many years the two tribes occupied different roles in a trade chain that extended from Hudson Bay to the Rocky Mountains. But at the turn of the nineteenth century, when the Cree started to lose their middleman position and to compete with the Blackfeet in the hide and provision market, war broke out between them (Lewis 1942:11, 31; Ewers 1969:11–12, 35; Milloy 1988:31–40).

The point is that although raiding and other hostile acts existed under war and symbiosis, and even though the activities appeared the same in both places, the aims were different. The differences, as Alan Klein (1977:217) notes, were recognized by traders and Indians alike. Under symbiosis, raiding was a strategy to adjust temporary imbalances in the flow of resources among tribes whose geographic positions were uncontested. Territorial displacement was not the goal. But under war, raiding was one instrument, among others, for altering the locations that tribes held. While warfare did not always result in dislocation, it was carried on with the intent to acquire favorable lands for production, to secure strategic places in trade and/or to increase the tribal labor force. To say that warfare between Dakota and Chippewa, Crow and Cheyenne, or Blackfeet and Shoshone was not a fight over the means of production, as Preston Holder (1970:117) seems to imply, is to make unintelligible the whole process by which tribes expanded onto the plains under the pressures of an advancing mercantile frontier.

The line between relationships built on symbiosis and those resting on war is thin and, in some cases, nearly indistinguishable. The point at which Plains tribes shifted from using raiding as a balance mechanism to employing it as a vehicle for change is not obvious. It is not easy to determine when symbiosis ends and war begins. Distinguishing between the two is especially difficult in the mid-nineteenth century, when most intertribal relations were in a state of flux. In fact, only in those cases where tribes were involved in long-standing and uninterrupted enmities does warfare appear as a discrete type of relationship. But even in these cases, its redistributive effects were not always clear. At this period in Plains history, warfare did not always result in the successful invasion of an enemy's lands nor the usurpation of a trade position. From about 1820 to 1870 warfare took on the appearance of a holding pattern in which there were few net gains or losses in territorial holdings. Yet in earlier times warfare did lead to territorial displacement and the rearrangement of trade locations (Newcomb 1950; Ray 1974; Moore 1988; Milloy 1988).

Making a distinction between war and symbiosis is complicated by the fact that tribes at war also engaged in trade. In the years before 1820 Plains Indians held large trade fairs at specified rendezvous points scattered over the entire region (Ewers 1969:215–16; Wood 1972:156–61). These fairs advanced an open and intense traffic in goods among multiple tribal parties. Often, tribes who attended were strangers or enemies. If tensions between enemy tribes could be quelled by overtures of gifts, a trade was conducted. Sometimes peace-keeping measures did not work, and treachery broke out in trade fair encampments (Jablow 1950:47–48). Arranging a trade among enemies, even if temporary, was a delicate undertaking, and it was the responsibility of go-betweens who had kinship connections with the hostile parties. Thus, when Shoshone attended trade gatherings where Hidatsa were present, they accompanied Crow who had close ties with these villagers. Similarly, the Cheyenne often acted as go-betweens in trade encounters between Arapaho and Arikara (Moore 1988:73). As a general rule, trade among enemies and strangers was indirect and sporadic, whereas in symbiotic relationships it was a direct and persistent enterprise.

More paradoxical than enemies trading was the fact that enemies occasionally visited without any intention to trade. The best account of such visiting comes from Thomas Leforge's narrative (Marquis 1974:99–101, 180–82) of the Crow who periodically hosted their arch-rivals, the Teton. Data on Cree relations with the Sarcee and Blackfeet also indicate that visiting and gift giving across enemy lines was conducted through kinship channels, established either in times of peace or through the widespread practice of abducting women and children (Thompson, in Coues 1908, 2:720, 737, 756; Jenness 1932:8; Milloy 1988:111). Similarly, the Hidatsa visited enemy bands where they had kin, and as Bowers points out, "no war party would have knowingly attacked a band from another tribe coming to the village to visit relatives" (1965:94).

Competitive Patterns of Alliance Making. Despite their apparent contradiction, trading and giving under the conditions of war created avenues for tribes to change their patterns of relationship when conditions warranted. In the Plains the possibility of enemy tribes redefining their alliances in terms of cooperation or complementarity was hinged directly on the preexistence of social ties. The emergence and reaffirmation of social ties among enemies had important consequences. Weist (1977:41–47) discusses how the Crow used such connections to negotiate an extended peace with their enemies, and Jablow (1950:46) mentions how the upper Missouri villagers kept enemy peoples in their midst to open avenues for trade.

When slaving was a dominant appropriation strategy, especially for populations on the central and southern plains, war captives were primarily an object of trade. In later years, however, captives helped to replenish a tribe's pool of social labor. Whether a tribe was decimated by war or by disease, the incorporation of enemy women and children into the social body of a community maintained a labor force necessary for surplus production aimed at trade and the organization of elaborate ceremonies (Malouf and Arline 1945; Jablow 1950:21; Kenner 1969). Indeed, Oscar Lewis (1942:50) argues that the Piegan ceased trading their female captives when they became fully involved in the commercial hide market. Captives not only established kinship avenues for peace, but they also guaranteed a group's dependence on the market through slaves' value as a form of labor and/or as a means of exchange.

On the Great Plains as well as in the neighboring Great Lakes region, it was customary for families to adopt outsiders to replace kin who had died (Albers and Kay 1987). Sometimes these adoptions took place in the context of symbiotic and merger relationships, but they also occurred in relations dominated by war. Among the Hidatsa (Bowers 1965:94–95), when warriors were able to bring captive women and children back to the villages without fear of counterattack, they did so. Children were given to households whose own offspring had recently died, and women were married to men of the villages. Here, as with the Cheyenne (Grinnell 1962, 1:345–48), Crow (Lowie 1956:229), Mandan (Bowers 1950:44), and Osage (Fletcher and La Flesche 1972:61–62), captives were incorporated into the kinship networks of their captors. In this light, the practice of abduction takes on new meaning, for not only did it contain the grounds for conflict, but it also embodied (quite literally) the terms of reconciliation. In other words, the capture of women and children was both a quintessential element of war, and a fundamental opportunity for peace. It maintained, yet rearranged, the social nexus through which tribes were able to rework their relationships.

Conclusion

Among historic Plains Indians, the existence of exchanges incongruent with a dominant mode of interdependence was characteristic of all intertribal relationships. In symbiotic relationships, where productive and distributive positions were specialized and stable, raiding and giving increased the elasticity of complementary alliances based on trade. When these positions were altered by local historical forces, the seemingly paradoxical exchange strategies of raiding and giving allowed groups to redefine their relationships and move either to merger or war. Under merger, these strategic positions were identical, and pooling as well as sharing advanced joint access to land and trade routes. Yet raiding and trading could coexist as exchange mechanisms to adjust labor and resources within a jointly held territorial space. When internal specializations developed in merger situations, trading could push groups to a symbiotic relationship. Similarly, when competition over shared resources increased, raiding could lead to segmentation and the emergence of war. With war, the productive and distributive positions of Plains Indian populations were also identical but contested. Raiding contributed to the displacement and reorganization of labor and resources over a given geographic landscape. Here giving and trading contradicted exchange strategies based on raiding, but they allowed for the possibility of alliances being built on complementarity or cooperation when material conditions changed. Thus, anomalous exchange strategies not only extended the flexibility of alliance making under a particular type of relationship, but they also ushered in and carried through transformations from one type of intertribal relationship to another when the conditions of interdependence were altered.

In the historic Plains, patterns of interdependence, alliance making, and exchange were not always defined nor differentiated along exclusively ethnic lines. Symbiotic ties, with their attending specializations in production and/or distribution, were established between groups from differing tribes as well

as among those of the same tribe. While members of one
tribe often competed with people from tribes other than their
own, hostility and warfare could erupt within the body politic of
a single tribe, leading to internal fissioning and eventual separation. Conversely, while coresidency and territorial sharing
linked people of the same tribal origin in a merger relationship, they could also join groups of differing ethnic backgrounds. The dynamic processes which united and divided
populations along single as well as multitribal lines were the
same because they were constituted in shared institutional
frameworks of kinship and sodality.

Arguments that resort to an ideology of ethnicity to explain
the united and divided actions of Plains Indians are inadequate. The fact that tribal members held a common ethnic
identity, or even spoke the same language, was neither a necessary or sufficient ground for them to unite and share in
some common political-economic interest. The River Crow
and Mountain Crow (K. Weist 1977) maintained different
kinds of relationships with their neighbors, as did the various
bands of Cheyenne (Moore 1988). The Assiniboin and Cree
who lived in the Qu'pelle and Assiniboin River region forged
relationships with outsiders in ways that were different from
their relatives living on the Saskatchewan River plains (Milloy
1988). The geographic distances separating bands of the
same tribe, coupled with internal variations in territorial environments and in access to commercial trade routes, created
different and sometimes opposing demands on how local
groups defined their own interests in relation to those of their
neighbors.

Nor were differences in ethnicity reason enough to keep
members of various tribes apart. When local bands and villages joined together and acted as a unified political body,
they did not always organize themselves along single ethnic
lines. Thus, when Cree fought against the Atsina, it was usually
in alliance with Assiniboin (Milloy 1988). Similarly, the nineteenth-century coalitions in which the Cheyenne were involved
frequently included bands of the Teton and Arapaho (Moore

1988). Importantly, there was not always a one-to-one relationship between the tribal identities of local groups and the ethnic composition of the wider political economic formations in which they participated (Sharrock 1974; Albers and James 1986).

Explanations that rely exclusively on various forms of ecological and technological reductionism to explain tribal cohesion and divisiveness are also inadequate (Oliver 1962; Osborn 1983). The patterns of social organization that evolved among "true" Plains tribes, for example, were not simply an epiphenomenon of local ecological or technological forces. They were an extension of the productive and distributive positions Plains tribes occupied in relation to a market and to each other during a time of intense buffalo hide production. The fact that some "peripheral" tribes, in Symmes Oliver's (1962) scheme, lacked the integrative devices of "true" Plains societies and were horse-poor was very much a product of the geopolitical and economic positions they occupied when the market shifted from fur to meat and, finally, to hide production (Albers and James 1991). The peripherally located Assini-boin-Cree-Chippewa of the far northern plains retained highly amorphous and segmentary social formations which evolved, in part, out of the conditions of this region's fur and provisioning trade (Ray 1974; Sharrock 1974; Thistle 1986; Milloy 1988). In contrast, the Cheyenne, as described by John Moore (1988), developed a strong sense of corporate tribalism that can be related to the historical position this tribe occupied in the nineteenth-century horse and gun traffic west of the Missouri.

Both the internal and external features of historic Plains Indian social formations become intelligible only when viewed against a backdrop of a regionally changing market whose relative influence shifted over time. The growing dependency of Plains Indian tribes on Euro-American commerce brought fundamental transformations in the direction and scale of their production. It altered how local environments were utilized and how labor was organized (Klein 1977; Hanson 1987). In time, the social relations of production were changed as well, creating a complex mosaic of shifting forms of interdependency within and across tribal boundaries. In the final analysis, these changing relations cannot be accounted for in terms of a single, monolithic form of determinism, either ideological or ecological. In this paper, we have attempted to understand intertribal relationships through a historical materialist methodology that, following the work of Karl Marx, rests on the assumption that history is an integrated political-economic process. It is only through an understanding of how articulations take place between historically specific material forces and their accompanying social formations that we can theoretically approximate the dynamics and contradictions which constitute human history.

Acknowledgments

This is a considerably revised version of an unpublished manuscript entitled, "Pluralism in the Native Plains, 1670–1870," that has been circulating among colleagues since 1978. I wish to express my thanks to Robert Anderson, Patricia Garrett, Dair Gillespie, Per Hage, Alice Kehoe, Alan Klein, Margot Liberty, John Moore, and Seymour Parker for their helpful comments on earlier drafts. I also wish to give a special acknowledgement to William James, who during a time of terminal illness provided me considerable inspiration and encouragement in its final revisions. And it is in memory of him and his dedication to the study of political economy that I dedicate this paper.

CHAPTER 7

Political Economy of the Buffalo Hide Trade

Race and Class on the Plains

Alan M. Klein

As students of Plains anthropology we have much to be thankful for. We are heirs to an ethnohistorical fortune including some of the best studies in the field of anthropology (for instance, Mooney 1896; Weltfish 1965; Ewers 1955). While those of us wanting to build on this tradition are challenged by the stature of our predecessors, there are gaps that we can productively seek to fill. One area in need of refinement is that of nineteenth-century trade relations between Anglo-American traders and Native Americans. Trade relations have generally been interpreted as one-dimensionally leading to Native American dependence at the hands of Anglo Americans (see Lewis 1942; Jablow 1951; Ray 1974). Anthropologists of almost every ideological stripe share the perception that initial native autonomy gave way to economic and political dependence. Implicit in this view is the sense that the trading post and its personnel were uniformly agents of change. Studying the two entities in dialectical interaction has simply not interested students of the trade. Our propensity to investigate only non-Western cultures has blinded us, in this instance, to what is a natural relationship between native hunting cultures and the trading post.

A related dimension, also widely subscribed to, examines the hide trade exclusively at the level of exchange rather than as a form of production. Here, changes in the social and economic independence of Native American trading bands would be interpreted as the result of the introduction and, later, dependence on trade goods such as guns and metal objects. Even a rare exception such as Thistle (1986), who interpreted the two-hundred-year trade between the Hudson's Bay Company and the Western Cree as occurring between independent entities, did so by focusing on the exchange of goods between groups rather than on the social relations of production. To break with this trend the present study seeks to: (1) examine the hide trade both at the level of production and exchange; (2) see the trade as running along a temporal continuum from an initial autonomy to a later state of dependency; and (3) propose a view which links the respective modes of production (precapitalist and capitalist) to interpret in a novel fashion the complexity of the political-economic reality behind extended trade.

The Articulation of Modes of Production

Studies purporting to examine Native American sociocultural change have long held to notions such as "colonialism" to explain the nature and direction of change that Native Americans experienced for the past five hundred years. While these approaches reveal much, they are in need of several refinements. The following observations are offered in the spirit of a constructive and collective amendment to those who study the political-economic change that occurred in the wake of the "settling of the West."

The impact of colonialism, as well as that of capitalism, on aboriginal systems is often treated as unilaterally destructive, and such treatments tend to judge the political-economic interactions by the end result. Hence, one can speak of the Spanish impact on the Pueblos of the Southwest (Spicer 1962), the impact of the horse and trade on the Blackfeet

(Lewis 1942), or American impositions on the Iroquois (Wallace 1970) as occurring fairly uniformly throughout their respective societies. While much has been gained from these studies, there are major aspects that go unexplored, most notably the variety of entanglements between societies as well as the complexity of a society's response to capitalist penetration.

Largely as a result of the debates that have occupied Marxist social scientists over the past fifteen years (Wolpe 1980; van Binsbergen and Geschiere 1985; Patterson and Gailey 1987) we are in the enviable position of better examining the political and economic changes that were wrought by colonialism and capitalism. The term "articulation" was first used by Althusser (1969) to describe the political-economic meeting between capitalism and other systems. Now generally referred to as the "articulation of the modes of production," it has spawned yet a further round of debates which are beyond the scope of this paper (Hindness and Hirst 1975; Banaji 1980; Leclau 1973). A word or two should be said of the term, "mode of production," a key Marxist economic concept which has been contested for some time. It basically describes the system of production, distribution, and ownership within a society. Generally speaking, the mode of production encompasses the "forces of production," which include the technological base of society as well as the labor process (division of labor) by which goods are produced. What anthropologists have called "subsistence patterns," (all of the means by which people provide for their economic needs) is also included in the discussion of forces of production. The "relations of production" comprise the second basic component of the mode of production and include the social and political division of labor and the property relations (ownership) which distribute basic and prestige goods throughout society. As used in the present study, modes of production have to do with the labor process, the political economy of production, and the property relations which imply ownership of key goods and their principle distribution as an outgrowth of production. Secondary forms of exchange having to do with the individual's interests and needs are not relevant here.

The "articulation discourse" has yielded some fruitful results, particularly in Africa. Here, colonialism's roots run deep. Studies to examine the articulation between European mercantile-colonial ventures and African societies have found a variety of linkages between systems (van Binsberger and Geschiere 1985; Wolpe 1980). The work of French Marxist anthropologists in particular have been significant. Meillasoux (1975), Terray (1972, 1975), Godelier (1972, 1977), and Rey (1975, 1979) were at the forefront of studies seeking to provide a model by which to assess the political-economic and cultural interactions of capitalism and various precapitalist systems. More recently the work of van der Klei (1985), de Jonge (1985), and their Dutch colleagues have added to the corpus of data accumulating on Africa. Most useful is the view that precapitalist relations of production play an active role in the transitions to some sort of capitalism, rather than the view that the simpler forms merely crumble. Rey's work on the active role of the African lineage system and age relations illustrated how intersystemic relations are many layered and complex. Following his lead, I will look at Plains Indian hunting societies and their relations with the trading posts in their areas in an effort to document the articulation and its implications.

The Plains ethnohistorians who have written about the impact of the hide trade on Plains Indian societies have been much more sensitive to the kinds of political and economic issues that interest Marxist analysts (Klein 1980). Their works rank among the best in North America and chronicle the effects of trade in economic detail (Ewers 1955; Jablow 1950; Lewis 1942; Goldfrank 1945). Yet the same criticism leveled at world systems thinkers such as Frank (1969) and Wallerstein (1974), namely that treating economic change in the context of exchange (as the socioeconomic movement of trade items and their political consequences) applies to this otherwise impressive collection of studies. What is needed is an assessment that looks at the impact of trade on the forces and relations of production both for the trading post and for equestrian hunting peoples.

Buffalo Culture: The Hide-Trade Period

Once trade reached the classic proportions of the 1850–1880 period, the political-economic and cultural sovereignty of both Native American and trading post no longer fully existed. Sovereignty, as used here, is interpreted as political and economic independence. Two points must be made: Native American dependency on European trade was not one-dimensional; and cultural and political sovereignty tended to last longer than did economic autonomy. A more complex understanding of the hide trade can be gained by treating it as part of the social relations of production as well as exchange between groups. Such a view shows the early outlines of a single stratum of people (Native American and working whites) organized by a complex division of labor into an unstable class crossing both racial and cultural lines. Indian and white alike were as dependent on the hide trade as they were powerless in the face of the larger and more distant capitalist interests that controlled it. In losing their respective autonomy, however, these dissimilar cultural entities inadvertently began creating a new social formation. I give this cultural phenomenon the working title "buffalo culture." Its heuristic value lies in helping us look at two hitherto relatively ignored aspects of the hide trade: its intersystemic quality, and its intrasystemic quality (being the nexus between race and class on the plains). Analytically, such a view of economic trade shows how racial and cultural differences obscure economic similarity. Politically, this analysis has practical consequences by showing how the potential for class solidarity is hindered by racial-cultural separation.

I must begin by outlining the key economic-political features of equestrian Plains Indians and trading posts. For each society to carry out its economic goals the functional interdependence of political and economic components within each system will be outlined. In a later section the mutual dependence between trading post and hunting tribes will be shown, but it is important first to document the early economic articulation between native hunting society and European (Spanish, English, American) presence. The final stage of hide trade history shows these modes of production merging into a new social formation.

The Native Americans discussed here are all Indians of the northern plains: Teton Lakota, Blackfoot, Assiniboins, and Gros Ventre. For trading companies, I have concentrated on the trading posts of the northern plains, particularly the American Fur Company; however, Bent–St. Vrain Company (Bent's Fort), a trading empire in the southern plains, also is used. The former is the largest and best known, but Bent–St. Vrain Company is exemplary of a firm owned and operated by someone intimately connected with the day-to-day workings of the post and offers a good comparison with the relatively larger and more impersonal American Fur Company of John Jacob Astor and his later successors, Chouteau and Crooks.

Political-Economic Prerequisites

The main points of articulation between the native and foreign trading posts revolved around processing and exchanging hides and meat for an array of trade goods (guns, metal goods, etc.) and assuring the respective modes of production needed to maintain key economic variables in some sort of equilibrium. To avoid a static functionalist-ecological model, these traits will be viewed as parts of systems that respond to changes in political-economic climate and to the requirements each has. These conflicts, documented in Moore (1974, 1988), Albers (1974, 1985) and Klein (1977, 1980, 1983a), are based on the fluctuation in the importance of social-economic relations and the ability to respond to shifts in the Plains hide trade.

Plains Equestrian Hunters. It may seem completely self-evident, but the single most important variable in all of the following discussions is the presence of buffalo in an ever-increasing supply. There are many variables to consider, but the buffalo is bedrock—without it there is no plains hide trade or even plains life as it was known in the nineteenth century. Searching for buffalo forged the nomadic patterns for those groups who had come to rely on the hunt, but other variables had to be factored into the economic equation: horse herds, pasture and water, size of encampments, proximity to enemies, relations of production, and forces of production.

Whether we are looking at the micro-band of the Dakota *Tiyospaye,* the macroband of the Cheyenne, or the tribal-wide gathering of the Piegan, each kind of collection of people had to ensure that their *horse herds* were numerically adequate to the task of hunting buffalo as well as for the socioeconomic requirements of a society increasingly dependent on accumulating and circulating horse wealth. Hunters sought to have at least one good "buffalo runner" (a horse trained to chase buffalo), and also enough horses for travel, for presentation as bridewealth, and as upwardly mobile status symbols in giveaways. Too few horses obviously diminished one's social status and hurt a hunter's ability to get at the best buffalo in the chase. In the extreme, the lack of a sufficient supply of horses could, as it did for the Assiniboins, force the retention of old, inefficient methods of hunting such as the cliff drive (Denig 1929:504). Politically the chronic shortage of horses also compromised the Assiniboins' ability to make territorial gains at the expense of their neighbors. By the same token, too many horses also created problems of managing the herd and finding adequate *pasture and water.* The Fort Laramie treaty of 1851, for instance, posed real problems of pasturage as thousands of Indians congregated there with their horse herds. Twenty-five years later the same situation was found at the gathering of tribes at the Little Big Horn River.

The *size and composition of the encampment* also set

limits on subsistence and surplus goods. The larger the encampment, the greater its basic subsistence needs as well as its demand for trade goods. Hence, more buffalo were needed to produce surplus hides. Given the overall reduction of buffalo herds and their shifting migratory patterns during the second half of the nineteenth century, the proximity of other encampments posed potential problems of access to buffalo in a given area. The buffalo range was changing, making territorial control a key political issue. If nearby encampments were of one's own people, access could be negotiated fairly easily; but if an unaffiliated *hostile encampment* inhabited the margins of one's tribal territory, hunting could become dangerous. In these situations adequate measures for defense needed to be factored into a group's composition.

The composition of the encampment could shift in response to political-economic changes as well. Moore (1988) documents how Cheyenne encampments shifted focus away from matrilocal organization to highlight soldier societies in response to increased needs for internal economic requirements and external defense. Similar occurrences were found among the Teton Lakota, when in the 1870s Sitting Bull's camp swelled in response to the decision of various bands to resist white encroachment into the Black Hills. The Teton camps of the 1870s were composites of Tiyospaye, larger than traditional camps, and organized on the basis of military defensive strategies. In the period after 1870 armed conflict with whites was not simply a response to the presence of the United States Army, but to the swelling numbers of homesteaders, gold-diggers, cattlemen, and railroad personnel who encroached upon the plains and accelerated the already rapid disappearance of the buffalo herds (Bartlet 1975).

The social relations of production and overall division of labor had also become a contested terrain. Based on the Plains collective mode of production and the innocuous economic position of raiding and trading in the pre-trade, pre-horse eighteenth century, women's status was relatively higher than it subsequently would be. The mode of production of the pre-horse and pre-trade period included a wide range of subsistence strategies. Hunting and gathering dominated the list, but also included were trading with and raiding other tribes. The array of hunting techniques utilized at various times included the buffalo pound (or its variant, the cliff drive), individual hunting, or hunting in small groups. Ownership of the kill depended on which of the above was carried out. Individual kills were privately owned, while collective endeavors were collectively owned and distributed (Henry and Thompson 1965 [1898]:520). The collective drive was the most important. Resources were collectively owned in Plains Indian society. Game, other foodstuffs, and raw materials for manufacture were all collectively owned. That the complexity of the cliff drive or buffalo pound method of hunting necessitated the cooperation and work of the entire band underscored the collective nature of this society. Even though hunting and gathering were the mainstays of the buffalo hunting tribes of the northern plains, other strategies such as trading and raiding were supplementary.

Some trading was collectively carried out (Ewers 1955:121), but most often it was the household that conducted the exchange (Denig 1929:456). As a result, trade goods were individually owned. Raiding, too, was best carried out in small groups and, though one was encouraged to share or distribute the loot taken on a raid, spoils were essentially owned by the taker. These strategies were relatively unimportant to societal well-being; hence, the benefits derived from them could be left to the individual rather than the group. The relative unimportance of trade is linked to the absence of need and is found in M'Gillivray's early nineteenth-century comment, "The inhabitants of the Plains are so advantageously situated that they could live very happily independent of our assistance" (1929:47). Prior to the introduction of the horse, raiding also had relatively limited value, being confined to garden products from horticulturalists or, occasionally for captives (Henry 1966 [1809]:299; Chardon 1932 [1834]:9).

The introduction of the horse on the plains altered the

mode of production. Through their monopolization of access to horses (they entered via raiding and trading, both of which are male dominated), Plains Indian men came to dominate the sphere of horse ownership and buffalo hunting. Women's labor, previously tied to the collective hunt, was eliminated, and their societal position was increasingly confined to the processing of hides (Klein 1983a, 1983b). With the increased importance of individual property (in buffalo, their hides, and the trade goods obtained in exchange), men and their dependent households grew more central to the trade, first as producers and owners of traditional use-goods, later as pillars controlling exchange within and between societies.

The increased importance of individual ownership exacerbated the increasingly "gendered" division of labor and control over production. Because ownership of goods derived from raids had traditionally been individually controlled, and because the horse first entered plains society via raids, ownership and access to this most valued animal was individual. Private ownership of horses dovetailed nicely with the individualized way in which the hunt was carried out, which in turn influenced property rights (that is, the buffalo chase method resulted in individual ownership of the hide, tongue, and choice cuts of meat [Denig 1929:531]). Social relations of production changed as well. Only men who could successfully gain access to horses could procure hides. This practice, so entrenched by the mid-nineteenth century, represented a societal shift which worked to fracture communal relations. Rey's work in West Africa (1979) and de Jonge's work in Tanzania (1985) also point to the age-related classes which formed in reaction to colonial penetration. Goldfrank, among others, talked of nascent classes being formed among the Blackfoot during this period: "Eager to participate in a hunt or raid, but lacking a fast horse, he was forced to borrow from a wealthy patron, sometimes handing over as much as one-half the game killed or one half the loot captured. . . . [A] poor boy, even when he was well endowed with these admirable qualities, might never become a man of substantial wealth or a leader in the community" (1945:7).

Hence, ownership, distribution, relations of production, gender, presence of other groups in the buffalo range, and composition of the encampment all factored into the equilibrium of the Native American buffalo hide trade. This in turn was a function of the growth of dependence on European trade.

Dependence upon the Hide Trade

"Now that he is acquainted with articles made of steel, such as knives, axes, rifles, etc., with tinder boxes, blankets, all sorts of materials for clothing and ornamentation, and with the taste of coffee, sugar, etc., he regards these things as indispensable to his needs; he is no longer content with his former implements, but regards ours as incomparably more profitable to him," said Rudolph Kurz, an employee at Fort Union in the 1830s, summing up the growing state of Native American economic dependency upon Western goods (1970:149). It was, for the most part, an accurate assessment. Oscar Lewis (1942:36), chronicling the trade relations of the Blackfoot of the northern plains with Euro-American interests, noted that the Indians could not remember how to make pottery a scant ten years after taking on the iron pot from British traders.

In short order, trade items went from being desirable luxuries to necessities. This shift evolved from more than just a lengthy relationship with whites or from the social benefits bestowed by the items themselves. Given sufficient quantities of buffalo to hunt, the importance of the trade is most tied to the impact of the horse upon Plains Indian culture.

It is important to see the horse as both a precondition for and a consequence of the hide trade. A spiraling relationship grew up in which access to horses meant increased hunting proficiency which, in turn, meant more hides taken, increased likelihood of polygyny, more processing of hides again, and

ultimately more European goods. All of this translated into
political power and social prestige, in turn requiring more
horses. Interestingly, only two groups (Comanche and Nez
Percé) were successful enough to raise horse herds in sufficient numbers for their needs. The chronic shortage served
to institutionalize and elevate raiding to unprecedented importance.

Elsewhere (Klein 1977) I have shown that, as compared
with the eighteenth century, all of the basic Plains Indian economic strategies of the nineteenth century (raiding, hunting,
foraging, and trading) changed; some declined in importance,
others intensified. Central to them all were the horse and the
hide trade. Clearly, the horse made possible the regularized
and selective hunting of large numbers of buffalo. However,
the impact of the horse on buffalo hunting and taking of hides
alone would have been restricted by a communally based
hunting economy geared to production for use. It was only
after the needs of plains equestrian peoples escalated to
include production of hides for external exchange (petty commodity production) that the complete range of economic
strategies altered in any real sense. The hide trade lifted the
economic ceiling. With the introduction of a strong and
irreversible bond between plains hunting groups and Euro-
American traders, one expects to see similar dependency-
generated processes occurring among the hide traders.

The Hide-Trade Company

The fur trade comprised primarily capital, traders, and
employees, a combination not always found together. The
American Fur Company under Astor's direction was split
between the capital source located in New York and the actual
enterprise found throughout the West. Later, when Chouteau
bought the company, he was more directly involved with running it, centering his operations in St. Louis. The Bent brothers represent an even more direct operation, being both the
source of capital and the operators in the field. The sole pur-

pose of the all these operations, be it the Bent brothers or John J. Astor, was to *secure as substantial a profit* as was possible. Hence, capital was logically the starting and ending point:

Capital is said ... to fly turbulence and strife, and to be timid, which is very true; but this is very incompletely stating the question. Capital eschews no profit ... just as nature abhors a vacuum. With adequate profit, capital is very bold. 10 percent will ensure its employment anywhere; 20 percent will produce eagerness ... 100 percent will make it ready to trample on all human laws, 300 percent and there is not a crime at which it will scruple, nor a risk it will not run. (T. J. Dunning 1860:35)

Kurz adds:

The Fur Traders' principal reason for wishing whisky back again as a commodity for trade with Indians, notwithstanding the attending peril to their lives, is the tremendous profit they derive from the sale of it. ... This made a gain earlier ranging from 200 to 400 percent. (Kurz, 1970:177)

Juxtaposing these quotes, we see the amoral rationale for the variety of risks taken by traders to push the fur trade west. If he acted prudently and had a healthy dose of good fortune, the trader-owner would realize a handsome profit. Prudent handling of business however, involved carefully managing a range of variables: some at the *general* level of the enterprise (owners); others at the *local* level of the trading post. A distinction between these two aspects of the hide trade is essential for this analysis. The requirements of capitalists are fairly simple and straightforward (one must realize a profit at any cost to oneself or others, control the market, and destroy the competition). The trading post, on the other hand, while less economically powerful, is more socially and culturally complex.

The *outlay of capital* needed to get the enterprise off the ground was initially concerned with finding requisite labor and buying trade goods. Purchasing trade goods involved not only the outlay of capital, but the knowledge of how many and what kind of goods Native American groups would want. In some cases the records note that goods bought and transported at great expense did not appeal to the groups and were commonly passed over by tribal peoples (Ray 1974:312).

Once secured, the company had to assure the *safe transportation of goods and men* from the eastern points of purchase, to St. Louis, then to the post and back. The use of the steamboat after the 1820s greatly reduced the turnaround time on the shipment of goods and hides, which in turn increased profits (Chittenden 1954, 1:36). Denig (1930:460) points out the risks attendant to the shipping of goods up and down river even in the era of the steamboat. While the company might have been insured, the cost of insurance was exorbitantly high, according to the remarks of his Ft. Union neighbor, Rudolph Kurz (1970:234). Profit margins were more impacted by this cost than any other.

Finding and keeping employees was, at every level, critical for the capitalist–fur trader. Bent–St. Vrain Company, for instance, employed over one hundred men of varied nationalities and races, while the American Fur Company listed three hundred during the 1840s. The workers at these posts included not only the managers and accountants, but blacksmiths, hunters, teamsters, tanners, interpreters, and agents as well. Often these employees would constitute a racial and ethnic potpourri.

Engendering trust and loyalty between employees and post managers was much more difficult for authoritarian and impersonal firms such as the Hudson's Bay Company or the American Fur Company than it was with companies like Bent–St. Vrain. Desertion, caused by mistreatment or by chronic and ever-growing employee debt, was common. Umfreville, writing of the Hudson's Bay Company in 1790, makes such a point (1954:60), as does Kurz on the Upper Missouri: "Indeed, for the purpose of chaining to the fort so to speak, those who are capable and those who are indispensable, the bourgeois endeavors to bind them down for the next year by advancing sums to them on credit" [Kurz 1970:236].

This one point of conflict within the post has been under-reported. Conflict between employees and employers on the post was also visible in the suspicion and distrust each had of the other. Umfreville (1954:60) reports that employees of "The Bay" were forbidden to possess skins and that they were warned to be alert to any of their numbers that might have any skins. Chittenden (1954, 1:62) mentions the high incidence of desertions at the American Fur Company, a situation occasioned by growing employee indebtedness.

Far and away the most problematic aspect of the hide trade, both for equestrians and fur traders, was competition from other Indian groups and fur traders. Without competitors there was stability. Competition eliminates the stability that comes from having a degree of control over trade relations. Chittenden's classic history of the fur trade lauds the Hudson's Bay Company, a crown-chartered mercantile monopoly, for being more successful than American counterparts at removing "the ill effects of competition." For Chittenden, it was laissez-faire capitalism that fostered the intense competition so characteristic of the nineteenth-century plains. At its most extreme, unhampered trade was seen among the Rocky Mountain fur traders, a collection of mostly white, solitary beaver trappers who both manufactured and traded on their own. Although this small fraternity of trappers lasted a scant thirty five years in the first half of the nineteenth century, it accounted for an inordinately large share of trade in the Rocky Mountain region.

Most trade, and hence most competition, was between companies using both local traders and Indian equestrian hunters as procurers of hides. This relationship established a structure for the trade that enabled Native Americans to function in a semi-independent way by performing traditional production with new, improved methods that allowed for surplus and for exchanging surplus value for foreign trade goods. Here is where the notion of cultural and economic sovereignty is based: white traders depended on the specialized labors of skilled Indian hunters and dressers of hides. Because it depended on a variety of factors, this relationship was very precarious and, with time, declined. Whites never really competed with Native Americans for direct access to the buffalo until the early 1870s.

Competition Among Equestrian Groups. This type of competition, both a precondition and consequence of holding on to favored trade status with a particular trader and/or company, centered on claiming choice buffalo hunting territories. The frequent mention at Bent's Fort, Fort Union, and Hudson's Bay Co. posts of various bands of Native Americans complaining, cajoling, and threatening war were as much to assure continued defense of a tribe's territory as to gain or keep a monopoly over a trader. This might involve, as it did among the Dakota, frightening traders traveling through Dakota territory to keep them from visiting a neighboring tribe. Among the Assiniboins and Blackfoot, it entailed keeping all the buffalo away from the vicinity, thereby raising the price of hides by convincing traders that there was a shortage.

Competition Among Hide Traders. From the perspective of the traders, competing fur companies were the most problematic element of the trade. Competition was difficult to control, it diminished profits by raising the prices paid for hides, and it threatened companies with bankruptcy. For Native American groups actively engaged in the trade, competition of this sort was a windfall that they encouraged. Competition in the Fort Benton trading post in 1870 caused the price of a single hide to temporarily double to six dollars (Branch 1973:204). To control the runaway nature of prices and to prevent loss of band loyalty to the trading post, managers would seek to dispense liquor to groups coming in to trade. Reports from Kurz at Fort Union in 1840, Lewis and Clark in 1806, Larocque in the 1820s, Denig from the 1830s through the 1850s, and others all frequently comment on the deplorable effects of alcohol on Native Americans.

Nevertheless, the use of alcohol as a lubricant in the trade remained common. This became more than a means of establishing a congenial climate for the trade because as some Native Americans grew addicted, alcohol itself became the reason they traded. However the traders may have lamented its effects on native populations, promulgating its use was an acknowledged strategy for dealing with competition. Such longtime plains residents as Edwin Denig exemplified this mind set as he complained about yet condoned the use of alcohol: "The usual consequence of drinking spirits is poverty, as they will sell or give away everything they possess . . . to obtain liquor" (1929:530). Others concur that although it had the long-term effect of addicting large numbers of people and destroying their ability to function in the trade, in the short run it proved a very effective way of securing all the hides a group had (Neihardt 1961:80 ; Kurz 1970:292, 177; Dodge 1970:233).

Not everything about competition boded ill for the equestrian. The ability to get a high price for hides is also widely mentioned (Maximillian 1966, 23:34; Boller 1972:59–60). All Plains groups were experienced at jockeying between traders for the highest price or the most extravagant goods. In fact, Ray (1974:63) points out that the Cree and Plains Ojibwa who were trading with the Hudson's Bay Company would not abide by the market-derived price for their goods, at times refusing to deliver until they got what they wanted. Their threats to go to the rival French companies were clear and often carried out.

Company Relations with Employees. The way that profits were assured went beyond competition and haggling over trade prices with native groups. Less well known is that fur-trade capitalists also dealt with their own employees in a variety of underhanded ways: "The less a bourgeois has to pay for the upkeep of his fort in salaries for employees, and for skins and furs, the greater will be his profit and that of his agents" (Kurz 1970:235).

Strategies to cut costs internally normally resulted in the owners' fostering indebtedness with their employees as well as charging the same inflated prices to employees (whites) as they did to Indians. Echoing the manager's view of trading-post employees, Kurz cites the regular source of indebtedness (referring to employees at Fort Union): "Indeed, for the purpose of chaining to the fort so to speak, those who are capable and those who are indispensable, the bourgeois endeavor to bind them down for the next year by advancing sums to them on credit" (Kurz 1970:236). Chittenden, on the other hand, blames the victims: "The lower class of employees were generally in the company's debt, and this may account in part for the desertions that were always taking place" (Chittenden 1954, 1:62).

Such strategies might also entail outright piracy. Chittenden reports that the American Fur Company would waylay employees who had gotten annual salaries and were taking their leave (Chittenden 1954, 1:347). Small wonder, then, that the American Fur Company's steamboat *Frolic* lost most of her crew to mass desertions in an 1844 trip up the Missouri or that an employee who was intractably in debt to the company robbed the store at Fort Union in 1840 (Sunder 1965:59). In their relations with owners employees often found themselves in situations of dependency and exploitation every bit as unfortunate as those of Native Americans.

One important impact of competition is that all competition, good and bad, worked to intensify the relationship between Native American hunting peoples and white employees at the trading post, ultimately forging a set of bonds that were as strong as they were ambiguous and unacknowledged.

Interdependencies Between Systems

As the hide trade grew dramatically through the 1860s and 1870s, the trading post and equestrian hunting systems grew increasingly interdependent. Of the two social formations, the American-controlled trading post clearly was dominant and, from the late 1860s, was growing in direct proportion to Indian dependence on trade goods and European weapons. Commissioner Parker, in his 1869 address to Congress, said that "Great injury has been done to the government in deluding this people into the belief of their being independent sovereignties, while they were at the same time recognized only as its dependents and wards" (Branch 1973:173) The key to understanding this growing imbalance has to do with changes in the buffalo hide trade itself. In 1870 a Pennsylvania tannery experimented with buffalo hides, which had until that time been too thick for many uses, and found that they could be treated for use as conveyor belts in the fast-growing factories of the east (Branch 1973:153). The new use for these hides involved "summer hides" normally not taken because they made poor-quality robes. With this new process for curing hides hunting would go on year round and, as Branch says, "the slaughter was on" (Branch 1973:153).

In the course of their growing economic interactions with trading posts, Plains Indian hunting peoples came to occupy economic roles within the post itself. Equestrians were first and foremost primary procurers of hides. As a result early on, Plains Indians, the provisioners of trading posts, brought in large quantities of meat for less mobile whites at the post (Ray 1974:124–31; Umfreville 1954:20; Harmon 1922:103). Interpreters from among the various tribes were also hired (Parkman 1911:122). Smart traders would also hire young men, members of soldier societies, in the capacity of policemen to protect stores of goods at the post and keep trouble to a minimum (Kurz 1970:253). This was particularly advisable where the groups were hostile to each other (for example, among the Blackfeet and bands of Dakota). Young men also were middlemen, running European goods between traders and tribes farther removed from the posts (Jablow 1950). Profit from the goods moving in both directions fueled the middlemen's desire to monopolize the white traders in their areas.

In all these ways, not only did Native Americans become more dependent upon the trading post and the trade, but the traders grew to rely on the performance of intermediaries as well. For instance, equestrian hunters grew so dependent on iron points and other goods that not only was the blacksmith the post's most sought-after man by equestrian peoples

(Lewis and Clark 1969, 1:98–99), but his profit increasingly depended on his new customers. The bourgeois at the post also depended on native labor, and so, among other things, he needed to supply Indians with metal points so that they could more effectively hunt buffalo. Bourgeois and Indian alike depended on the same resource, with one acting in the primary role of provisioner and the other as buyer.

Additional interdependencies served to bind native hunters with post employees. Some bands periodically used the fort as a repository for their aged and infirm. Denig (1929:460) complains of Assiniboins and others using Fort Union as a hospital. The presence of significant numbers of Indians residing at the post on a fairly permanent basis seems to be a direct function of the social and cultural bonds between a particular band of equestrian hunters and the people residing in the post.

Many agents and bourgeois as well as other employees took Indian wives, the result of which was to undercut competition for Indian trade and form more substantive bonds between the two cultures. Intermarriage was a key factor in the fashioning of intercultural relations between Bent's Fort and the Southern Cheyenne, as it was with the Assiniboins at Fort Union, at Fort McKenzie, and at other places (Lavender 1969:190; Denig 1929:289; Chittenden 1954, 1:384; Schultz 1970:111). Respected traders such as Bent, Lisa, Denig, McKenzie, Culbertson, Schultz, and others all had Indian wives and families. The Red River Colony of Canada was the result of numerous intermarriages between fur trade employees and Indians. In this more than any other area we can see the potential for racial and cultural differences to be ameliorated.

In summary, for Native Americans to become enmeshed in the hide trade provided favored trade status, kinship bonds, a haven for their immobile kinsmen, an opportunity to be employed at the fort, as well as a place to meet for gifts. Dependence upon the trade also culturally conditioned the people at more than 150 trading posts. Whites at the posts took for granted the established and long-term presence of bands coming to trade as a prelude to forming long-term bonds.

Some research in this area of cultural relations has been carried out, so there is sufficient evidence to suggest that bonds between whites and Indians were common and long-standing, keeping many employees at the post long after they might otherwise have left. Bent's Fort, in Colorado, or the trading post called Pueblo, now a city in Colorado, are typical of the interracial and cultural unions that sprang up during the hide trade period. Writing of the latter, historian Paul Phillips describes it as "The strangest trading establishment in the West. . . . The crude adobe fort known as Pueblo was "home" to a bizarre melange of American adventurers, French coureures de bois, Canadian Iroquois, Mexican trappers and traders, Negroes, and European immigrants" (1961, 2:536). In seeing these concentrations of diverse cultures and the frequent intermarriage that resulted we have a set of important cultural and psychological circumstances that potentially work to blur racial-cultural boundaries.

While Native Americans were influencing the daily life about the post, traders effected changes in the social organization of Plains Indian groups as well. Through their ability to place large quantities of trade goods in the care of influential members of the Indian community, traders could enhance the political position of the local "big man" (Culbertson 1952 [1850]:83; Hamilton 1900:61; Kurz 1970:219). The latter in turn, could distribute these goods to underscore his status as big man or generous man.

The intricate and sensitive set of subsistence strategies devised by equestrian hunting groups increasingly became tied to the trading post. With greater reliance on trade goods and alcohol, some groups maximized political-economic strategies that had been previously unimportant. Chief among these was the strategy of "smoking," a political act carried on between two groups seeking to make peace and involving the generous bestowal of gifts on each other (Thomas 1940:43; Boller 1972:39; Ewers 1937:18; Bradbury 1906:131; Neihardt 1961:135). While this tactic was utilized in the pre-trade era, as the buffalo range shrank and trade dependence increased, reliance on this stopgap measure as a political foil became part of the overall mode of production for Plains Indians after 1850 (Klein 1977). The resurrected and stronger economic bonds that followed such a ritual were also sought by the managers of the trading posts who stood to benefit from the stable and dependable relations. Smoking worked in two ways: between plains groups and trading post, and among Native Americans groups. Writing of the latter, the trader Edwin Denig astutely describes its economic as well as political character:

Peaces are made between wild tribes by the ceremony of smoking and exchanging presents of horses and other property, sometimes women. The advantages and disadvantages are well calculated on both sides before overtures for peace are made.... The Crows, a rich nation, five years ago, through the writer as the medium made peace with the Assiniboines after a half century of bloody warfare.... The points the Crows gained were these: First, liberty to hunt in the Assiniboines country unmolested and secure from the Blackfeet... two enemies less to contend with.... The Crows having large herds of horses and the Assiniboines but few, the latter stand to gain ... (1929:404)

This same strategy used with whites brought many of the same benefits, only the term "smoking" was changed to "peace treaty," and "gifts" was translated to mean "annuities". The use was identical however, designed to see a tribe or band through difficult seasons or times. Writing of the Teton, but equally accurate for other trade-dependent plains groups, Ewers writes that "in the 1860s, the Teton were able to subsist by receiving government rations at the Agencies during the hard winter months, and then, supplied with arms and ammunition, to continue their free existence by the chase until the return of next winter. It was the rapid extermination of the bison that soon made even a periodic reliance on the chase an impossibility" (1937:18–19).

Denig, an interested party in the hide trade of the nineteenth century, understood the implications of "smoking-for-peace" as a tribal policy for the government: "With the Blackfeet a peace must be made in some way, and that at Laramie having proved successful, why not in the same way? They are very numerous and hostile, and nothing but a large appropriation judiciously distributed in merchandise would gain the point. Afterwards, it might be kept up for a series of years by smaller annuities, and when the general end is gained these could be discontinued" (1929:467).

It is in "smoking" or "suing for peace" that we most clearly see the interconnectedness of politics and economics in a changing milieu.

Termination of Trade: Class and Culture

Social historian Richard Bartlett quite humorously character-ized the mass migrations of whites through the West as a con-sequence of life east of the Mississippi having become routinized, hemmed in, and "boring": "By the 1840s everyone east of the Mississippi could pretty well plan on dying misera-bly in bed" (1974:109). Bartlett and others who study west-ward expansion know the real reasons to be more economic and political; the dramatic nature of all these upheavals resulted in the sudden and dramatic termination of the hide trade after 1883. A number of factors brought about the exter-mination of the buffalo herds, not the least of which was the untrammeled pursuit of hides for the trade. The building of the transcontinental railroad, the rise of the cattle industry, mining, and a conscious government policy to destroy the herds also hastened the movement of immigrants onto the plains beginning in the 1850s.

The dramatic rise in sales of buffalo hides during the 1870s was matched by a rise in the market for buffalo meat and, later in the decade, for buffalo bones (Burlingame 1940). This necessitated larger numbers of hunters, skinners, and other personnel, and companies sought to hire more whites from the East. Of the 1.2 million buffalo skins shipped east by vari-ous railroads during the years 1872 and 1873, only 350,000 (roughly 28 percent) were supplied by Indians (Branch

1973:169). Simply put, Native Americans were no longer the sole, or even the primary, providers of buffalo products in the hide trade. Unemployed railroad workers, nesters (homesteaders coming through the plains), and others were swelling the ranks of men trying to earn a living by what promised to be something better. By the end of the buffalo trade period (early 1880s) there were some five thousand white hunters on the plains, not to mention thousands of skinners, all armed with the latest Sharps buffalo guns and focusing exclusively upon the act of killing animals.

During this last period, while Native Americans rarely got more than six dollars in inflated trade goods per hide, salaried post employees were receiving substantial wages. Skinners might get fifty dollars a month or thirty cents a skin, and as Branch (1973:168) reports, a skilled worker could skin fifty animals a day. Compared to the amount of time a Native American woman took to produce a skin (untanned), or the amount of skins a Native American man could secure (eight to ten in a good hunt [Klein 1977]), skinners were earning significantly more. White hunters could earn even more than skinners.

Because most Plains tribes were alarmed by these events to the point of defending their territories, increased hostilities between Indians and whites characterized the period after 1870. At that historic juncture the hostility between cultures (races) obscured the economic competition of one set of skilled employees replacing another: this was a political manifestation of an economic problem.

Changes in Native American Socioeconomic System. The destruction of the Plains Indian economic base through the extermination of the herds has been well documented (see Hornaday 1869; Goldfrank 1943, 1945; Ewers 1955; Flannery 1953). My work (Klein 1977, 1980, 1983a) and that of other ethnohistorians seeks to focus more closely on changes in the social relations of production of plains equestrians. One issue raised by Goldfrank (1945), Ewers (1955), and others shows dependency on the horse and hide trade spurring individualism. Individual social mobility based more on accumulation of wealth than on traditional giving away of wealth became pronounced among all four of the groups I studied. In its most extreme an accumulation of wealth engendered dependency among tribespeople who were previously egalitarian. Hence, Goldfrank, writing of the Blackfeet, comments on the wealth differences, notes that "The Chasm between rich and poor was widening. When an old medicine man was asked, 'Who gets respect?' he answered, 'those people who are born of rich people and maintain their riches" (Goldfrank 1943:18).

Increased reliance on individualism also strained the traditional collective forms of distribution (based on the earlier buffalo pound–drive method of hunting). Private ownership (albeit mediated by kinship considerations) of killed animals (Ewers 1955:305; Denig 1929:504) reflected the emergence of hunting on horseback. It mattered not that hunting in groups was enforced when necessary. Previous forms of distribution, such as the Dakota hunka ceremony, Blackfoot tail-tieing, or challenge sticks, all ritualistic forms of assuring someone in need, became very necessary to provision those who were without requisite goods. Here, the use of older relations of production and distribution plays a key role in the emerging economic order.

These changes also affected gender and age relations. No example of age-related tensions better reflects this than the Cheyenne incident involving the old medicine man Grey Thunder and the Kit Fox soldier society (Hoebel 1961). Throughout the plains, egalitarian gender relations fluctuated, then gave way. The rise of male political-economic fortunes and social formations rose in direct proportion to the decline of women's (Klein 1983a).

Changes in the Socioeconomic System of the Trading Post. Changes in the trading post sector of the hide trade are less well documented, but in many respects they parallel the fortunes of Native Americans. For the members of the trading post and fort, the loss of the buffalo herds also spelled an end to life as they had come to know it. Only the larger and suddenly absent capitalist could escape without a sense of loss beyond the removal of capital.

The employees' responses to the end of the hide trade and trading posts ran the gamut from desperate to dignified, including taking a turn at hunting (Chittenden 1954, 1:43), cattle raising (Norwood 1852:359), and homesteading (Wheeler 1990:245). Branch notes that with the sudden disappearance of the buffalo in Wyoming, the effect was a sudden rise in the rate of horse theft (1973:197). Others turned to the railroads, working a variety of jobs including "hired guns" (Branch 1973:199). More commonly, a dispossessed employee of the trading post turned to homesteading or ranching (Norwood 1852:359; Denig 1929:515).

Employees, agents, and other members of the trading post understood the inextricable ties between themselves and the Native American; perhaps that is why in 1883 a large group of white hunters was joined by none other than Sitting Bull's band of Hunkpapa Dakota to jointly and peacefully hunt one of the last remaining herds in North Dakota (Branch 1973:219). While at Fort Union, Rudolph Kurz came to see this as well:

Fur traders regard civilization of the Indian with detestation, because that means the end of their traffic. . . . They will no longer follow the chase as their chief occupation, consequently there will be no longer a supply of furs and skins, the present source of the trader's ready money. Anyone who investigates the history of the dispossessed Indians will find fur traders always among them warning the tribes against the whites, their own countrymen, and yet at the same time abetting the plunderers. (1970:177)

The political-economic tension in the relative positions of native hunters and trading posts, the potential for cross-cultural class ties, and racial-cultural differences are all clear from this statement. By short-circuiting class identity in favor of racial-cultural antagonism, those members of the capitalist class seeking westward expansion and maximum profits (railroad and real estate companies and politicians) could get whites to help "settle" the West. This was seen most dramatically in the railroad companies' use of foreign immigrants who were lured west with the promise of free or cheap land to act as unwitting buffers against outraged Native Americans (O'Conner 1973:125).

The many whites thrown out of work by the termination of the hide trade could seize on their cultural origins and become engaged in other aspects of Anglo-American presence on the plains (the Homestead Acts, the setting up of towns, and employment therein) all of which was premised on the seizure of Indian land. Hence, racial and cultural antagonism was adaptive for ex-trading-post whites seeking to dispossess their former, and never quite acknowledged, Native American partners. By viewing the hide trade as both a system of production and exchange—crosscutting cultural lines—we can glimpse at the way in which race and culture aborted the formation of class consciousness and identity.

Examining the hide trade in the context of articulating modes of production allows us to fashion a sociocultural model that simultaneously flashes the dual and singular nature of the cultural encounter. What this particular assessment contributes to the "articulation" perspective is a political-economic view of the two systems that is somewhat different. By delineating between the system of capitalism and its outposts, I can create a paradigm sensitive to the system it seeks to influence (Plains Indian hunters) but at the same time remains true to its internal logic. Capitalism, in the guise of the fur company, operates in accordance with the laws of the market and the search for profit. The capitalist's view of precapitalist system is, here, phasic: initial sovereignty and mutual beneficence, later dependence and subordination.

However, in the hide trade we see a peculiar twist. The equestrian hunters represent a skilled, complexly organized labor force already in place and politically capable of backing their claims on land and lifestyle with force. On the other hand, the establishment of the trading post to carry out the business of trade is far removed from the influences of the parent firm, and as such is susceptible to "frontier" influences. Rather than systematically subordinate as a precapitalist partner, the trading post becomes, on some level, an entity that seeks to replicate precapitalist relations because they make more sense in the context of the plains. Much of this is played out on a cultural rather than on an economic level, yet even the latter shows signs of being sensitive to Plains Indian ways of doing things (extending lavish credit resembles gift giving more than the rational notion of credit, turning the post into a multipurpose community center rather than a business establishment, and intermarriage). Over time the hide trade effected changes in a complete range of Plains Indian institutions (capitalism subordinated the precapitalist system), but the agent of this change, the trading post, was also transformed into something that more closely reflected the precapitalist structures it sought to alter.

This is a more dialectical rendering of the "articulation of modes of production" model. It allows us to refine our view of the entanglements between cultures, and between culture and political economy, to include subtle shadings and shifts. It also allows us to see precapitalist forms as capable of influencing the more dominant colonial power as that power became more rooted in its mission. Most importantly, it allows us to talk about entities that are at once constituent units of disparate cultures and elements in an emerging culture made up of their mutual and repetitive interaction.

CHAPTER 8

The Quest for Indian Development in Canada

Contrasts and Contradictions

J. S. Frideres

For nearly two centuries scholars and journalists have recorded how Indians in Canada have experienced physical and cultural genocide. They have provided vignettes of personal tragedies of Indians as the full impact of European society was felt. Academics have noted with facts and figures the marginalized status of Indians in Canadian society. In an attempt to deal with these issues, both the federal and provincial governments have taken action with regard to the social and economic problems facing Indian people. What has been the impact of these policies and programs? Have they increased the number of Indian people integrated into the socioeconomic structure of Canadian society?

Indian affairs in the late nineteenth century emerged out of a period of colonization, racist beliefs, and the ideology of Christianity. The dominant society's belief in the "white man's burden" and the superiority of whites over Indians was predominant. Few Canadians believed that Indian culture was worth saving. The policies and programs of the early twentieth century were directed toward assimilation—at times seemingly benign, at others coercive. Not until after World War II did a new era characterizing Indian-white relations emerge. The paternalistic ideology of the government began to give way to a more democratic philosophy. As Canada moved into the 1970s, new views emerged, a multicultural perspective developed, and new policies and programs resulted. Yet the marginalized position of Indians has changed little.

Traditionalism, and all that goes with it, was the basis of Indian culture. A strong sense of familiarity, kinship bonds, and communalism were an integral part of their way of life. These cultural values had been challenged by Euro-Canadians since their arrival in North America. The force of change had its roots long before World War II, but its impact was direct, severe, and unrelenting after the war. Now, after two postwar generations, Indians have been subjected to factors that brought about a rapid change in their way of life. The social, economic and political structures of Indian culture have been affected, but the impact has been most direct in the economic sphere.

For example, the number of Indians with incomes below the poverty line has increased to about 60 percent during the past half-century. Per capita income for Indians is about half the Canadian average. Furthermore, nearly half of Indian income is unearned—welfare, family allowance. Why this lack of success? The usual explanation is that insufficient funds have been set aside to support natives or that the funds set aside for economic development are inadequate. Given that more than $3 billion was spent by Indian Affairs in 1989 and that in 1992 the cost is expected to exceed $5 billion, it would seem that direct financial constraints are not the answer. Three major factors, however, do contribute: (1) failure of government policy to reflect the economic realities of reserves; (2) adoption of conflicting goals in attempting to achieve economic development; and (3) emphasis on a singular strategy to achieve economic development.

Before we address these issues, however, we must (1) review the geographic context in which Indian people find themselves and (2) assess their demographic and cultural characteristics.

Indian Reserves

The physical characteristics of each reserve constrain economic development strategies. The location of each reserve also affects development plans. For example, remoteness affects transportation costs and, thus, commodity prices.

"Indian land" comprises approximately 2,242 reserves spread throughout Canada. The smallest is less than 50 hectares and the largest covers 900 square kilometers. All together, Natives reside on nearly 26,000 square kilometers of land. Much of the land set aside for reserves lies in the subarctic region, although a considerable area lies within the productive Great Plains region of western Canada.

Reserves in the eastern woodlands comprise deciduous forests in the south and a mixed deciduous-coniferous canopy in the western boundary. To the north the boreal forest zone, consisting of spruce, fir, pine, and larch, covers the landscape. This northern terrain is characterized by many small lakes and extensive parklands. The region has short, cool summers and long, cold winters. The Canadian Shield, which dominates the area, lacks both renewable and nonrenewable resources. The plains area covers the provinces of Manitoba, Saskatchewan, and Alberta. This region has a continental climate. Most of the vegetation is grasslands, with few trees. Better than one-half of the area is under crop, summer fallow, or communal pasture. The northwest coast varies from mountains to deep fjords. Temperatures in this region are moderate, usually above freezing. Annual precipitation is at least 65 cm; some areas receive over 600 cm. Heavy coniferous forests with dense undergrowth dominate this region.

Cultural Characteristics of Indians

Six broad cultural areas differentiate Indians in Canada. They are the woodlands, the plains, the northwest coast, the subarctic, the arctic, and the northeastern area where Algonquian people live. To add to the complexity, ten major linguistic

groups crosscut these cultural areas. People's behavior, attitudes, and modes of thinking are determined by the cultural
context in which they grow up. These socializing experiences
set the stage for behavior in later life. Whether or not a person
sees a particular object or phenomenon, how one interprets
what one sees, and how one responds are determined by the
culture within which one is raised. However, it must be
remembered that humans are not passive individuals acting
under more or less complete constraint. Of course, they also
act upon the complex machinery of culture (Douglas 1986).

Indians tend to be categorized as culturally a homogenous
group, different from non-Indians. At a macrolevel this is an
appropriate characterization, but to implement policies and
programs on the basis of such an assumption poses many
problems which, until recently, have gone unchallenged.

Demographic Characteristics of Indians

Of the estimated 425,000 Indians in Canada, about 65 percent live in approximately 577 bands of varying sizes. Slightly
more than half are treaty Indians (have signed a treaty with the
federal government).[1] The Indian population is significantly
younger than the national population; more than one-half of
the Indian population are under twenty years of age—as compared with less than one-third for Canada. Only 3.5 percent of
the Indian population is sixty-five and over; the national average is more than 10 percent. The age structure has important
short- and long-term labor force implications. For example,
the annual increase in the working-age population for Native
people is about 3 percent—three times that of the remainder
of the population. Seventy percent of Indians have less than a
high school degree—as compared with 45 percent for the
national average. Of those attending school, fewer than 20
percent of Indian students complete high school; the national
rate is 75 percent. In addition, accessibility to secondary

schools is restricted for much of the aboriginal population because they live in remote or rural communities.

Unemployment in Native communities averages 32 percent; those who are employed are underemployed or employed as seasonal or part-time workers. Indians generally take jobs in the service and nonskilled areas. Related to level of employment is income. As noted earlier, individual Indian income averages less than one-half that of the nation.

Housing units on the reserves are crowded and in poor condition. One-third of Indian housing is considered overcrowded; the figure for all of Canada is 2 percent. Few Indian houses have facilities that are taken for granted in other Canadian houses: indoor plumbing, central heating, electricity. Health is affected by poverty: Indians, particularly younger children, use hospital facilities more than twice as often as does the general population. This has produced a mortality rate for young people three times that of the general population; the average life expectancy is only forty-six years—as compared with more than seventy years for the nation (Canada 1990).

Indian Dependency

Reserve Indians occupy a position of "domestic dependency" (Jorgensen et al. 1978). Major decisions affecting socioeconomic development on a reserve (for example, regarding commodity prices and investment patterns) are made by individuals and institutions outside the reserve. This domestic dependency is a form of political and economic domination.

Initially, Indians were treated as "domestic" nations with whom only the federal government could deal. This relationship was primarily limited to the carrying out of treaties. However, the creation of the Department of Indian Affairs, after the signing of treaties toward the end of the nineteenth century, continued the federal primacy over Indians. This department continues to control and monitor many facets of Indian people's lives through the implementation of the Indian Act of 1951, and today Indians are further controlled by legislation implemented by provincial governments.

The development strategy employed by Canada over the past century has been to view investment, production, and consumption as engines of growth. As the Saskatchewan Cluff Lake Board of Inquiry pointed out when it assessed the impact of mining on Indians, "the intrusion of the twentieth century into all parts of Canada is inexorable and the accompanying force of industrial expansion in its diverse and sometimes forms is irresistible." Thus, the industrial sector is given prime consideration in plans and programs usually concentrated in cities. While the industrial sector is being promoted, other sectors such as services and the more traditional sectors (for example, agriculture and cottage industries) are ignored. Agriculture has seldom been integrated into a development plan. Agricultural activities continue to be viewed as simply a way of increasing exports and balancing trade as well as supporting the increasing urban population (Kuznets 1972). Reserves, characterized by subsistence agriculture and domestic production, have become integrated into the larger national market through the establishment of various patterns of trade and development. As a result, national demands determine what Indians produce and, eventually, how they live.

Driben and Trudeau (1983) have evaluated the failure of the federal government's 1970s economic development programs. Analyzing a number of case studies, they point out that instead of beginning with a clear set of workable objectives consistent with the wishes of the local people, government agencies (at federal and provincial levels) worked at cross-purposes. Nor did they monitor or assess their programs once they were put in place. Driben and Trudeau conclude that the bands were rewarded for becoming dependent. Any attempts on their part to become independent were stymied. In the end, Native communities were left economically dependent upon government and thus vulnerable to fiscal restraints (Miller 1989).

Role of Technology and the Decision to Modernize

The role and commitment to technology in modernization is crucial. Technology implies a systematic approach to control of production through labor-saving devices and a sophisticated communication and transportation operation. The influence of technology is not neutral. If technology is embraced, then certain societal structures and orientations must be accepted; new values are created; and existing traditional values are challenged. Three major aspects of modern technology have had particular importance when introduced to reserves. First is the belief in the value of rationality. This means that an idea or phenomenon can be broken down into component parts, put together again, and verified. Rationality also implies the belief that if we change things, we will be able to extract more out of nature. A second value is efficiency. This means that by organizing our efforts, we will be able to increase our productivity. In short, the final output is all important. Third, and finally, modern technology promotes problem solving in a unique fashion. In other words, technology does not view nature as something to live in harmony with; rather, the goal is to manipulate and dominate nature (Wilber 1977).

When technology is brought to undeveloped areas or traditional cultures, value conflict emerges. For example, there is a difference in how technology is viewed. Developed economies view it as a marketable commodity while in undeveloped areas it is considered a free good. Another conflict focuses on the issue of standardization. Developed economies want to standardize commodity production in order to take advantage of economies of scale and efficiency. Undeveloped areas prefer cultural diversity and pluralistic social patterns which can accommodate individual needs. Finally, underdeveloped areas generally want to develop "low tech," which is inexpensive, labor intensive and small scale, while developed areas want "high tech," which is expensive, large scale, and capital intensive (Schultz 1972).

One further difference between the two cultures centers on land. We know that many reserve Indians continue to evaluate land as space where livelihoods are obtained and places where present and future generations will reside. They believe that spaces are part of nature and are of special consequence and meaning for the past, present, and future. Non-Indians do not view land in such a manner. To them, land is an economic interest. Furthermore, Indians define natural resources differently from non-Indians: non-Indians view resources as commodities; Indians do not (Jorgensen et al. 1984).

The overall goal of modernization (development) for Indians is to raise their standard of living (increase their quality of life) and to provide them with the opportunity to develop their potential while still being able to retain the more salient components of their culture. The concern Indians have with industrial development has been based on a disenchantment with the form that previous economic growth has taken. But Indians have found that modern technology has produced an income distribution and a style of development seldom in alignment with their expectations of development (Whyte and Williams 1968).

As noted previously, industrialization and modernization bring about a radical change in the social structure, and Indians are cognizant of this. Because social institutions encode information, they allow us to make routine decisions, solve routine problems, and carry out a considerable amount of regular thinking on behalf of individuals. The question Indians face is whether or not they want (or need) to move from a traditional set of institutions to those created by an industrialized society. In short, Indians are faced with two major issues which affect their decision to modernize: (1) How difficult or costly it is to obtain the necessary information about an industrialized society and (2) Which institutions (and how many) provide the individual with important information (Douglas 1986).

Obstacles to Modernization

Factors creating resistance to modernization are more complex than the "dead weight of tradition," "customs suppressing individual initiative," or the "lack of work ethic" (Myint 1972). Usually a combination of contradictory desires includes unbridled enthusiasm for economic development and exaggerated expectations from modern technology offset by resistance to the changes necessary to accommodate technology.[2] However, there are many other specific obstacles which impede Indian participation in modern society.

It is generally accepted that economic and technical advancement depend upon social and residential mobility. While Natives move from reserve to city, their mobility is best characterized as that of a sojourner. This unwillingness to take up permanent residency in a city or establish roots in another area of Canada works against Indian participation in modern society.

Many economic plans developed both by Indians and by the federal government are not realistic, given the needs, resources, and productive capacities of Native people. Conflicts between short-term and long-term goals are a third obstacle. Because different strategies are required to achieve short-term and long-term development projects, these may come into conflict. Indians want greater diversification in production in the long run, but the short-term activities (for example, nonrenewable primary resource extraction) must be supported at the same time. Finally, Indians need to develop new social institutions and to accept new values which can be integrated and adapted to their existing cultures, that is, changes in methods of work and skill levels to accommodate the new technology. Indians also need to increase their rate of capital accumulation and widen the margin between consumption and total output. This means they must reduce consumption on nonessential goods so they can save money which can be used for investment (Anders 1980).

For the past century and a half, non-Natives have developed

the natural resources on reserves to support the expanding urban centers. In doing so, they have aggravated regional disparities and rendered the exploited areas uninhabitable through, for example, deforestation and the destruction of wildlife. Indian people have not been allowed to participate in the economic development of Canada because they lack capital and relevant skills. Developments placed on or near the reserve by outsiders have disrupted and displaced Indian people in many regions. In those cases where Indian people have been involved in resource development, they have played a subordinate role such as low-paid transient labor (Barsh 1985). Egbahl (1983) calls this process "development exclusion" and notes that anytime the modern industrial segment of society initiates a large scale project, peripheral groups such as Indians have little choice as to how they will participate. Finally, experience has shown that after development has proceeded, rising prices and ecological deterioration make Indian people more dependent on cash and food imports (versus food from the land) (Waldram 1985; Collins 1986).

The results of such a development strategy are threefold. First, these projects enrich multinational organizations as well as a large cadre of personnel that are supported by this structure—consultants, banks, contractors. A good example of this is revealed in Harding's (1988) analysis of uranium mining in northern Saskatchewan. Second, regional and ethnic economic disparities widen. Indigenous people become impoverished, powerless, and increasingly unable to break the cycle of underdevelopment. Third, these development strategies increase ethnic tensions by adding highly visible economic factors to already real or imagined cultural and historical grievances (Hoselity 1972).

The current Indian economy is a unified entity of a complementary set of small-scale productive activities vested around stable production in agriculture, cottage crafts, and fur production. Indian people are at the edges of the industrialized world, although they participate in the modern economy at several, albeit limited, junctures (Asch 1987). Nevertheless, involvement is increasing. Today they have a large subsistence and a small capitalistic sector. This marginality in modern technology has kept them from entering the middle class and engaging in such activities as saving money for capital investment. Their poverty does not allow them to alter their way of life as their income remains fixed and directed toward customary expenditures (Henriot 1977).

Indian communities have been economically stagnant for decades. Personal and tribal resources are allocated in much the same way they have been for years. Over time and through experience, members of the community have developed a body of information about how to produce goods and about the contribution each will make to one's income. Similarly, people have adjusted to certain consumption and savings preferences (Chartrand 1987). How does a community free itself from this very unproductive equilibrium in which it is caught? Getting more land or making more money will not solve the problem. Superior skills—education and training—and equipment are available and must be incorporated into the Indian way of life. It also means that Natives must create a diversified and stable reserve economy (Cox 1987). Indians can no longer use an apprenticeship model to develop their skills; they must use education (Owen 1978).

Native people are seeking to achieve economic development through the enhancement of their commercial efforts. However, they are beginning to realize that long-term benefits are the basis for negotiation. In order for Indians to meet long-term as well as short-term needs, they must maximize their control over the events that take place on the reserves. This means that jurisdictional, financial, and managerial control must be exercised. For example, Indians have used the forests in many ways in the past, and most Indian communities would like to engage in forestry activities. However, they wish to take a larger role in accessing, developing, and managing resources which are presently being developed and managed by non-Indians.

Intense lobbying has been carried out by large corporations who are afraid that their own access will be limited if Indians gain control over land and forests. Today there are a few examples where Indians have begun to develop their forestry potential. Cariboo Indian Enterprises is a corporation jointly owned by fifteen bands in central British Columbia. Another example of Indian development in the forest industry involves a co-venture between an Indian enterprise and a small non-Native company which had technology and machinery but no access to timber. Hecate Logging developed a working relationship with the non-Native company and has established hiring, subcontracting, and revenue contracts. Other examples of Indians becoming involved in forestry activities, while at the same time controlling land and natural resources, are the Matsqui Band–Scott Paper agreement, the Tanizal Timber Company, the Nuu-chah-nulth Tribal Council Forestry Program, and the Musagamagu Demonstration Project.

These examples show that Indians have the ability to regulate activities of people and businesses on the reserve through negotiations and enforcement of appropriate laws and codes. This means that Indians must have control over both Indians and non-Indians on the reserves and that they will not undertake developments which increase the number of non-Indians. Finally, this means that they must control all business activity on the reserve.

The ability to generate capital for investment and to control the rate of return is an important issue that Indian communities must address. As noted earlier, previous economic development on the reserves has not produced any significant multiplier effects. This is particularly true when the development is in the form of an "export economy" or concentrates on nonrenewable resources. For example, the Fort Nelson Band receives royalties from petroleum companies for natural gas being pumped out of their reserve. Although they receive over thirty million dollars a year, they have no say over ownership, administration, or control. There is very little involvement in the industry by Indians because of their lack of education and occupational skills.

Taxation also falls under the rubric of financial control. Economic development on reserves should not be encumbered with federal or provincial taxes since Indian reserve land has been exempt from taxation since the early nineteenth century. These tax exemptions are not part of a treaty but rather are embedded in legislation.[3] The principle of taxation allows a government to finance its own activities by requiring businesses that are not producing wealth to share the costs of government services that support the needs of both business and the general population. The attempt to implement taxation procedures on reserves today further enhances the federal government's ability to regulate the economy on the reserve. In order to break this control, Indians need to establish their own taxation system. Two types of taxes have been identified as potentially appropriate for reserves: (1) possessory-interest tax, on the value of leased property and (2) business-activity tax, on the gross receipts of a business.

In addition to control over taxes, Indians should be able to provide incentive reductions to these taxes. For example, if a non-Indian business buys Indian goods and services, the taxes would be reduced. All the above factors point to the need for financial control on the reserves.

There is also a need for managerial control. This is the ability to conduct research, promote and manage business activity, and provide training programs. It is clear that when Indians have given up control of their resources to outsiders, they have lost economically in both the short and long run.

Finally, tribal control is necessary in order to create a stable and diversified economic base. The multiplier effect has been absent on reserves in the past because most purchases (at any stage of development) are made from outside the reserve. In addition, nearly all businesses on or near the reserve are owned by non-Indians. As such, there is a need to develop vertical integration of tribal economics. Take the following examples: timber (raw material–primary industries); finished wood product (secondary manufacturing); houses, furniture (retail-wholesale-commercial); and banks, loans (financial services).

Indians need to emphasize production for local needs as well as for export. In this process, the following conditions should apply:

1. Development must be on a scale that can be controlled by the tribe.
2. Development should be labor intensive, not capital intensive (it is better to create more jobs at moderate pay than a few at high wages).
3. Jobs should be consistent with Indian lifestyle and kinship obligations.
4. Development should be oriented toward the "inner economy" of reserve.
5. Development should not focus on individual businesses but rather on tribal businesses.

Tribal members must be encouraged to relate economically to the tribe; the tribe could then relate to the larger economy. Then the tribe would have more power and be able to compete against outside developers.

The short introduction to this essay suggested that there are variations in the resources, needs, and goals of Indians residing in different parts of Canada. Each group's history, regional milieu, and contact with the capitalist system has had a differential impact on needs, resources and goals. Present Indian communities range from isolate and traditional to modern and assimilated. The largest number of Indians fall at the isolate, traditional end of the continuum, although a small number are well integrated into the capitalist system. The federal Department of Indian and Northern Affairs has failed to acknowledge this diversity.

In addition, Indian Affairs has, persistently, taken the position that there is only one type of Indian development and has promoted only one type of program to help Indians develop and modernize. The one program type developed by Ottawa has assumed that Indians are at the "modern-assimilated" end of the continuum, and all policies and programs emanating from Indian Affairs are developed for this type of Indian community. What needs to be developed, at minimum, is a dual strategy with policies and programs geared to Indian communities that represent both ends of the continuum. Finally, Indian Affairs seems unwilling to be innovative in developing alternative programs for Indian people. It has long been a sine qua non of Indian Inuit Affairs Program procedures to interpret policies and programs for bureaucratic convenience, not on the basis of reality.

Natural Resource Development Strategies: Some Alternatives

The following section will identify several approaches that Indians might take in the development of one component of their economy—natural resources. It clearly demonstrates that there are many alternative development strategies. Furthermore, given the diversity of Indian communities, each must have the option of customizing a development plan. This accomplished, each will be able to generate a modest cash flow and further develop the overall economy. However, as in any development, a cost is incurred. The actual cost of developing a natural resource is directly related to the type of agreement Natives enter into with government or private industry in order to proceed.

What can Indian people do to deal with their marginal status in the Canadian economy? How can they deal with the increasing pressure to develop their natural resources? When the resources are gone, will the reserves be more impoverished? What will be the fate of their children and grandchildren? On the other hand, as the need to support the present population is great, how can they resist the promise of jobs and money?

While we focus on one aspect of the economy for illustrative purposes, it should be remembered that the present paper takes the position that there is a need to develop selected aspects of various sectors of the economy. This rejects the notion of balanced growth because: (1) it is too costly and politically impossible to develop all sectors of the economy equally, and (2) since even a developed economy is not balanced, why should a reserve economy be balanced? Natives, like other organizations, should build on their strengths.

Undeveloped areas such as reserves must search for and invest in some intermediate or basic industry whose products are distributed as inputs through industrial sectors. That is, they must set up heavy/capital goods industries rather than consumer goods industries (Anders 1980). However, most reserves do not have the ability to undertake large-scale natural resource development on their own. The capital requirements are too high, domestic economic funds are not enough, and banks will not loan money to Indians on reserves. Tribes do not have the necessary expertise to manage large scale developments. In addition, the energy industry is tightly controlled by existing multinational corporations, making it difficult for Indians to cut into the market. Finally, access to major transportation routes from many reserves is problematic (Robbins 1984).

However, there are many different types of agreements that Indians could utilize in order to develop their economic base. Because of space limitations, we will discuss only six of these here: the concession, the joint venture, the service contract, the management agreement, the development corporation, and the local producer's cooperatives.

The Concession. This strategy has been the traditional way in which Indians have become involved in nonrenewable resource development. Indians, through the federal government, grant a company all the mineral production rights. The company then makes a direct equity investment for the sole purpose of extracting a resource (Bankes 1983). The Fort William band example, mentioned previously, is an example of this type of economic development. Asante (1979) claims that in many cases the concession amounted to a virtual assumption of sovereignty over the Indians' resources by transnational corporations. Under these conditions the corporation asserted ownership of not only the fixed assets but also the natural resource itself (Bankes 1983).

Under a concession agreement there is very little direct "up front" cost for the Indian community, nor are there operating costs. In addition, these agreements are easy to administer, since the need for supervision, auditing, and training is minimal. All of this is provided by the company agreeing to exploit the minerals. In short, the cost to the band is minimal. Correspondingly, the return to the Indian community is also minimal. Indians have also found that this type of agreement does not encourage industries to train local residents to assume jobs that would thereby introduce them to the wage economy.

Indians also suffer when companies unfairly determine royalties by the price received by a wholly owned subsidiary from a refining or distribution subsidiary of the parent company. Evidence in court cases in the United States also shows that many such ruses have been used to cheat Native people. The following list identifies only a small sample of techniques employed by companies over the past decade: bypasses on wells, adjustable meters, unreported oil sales, unapproved "sales" that are fed directly into pipelines, and movement of oil from a higher royalty lease to a lower one.

The Joint Venture. This means that there are two (or more) parties who pool their interests (money, technical expertise, land) in order to develop a project. There are two variations. In the first, a separate legal entity is created which would be jointly owned by the parties involved (Indians and a development company). The second type does not involve the formation of a separate company; rather, the parties to the venture have a direct undivided working interest in the project (Bankes 1983). For example, a joint venture called Shehtah Drilling was formed among Esso (50 percent) and the Dene (25 percent) and Metis (25 percent) development corporations in 1983 to conduct drilling and service rig operations in the Northwest Territories. Chevron and the Fort Good Hope band have negotiated a joint venture agreement for oil and gas exploration, as have the Tahltan Tribal Council and Gulf Canada Resources. The ATCO/EQUTAK drilling joint venture organized between Atco–Mustang Drilling and the Inuvialuit Development Corporation (with the assistance of Petro Canada) and the Beaufort Food Services, a joint venture between Beau-Tuk Marine and the Inuvialuit Development Corporations are other examples of negotiated ventures which have been relatively successful.

The joint venture type of agreement requires that Indians (1) have some technical expertise and (2) have some "interest" which is considered valuable by the other party (for example, land and mineral rights). There is both a direct and indirect cost to this type of development. Conversely, the joint venture generally presents an opportunity for local people to increase their control over development, may increase revenues to Indians, and allows for a flexible method of collecting revenues (Bankes 1983; Asante 1979).

The Service Contract. Under agreements of this type, the status of Indian ownership over the natural resource is reaffirmed. Thus, rather than transferring the title of the resource (as in concession) to the developing company, the Indian community simply hires the corporation as a contractor or business partner to perform a specific task for a specified amount of money. A major implication of this strategy is that Indians have to have a substantial cash flow in order to pay for the "up front" cost of the development. Given that mineral exploration and production is highly capital intensive, this means that substantial monies would be necessary and must be available to Indians prior to the actual development. Both Zakariya (1976) and Bankes (1983) point out that under this type of agreement the band would have no internal control over the project, and there would be minimal opportunities for Indians to gain employment or technical and administrative skills. Careful monitoring of the project would be required by the Indians to ensure that maximum benefits would be derived. The benefits of such an arrangement would be that Indians would retain total ownership and jurisdiction over the

natural resource. Other firms would supply the technology
(and risk capital) to explore, develop and market the resources.

Management Agreement. This is a strategy whereby Indians purchase expertise for a specified period of time. The contracted consultants can act as advisers while management
(Indians) retains sole control of the company, or it can relinquish control to the consultants.

The Development Corporation. These corporations are
created to help plan and implement the development goals of
a community or region and to assist business development.
The Fort Nelson band's Eh-cho-Dene Enterprises, a firm spe-
cializing in oilfield facilities and land development, is a good
example. This band and other bands in the area have formed
an agreement to further develop tourist facilities in the area.
The corporation may involve itself in risk capital, or it may be
an advisory body. A variation of this strategy is referred to as
a local producers' cartel. This is a business strategy which
involves the formation of a syndicate or trust that is able to
take over a business venture from the original developer and
carry on all negotiations with developers. The cartel takes over
from the traditional developers and controls the operation.
When twenty five American Indian tribes created CERT
(Council of Energy Resource Tribes) in order to control all
mineral development on the reserves, they established a
cartel.

Local Producers' Cooperative. These are usually voluntary
nonprofit societies incorporated to run a business. The members of the cooperatives own shares of the business, and each
has one vote at every general meeting. A board of directors
usually is elected to operate the business and carry out day-to-
day activities. In effect, a cooperative is a business owned by
its customers.

In 1959 the government began to encourage and support a
number of locally owned and operated cooperatives. This idea
seems to fit particularly well with one of the elements of Indian
culture—sharing. The first Native cooperatives were producer

oriented—art, fishing, crafts, and the like. Then consumer cooperatives emerged where both importing and exporting activities were carried out. In many communities, cooperatives and other private enterprise businesses (for instance, Hudson's Bay Company) exist side by side—selling and buying many of the same products.

The Native cooperatives have two major problems in continuing their operations. First of all, they often lack managers with good management skills. Second, they find it difficult to engage in direct competition with other integrated multinational companies. Nevertheless, they have provided employment for Native people. Today they are the largest employers of Natives in the North with annual sales of $30 million. Today there are about fifty co-ops employing about six hundred people and generating nearly $10 million in annual income. Nevertheless, an infusion of government monies is still required for many co-ops to continue operation. Over time various government departments have contributed more than $10 million to the development of cooperatives. In 1983 the federal government set aside an additional $10 million for a continuation of its Co-op Development Program. Much of this has been directed toward the training of directors, managers and staff to ensure their competence in running the co-ops. An additional $2 million was set aside to help with the new production techniques and marketing strategies.

To date, the concession has been the most widely employed development strategy used by Indians. However, recently the joint venture has become a more attractive alternative arrangement by which Natives can participate in the ongoing modern economy. This strategy has been made possible because of the federal government's involvement. They have loaned money to Native companies and have guaranteed their backing. However, with no control or ownership of the natural resources and little capital to invest in vertical linkage, it is unlikely that these joint ventures can continue or be made a viable economic strategy by Native people.

Each of the development strategies discussed will have

both benefits as well as costs. Hence, the type of agreement that a Native group might wish to make is ultimately determined by the group's needs, resources and goals. For example, if a Native group (for instance, the Cree, of James Bay) wanted to maintain a subsistence way of life and still allow development of natural resources, the concession type of agreement might be appropriate (Owen 1978).

Conclusion

Notwithstanding their goals, Indian people have three major problems that confront them in trying to make a decision as to whether or not to develop their natural resources. First of all, and unique to our case study, many of these resources are nonrenewable and thus are a "one shot" event. What happens when the natural resource runs out or is no longer a valued commodity?

A second major concern for Indian people is the impact of the development (both short- and long-term) on their communities. There is increasing evidence and awareness of environmental damage, pollution, and disruption of Indian ways of life by industrial activities and recent major resource development projects. These environmental effects include an impact in rate and nature of cultural change (that is, a change to a wage economy from a subsistence economy), the forcing of Indians (individuals and communities) to relocate, the disruption of fish and game populations and, in some cases, the creation of serious health hazards. In some cases, multiple effects can be seen. For example, Harding (1988) has analyzed the impact of uranium mining in northern Saskatchewan and identifies the multiple negative environmental and social impacts on Indians by the development of mines.

A third concern relates to the view that Indians have of their reserve communities. Reserves are viewed by many Indians as their "homeland." As Pendley and Kolstad point out, "it is impossible to separate tribal attitudes and actions related to their homelands. To tribal members these are part and parcel

of the same thing" (1980:223). Once the development oc-
curs, the residents must live with the consequences.

Finally, Indian people are concerned about their ability to
negotiate agreements with private enterprise for the development of their natural resources. There is a great deal of suspicion on the part of Indians when dealing with the corporate
world, and a feeling often exists that the government cannot
be trusted to act on their behalf. Hence, Indians themselves
must obtain expertise in the area of development in order to
insure that they receive the best deal and are aware of the
impact of the development (Jorgensen et al. 1978).

The foregoing concerns (plus others) have forced Indians
to be cautious when making decisions about natural resource
development. It is an "ethos" that neither government nor private enterprise have taken into consideration when approaching Indian peoples. As Fudge (1983) points out, Indians are
conservative in strategic outlook, emphasizing loss avoidance
rather than risk taking. Indian community leaders are, therefore, often caught in a dilemma. On the one hand, they are
urged by local residents to assert a public desire for change;
yet at the same time, they are cautioned to express an intense
skepticism about any specific proposal to achieve change.

Indian people must convince federal and provincial officials
that they are not a single homogeneous group. Indian communities must be afforded the opportunity to develop according to their needs. Furthermore, Indian Affairs must develop
alternative programs to match the needs, resources, and
goals of different Indian communities.

Today most reserves have variations on a theme of "dual-
allegiance economic development." These adaptations have
been made primarily as a result of nondirected adjustments
by local residents over time due to opportunities made available by expanding economies. All were a result of dramatic
human population decline, resource decimation, or forced
relocation by government.

Socioeconomic indicators continue to reveal that there has
been little improvement in the economic status of Indians in

Canada. Employment and economic development opportunities of Indian people, collectively and as individuals, will continue to be fundamental concerns for the future. There are a number of initiatives in the area of economic development, such as the interest shown by Indian people and communities in developing new businesses and establishing their own trade and business organizations, exemplified by the Native Investment and Trade Association. The First Nation Technical Institute and the Aboriginal Economic Development Strategy have been created to develop new opportunities for Indian people and communities. The federal government will need to remove legal restrictions blocking economic development on the reserves so that Indians can properly develop and retain local control.

CHAPTER 9

Autonomy and Constraint

The Household Economy on
a Southern Ontario Reserve

Max J. Hedley

Throughout their encounter with the agents of colonization, aboriginal peoples in Canada have been inexorably drawn into the national and global processes of accumulation character- istic of an expanding capitalist society. The consequences of this have been well documented with respect to the fur trade (Bishop 1974; Ray 1974; Wolf 1982) and, to a lesser extent, in other areas of commodity production and wage labor (Knight 1978). The point to recognize is not only that cultural and social transformation occurred, but that the relationships aboriginal peoples entered into as commodity producers and wage workers incorporated their labor into the central eco- nomic process underlying the reproduction and transforma- tion of Canadian society. Despite this incorporation, it has been noted that many Native peoples retained a considerable degree of local autonomy (Brody 1975; Henriksen 1973; Tan- ner 1979). This has been particularly noticeable for those peri- ods during which Native peoples were living off the land. Here, the isolated character of camp life and a dependence on the land for trapping and subsistence allowed for the retention of control over processes of material and cultural reproduction.

The situation of Native peoples on reserves in the more

densely settled regions of southern Canada is different and, perhaps because it lacks the romantic aura of the north, has attracted far less attention. Not only were Native peoples historically involved in commodity production and wage labor (Knight 1978), but their affairs fell directly under the control of the federal government and its British and French precursors. With the formation of the Canadian state at Confederation in 1867, the federal government assumed responsibility for the affairs of Indians. In 1876 preexisting legislation concerning Native peoples was consolidated into the Indian Act which, with its subsequent amendments, continues to provide the legal framework defining the relationship between the federal government and registered Indians.[1] This all-inclusive legislation continues to grant the government extensive powers.

Administrative control was centralized in the Department of Indian Affairs,[2] represented on the reserves by the ubiquitous figure of the Indian agent. While various forms of local government, elected or traditional, have existed since the nineteenth century, they possessed little formal power and were unable to influence policy formulation. The situation on southern reserves was one in which an authoritarian and hierarchically organized bureaucracy administered its policies in accordance with its own interests, regardless of the wishes of Native peoples (Titley 1986). It is, then, with little surprise that we find a major study in the 1960s describing Indian Affairs as "a quasi-colonial government dealing with almost the entire life" of Indian peoples (Hawthorn 1966:368). This conclusion has been affirmed by many other writers (See also Carstens 1971; Lithman 1984; Frideres 1988; Titley 1986; Weaver 1981).

Federal control over reserves was used to pursue a policy which sought to destroy the traditional practices and patterns of authority, while with the assistance of missionaries, imposing a new social and cultural order. This was the policy of "civilization," or assimilation, which persisted at least until the 1970s. One of the objectives was to turn Native peoples into commodity producers and industrial workers. The Superintendent of Indian Education in 1911 provided a clear statement of this policy. The aim of Indian education was not only "scholastic," but also to instruct "in the means of gaining a livelihood from the soil or as a member of an industrial or mercantile community" (Canada, *Annual Report* 1911:273). While denying intent to "transform the Indian into a white man," the report stated that the objectives of education included "the substitution of Christian ideals of conduct and morals for aboriginal concepts of both" (Canada, *Annual Report* 1911:273).

The economic policies are of concern, for they sought to define the way reserve populations were to be incorporated into the capitalist economy. Of particular interest here are the policies relevant to reserves in southern Ontario. Once the bulk of the land had been appropriated for settlers, the policies of the pre- and post-Confederation governments were directed towards turning reserve populations into agriculturists. The policy ideal was of the self-sufficient pioneer household, in which production was based on family labor and the property regime was characterized by private ownership of the means of production. It involved production for both self-consumption and exchange. Nomadic habits were to be curtailed as Native people developed an appreciation of the virtues of private ownership and became self-sufficient farmers within the expanding Canadian state. A particular merit attributed to this policy was the protection it provided for the public purse. It would help to ensure that Native farmers financed their own subordination on the reserves.[3]

In general terms, concern here is with cultural autonomy on a southern reserve which, unlike the bush camps in the north, has been subject to the direct political intervention of Indian Affairs since the 1830s. The particular empirical focus is the agrarian household economy on Walpole Island First Nation just prior to its demise in the 1940s. There are two related issues which will guide the discussion. First, there will be an examination of the ways in which political and economic interests entered into the formation and reproduction of the

Fig. 9.1. Walpole Island First Nation Reserve, Ontario, Canada.

household economy. Second, there will be a delineation of the basis of cultural and economic independence which reserve residents associate with the time. The latter is a complex issue, for, unlike in the north where cultural continuities seem more obvious, we are dealing with a situation in which aboriginal lifeways have undergone extensive transformation. Under such circumstances it is easy to assume that people are without traditions or have retained only a little of what is authentically their own. This assumption does an injustice to the lives of many Native people, for it fails to recognize emergent traditions which retain a distinctiveness despite incorporating the experience of domination. The household economy of the 1920s and 1930s was part of such a tradition. For those who remember the time, it is described as being marked by economic independence and cultural autonomy. To understand this it is necessary to examine the ways in which the relations of production were linked to the social relations of household and community, and to assess the manner in which general political and economic processes were incorporated into household and community life.

The discussion to follow covers a period beginning with the emergence of an agrarian household economy on the reserve in the nineteenth century and ending with its demise in the 1940s. Emphasis is placed on the period between 1920 and 1940 and is based on interviews with people who remember the time, thus allowing us to develop a fuller understanding of the local economy and community life than would otherwise be possible. The primary source of historical data is the annual reports of the Department of Indian Affairs to the government of Canada. These contain the submissions of Indian agents until 1917.

The Agrarian Household Economy: Political Control

Walpole Island First Nation Reserve is located in southwestern Ontario, bordering the state of Michigan. Situated on the Canadian portion of the St. Clair River delta, the reserve covers approximately 58,000 acres and consists of six islands. The largest of these are Walpole Island (30,122 acres) and St. Anne's Island (10,834 acres). The low-lying topography includes extensive areas of marshland covering the southern third of the reserve and providing a major habitat for muskrat and large numbers of migratory birds. A third consists of woodland (bush), while the northern third is agricultural and residential land. The surrounding waterways provide a rich habitat for various species of fish. While the mode of exploitation has changed, the resources of land and water remain important to band members.[4] The band population in 1987, consisting of descendants of Ojibwa, Potawatomie, and Ottawa peoples, was 2,476, of whom 1,738 lived on the reserve.

The formation of Walpole Island as a reserve has its roots in several land surrenders (treaties) made with the British imperial government in the late eighteenth century. The area of the reserve was left under Indian control when the land to the east and south (1790) and the land to the north (1796) was surrendered (Surtees 1983:47–53). At the time of the surrenders the government sought to obtain land for European settlement, to ensure title to land which was already occupied, and to make provision for Indian peoples who were still considered to be valuable allies in war (Surtees 1983). Direct governmental intervention in island affairs dates back to the 1830s, when its occupants came under the jurisdiction of a superintendent of Indian affairs. They became a separate band in 1836, and two years later an Indian agent, located at Sarnia, was assigned to oversee their affairs as a distinct band (Taylor 1984:25, 28). Permanent European presence was secured with the arrival of missionaries. The first attempt to establish a permanent mission on the reserve, made by the Jesuits, ended in failure in 1849 (Nin.Da.Waab.Jig 1987:40). However, by this time the Church of England had established a church and school among the Ojibwa. A decade later the Methodists did the same among the Potawatomie (Nin.Da.Waab.Jig 1987: 41). As is well known, the interests of the missionaries and government were closely entwined, for conversion to Christianity was linked to the attainment of the "virtues of civilization" and the establishment of a sedentary agrarian population.

Control by the federal government became more direct in 1883 when the administration of the band was transferred to a resident Indian agent. About this time the traditional leadership structure was replaced by an electoral system. This involved the election of chiefs and band councils for both the Ojibwa and Potawatomie bands. Separate councils remained in operation until their amalgamation in 1940 (Nin.Da. Waab.Jig 1987:37). During this period the General Council met to deal with issues concerning both bands. In essence, band councils had little formal power, because they were part of the administrative structure of the Department of Indian Affairs. Despite the power of the Indian agent, there is ample evidence to suggest that councils were not always prepared to comply with the policies of Indian Affairs (see Nin.Da.

Waab.Jig 1987:52–54). This system of administrative control remained in place until 1965, at which time the people of Walpole successfully sought to free themselves from the excessive control of the agent. The band became the first in Canada to achieve self-government, as it was known at the time, under the terms of the Indian Act (see Taylor 1984).

Emergence of the Agrarian Economy

During the first half of the eighteenth century the movement of Euro-Canadian settlers into the region steadily eroded the resource base used to sustain nomadic Native lifeways. This loss of resources was associated with the emergence of Walpole Island as a place of permanent settlement. The initial Ojibwa residents were joined by Potawatomie and Ottawa Indians from the United States in 1839. With this influx the population rose from 319 in 1839 to 1,140 in 1842 (Taylor 1984:26). The population was 804 in 1869 and fluctuated between 769 and 852 for the rest of the century. Throughout this latter period those of Potawatomie descent formed between 25 and 30 percent of the total population.

By the 1840s the people of Walpole had started to incorporate a settler-styled agriculture into the round of subsistence activities (Nin.Da.Waab.Jig 1987:30; Taylor 1984:26). Cultivating about four hundred acres of land mostly retrieved from squatters, they seem to have been following farming practices similar to those of European settlers. However, the social organization of production remained distinct, for it involved separate bands working in enclosures under the coordination of an "inferior chief" (Nin.Da.Waab.Jig 1987:34). The significance of agriculture increased throughout the century. By the late 1870s the Indian Office could report that many of the farms cultivated by the Ojibwa were "pretty well cultivated", and that they participated in an "annual Exhibition of animals and farm produce" (Canada, *Annual Report* 1879:21).[5] It was also observed, despite their later arrival on the reserve, that a number of Potawatomies had their "farms in a tolerable state of cultivation" (Canada, *Annual Report* 1879:22). However, a few years later the agent could note that farms were too small and that for many the cultivated land was "evidently of less extent" than it had been a decade earlier (Canada, *Annual Report* 1883:5). Despite what was seen as slow progress, the area of land under cultivation was rising. It had reached 2,297 acres by the mid–1880s and a little over 3,000 acres ten years later (Canada, *Annual Report* 1886, 1897).

Within fifty years the people of Walpole were relying extensively on agriculture for self-provisioning and income. The extent of this transformation led the agent to report that there was a "general looking to the land" and that there were "very few men (heads of families) now on this reserve who did not farm to some extent" (Canada, *Annual Report* 1888:4). By 1895 any doubts about the success of agriculture seem to have been dispelled, for farming had become the "most important of all operations" (Canada, *Annual Report* 1896:13). A wide range of crops were cultivated: wheat, barley, oats, buckwheat, corn, potatoes, beans, peas, and other vegetables. Households also raised cows (for milk, butter, and some cheese), pigs, sheep, horses, and poultry. Moreover, many had orchards in which they grew fruits such as apples, pears, and plums. It should be stressed that farming was for both self-provisioning and for the market. A variety of products were sold, including "considerable fruit" (Canada, *Annual Report* 1885:3), grain (wheat) (Canada, *Annual Report* 1891:2), hay (Canada, *Annual Report* 1897:33)[6] and, for a brief period, sugar beet (Canada, *Annual Report* 1901:43).[7] The mixed farming that had emerged on Walpole Island was similar to that described for other reserves in Ontario (Christie 1976; Rogers and Tobondung 1975; Knight 1978).

There were marked differences in the size of Walpole farms. In the 1883 report the agent noted that there were 2 farms over 60 acres; 3 farms of 60 acres; 5 farms of 40 to 60 acres, 11 of 30 to 40 acres, 14 of 20 to 25 acres, and the remainder of 1 to 17 acres. The latter were described as "mere patches"

which, "ploughed from year to year," "soon become sadly
deteriorated" (Canada, *Annual Report* 1883:5). Inasmuch as
reserve residents were cultivating land, the figures suggest
that the bulk of the population, probably over 600,[8] was associated with these "patches". Evidence for continuing differences in farm size can be drawn from the 1890–1891 census.
Of a total population of 885, there were 193 people identified
as occupiers of lands on Walpole Island. Of these, 100 (52
percent) occupied 10 acres or less, 86 (44 percent) occupied
from 11 to 50 acres, and 7 (4 percent) occupied from 51 to
100 acres (Canada, Census 1890–1891:274, 278). The occupiers of the largest holdings are probably those described
as being comparatively wealthy with "surroundings equal to
many white farmers" (Canada, *Annual Report* 1888:4).

Even considering the general level of agricultural development at the time, Walpole farms seem to have been relatively
small. An indication of this can be gained through a comparison with the adjacent area of Dover Township, based on figures drawn from the census (Canada, Census 1890–1891:38,
50). It should be noted that the percentage of improved land
(not forested or woodland) occupied was about the same (85
percent on Walpole and 87 percent in Dover). According to
the 1890 census, we find 783 occupiers in Dover distributed
as follows: 21 percent occupying 10 acres or less, 36 percent
occupying 11 to 50 acres, 26 percent occupying from 51 to
100 acres, 17 percent occupying 101 and over (there were no
Walpole farmers in this category). The proportion of Dover
farmers with land holdings of 51 acres and over is 43 percent
compared with 4 percent on the reserve. At the other extreme,
only 21 percent of Dover occupiers are on 10 acres or less,
compared with 52 percent on the reserve. Another indication
of the relatively small size of Walpole farms is provided by the
average acreage per occupier of the land. For Walpole this is
16.4 acres per occupant and for Dover 66.3 acres per occupant. On average, farm size on Walpole was 24.7 percent of
that found in Dover Township.

A further indication of the limited size of Walpole farms is provided by a comparison of the area under cultivation. We find that the total land under crops per occupier is 6 acres on Walpole and 39 acres in Dover Township. For total improved land (under crops, in pasture, and gardens and orchards) the figure rises to 14 acres per occupier for Walpole and 58 acres per occupier for Dover.

The relatively small size of most farms points to the particular circumstances of reserve farming. A difficulty, at least for the agent, was the presence of a land shortage, as seen in the report of 1890, where it is stated that thirty members of the reserve had left for Green Bay, Wisconsin, where they could "get land easily among their own people...." (Canada, *Annual Report* 1891:3). There were also several reports of young men being forced to seek work elsewhere because they could not obtain land. The problem, from the agent's perspective, was not the amount of reserve land that could be used for farming, but the prevailing system of land tenure. In fact, the agent estimated that there was enough land, if surveyed, to support three times the reserve's population (about eight hundred at the time). The agent seems to have brought this issue to council in an attempt to make land available to young men who lacked it. However, when the possibility of a survey was raised, the "old men objected strenuously" (Canada, *Annual Report* 1887:20).

This "strange aversion" to changes in the land regime points to an area in which the band council was able to protect the interests of those who sought to preserve local tenure arrangements.[9] It also identifies a divergence of interests between those who had adequate access to land within existing arrangements, and those (the "young men") to whom existing rights constituted a constraint on their own aspirations. Consequently, when it was observed that "all the available land" was "farmed at capacity" (Canada, *Annual Report* 1889:1), the reference was not to the capacity of the reserve, but to the land made available through the reserve's tenure system.

We have noted that by the end of the century the agent

could assert that all were "engaged for the most part in agriculture." This statement requires careful interpretation, for the
extent to which households relied on agriculture varied and
was seldom total. Some of those who depended exclusively
upon farming were described as "very-well-to-do", because
they were "comfortable in their houses," and had "plenty to
eat, and something to sell" (Canada, *Annual Report* 1897:
33). However, the latter comment suggests that even the
"well-to-do", presumably on the larger farms, relied on subsistence production. It follows that the emergent agrarian
regime, which was encouraged and praised by the agent, was
primarily directed towards self-provisioning, though any surplus was sold. The overall strategy becomes clearer when we
turn to the other activities involving Walpole agriculturalists.

It is important to recognize that agriculture was not the only
means of obtaining subsistence or generating revenue for
Walpole households. However, a preoccupation with agriculture in the Department of Indian Affairs's reporting meant that
other activities were largely ignored. Hunting was dismissed
with condescending references to the persistence of an unde-
sirable love of the "chase." The production and sale of Indian
crafts were also treated with disdain. In 1882 the deputy superintendent general asserted that too many farms failed to meet
the wants of their families and, therefore, had to rely on
"basket-making, axe handle manufacturing, bead work" and
moccasin-making to meet their needs. Making matters worse,
Indians had to visit many places to sell their handicrafts. As a
result, "their old, and to them, congenial" nomadic habits
were encouraged, with their "morally and materially ... evil
results" (Canada, *Annual Report* 1882:xlvii). Again, at the end
of the century the agent for Walpole Island was still prepared
to suggest that too many depended on the sale of baskets, axe
handles, bows and arrows, and other souvenirs and could not
be induced to put crops in the ground (Canada, *Annual
Report* 1897:33).

Despite the tone of these comments, the agent's reports

indicate that nonagricultural activities provided important sources of income for reserve households. A closer examination of the reports makes it clear that the people of Walpole pursued a wide range of nonagricultural activities generating revenue. They were extensively engaged in the production of fish,[10] furs,[11] domestic crafts, and lumber, as well as in casual wage labor.[12] Moreover, there were times when these activities made a vital contribution to maintaining farm households. The 1886 report noted that when farming was supplemented by fishing, hunting, and the sale of handicrafts, households were placed in "very comfortable circumstances" (Canada, *Annual Report* 1886:xv). Eight years later the agent observed that no one suffered during a poor crop year, because necessities could be met with "extra exertion in the way of making baskets, axe handles and other things for sale" (Canada, *Annual Report* 1894:2). Even if we acknowledge the significance of these handicraft activities, the picture remains incomplete because there is barely an allusion in the reports to the use of the reserve's resources for self-provisioning by farming. Yet this was probably extensive. Instead, comments on what are defined as "supplemental activities" are confined to those generating revenue.

The tenuous nature of the household's commitment to subsistence agriculture became apparent during the first decade of the twentieth century. Within a very brief period male labor rapidly transferred from farming to wage labor, and agricultural output declined. By 1907 the agent could report that the "majority of Indians work amongst the whites in the beet-fields in the summer, and in the woods in the winter" (Canada, *Annual Report* 1908:37). The views expressed by the agent show little enthusiasm for these changes. In fact, there was a touch of disdain in such comments as they "would rather work out for the whites than farm their own land" (Canada, *Annual Report* 1908:37), or that their wages were good but they "live well and dress well and do not save any money" (Canada, *Annual Report* 1908:38). This echoed the government's continuing commitment to traditional agrarian policies. A clear enunciation of this position can be found in the deputy superintendent's report for 1908. Here it was stated that only in agriculture can "Indians as a class ... equally contribute to the commonwealth" and "to their own permanent material, and perhaps it may be added, moral benefit" (Canada, *Annual Report* 1908:xxiv). There was perhaps a sense of vindication for the department's commitment to its policy when, less than a decade later, it could be said that the "greater number" were once again returning to subsistence farming (Canada, *Annual Report* 1917:18). This renewed involvement in farming remained in place until the 1940s.

Agricultural activity, then, declined during the first decade of the twentieth century as off-reserve employment rose. However, it seems reasonable to assume that households remaining on the reserve (and not all did) continued to be involved in a broad range of activities. This could hardly have been otherwise in a context where most of the work was seasonal. There was undoubtedly a redeployment of labor within households, but small-scale commodity production and self-provisioning continued. This can be seen in the fact that revenue was still derived from fishing, trapping, and the sale of crafts [13] and agricultural products. Moreover, households continued to grow a variety of crops such as potatoes and corn and to maintain livestock such as cows, pigs, and poultry, all important components of subsistence farming. It appears, then, that there was not a major restructuring of the reserve economy, for households remained committed to a broad range of activities. The ready movement into the work force indicated both the labor-intensive nature of subsistence agriculture and the difficulty of raising incomes in a situation where most holdings were small. Conversely, the subsequent reemphasis of agriculture points to one of the ways in which general economic changes constrained household strategy and structured the reproduction of the subsistence regime. We now turn to a closer look at the organization of the household economy during the final years of its existence.

The Household Economy (1920s and 1930s)

The self-sufficient nature of reserve households, with their dependence on local resources, persisted until the 1940s. This was the final phase in the life of the household economy, for in the postwar years local production was replaced by a more thorough reliance on wage labor and a dependence on transfer payments. During this later phase the symptoms of social disorder, which typify many modern reserves, began to appear. But here we will turn towards developing a more detailed understanding of the household economy during the 1920s and 1930s and towards gaining a more thorough appreciation of the ways in which the experience of domination was absorbed into local culture. The practices of this period have undoubtedly changed since the late nineteenth and early twentieth century. Nevertheless, it is suggested that the basic structure of the household economy of the time was similar to that which characterized the earlier period. The analysis is based upon a series of interviews with residents of Walpole Island who personally experienced the decade.[14]

The 1920s and 1930s are portrayed as a time when people on the reserve were independent, and a time when households could meet their needs through their own labor. These views are conveyed by the following description of the 1920s: "We had independent people.... They made a living off a farm. They had horses, cows, sheep, chickens, ducks, planted their own gardens and what they produced from the gardens, that's what they lived on. And they had trees—fruit trees, all kinds of apple trees, pear trees, peach trees, and raspberries and strawberries" (Nin.Da.Waab.Jig 1982–1984a).

The self-sufficiency associated with the farm household underlies the observation that people were independent. This perception was widely shared by those interviewed. People were well aware of the political constraints of the reserve system. However, control over subsistence meant that the intrusive influence of the government, linked to dependence on transfer payments and the delivery of a broader range of services, did not permeate the affairs of the household in the way that it does today. The degree of material independence is indicated by the following comment: "I had a garden, 41 acres. Good many times I lose through water.... I planted potatoes, beans, everything that I need, what I want to use, I never bought nothing much, just the salt, sometimes pepper" (Nin.Da.Waab.Jig 1982–1984b).

Farm households possessed, or had ready access to, the means of production. These included farm implements, horses, an occasional tractor, and ownership of the land required for cultivation. Individual possession of farm land was well established by the late nineteenth century, though the configuration of rights associated with this are unclear. However, by the 1920s the land had been surveyed and a system of individual allotments was consolidated through the issue of certificates of possession.[15] The rights an individual acquired approximate those we associate with private property. It included the right of exclusive access and the right to dispose of the land in any way that the owner saw fit. The land could be bequeathed in a will,[16] sold, given away, or leased.

A major qualification to this was that possession could only be transferred to another band member. A further complication was that women were obliged to dispose of their land if they married outside the band, wedding either a male who was not a registered Indian or a registered Indian who was a member of another band. In essence, a regime of private ownership was in place to ensure that households, in that they had legal possession, could maintain access to the land required for cultivation.[17] In this we see the fruition of the Department of Indian Affair's policy, for throughout the nineteenth century the security offered by private ownership was seen as an important means of curtailing nomadic patterns and nurturing attachment to an agrarian way of life.

To varying degrees, households drew upon a rich array of resources which were available on the reserve. Those households reliant on wage labor were still likely to engage in subsistence fishing and hunting, particularly when employment was seasonal. As one informant from such a family put it, there was "not much gardening," though "mother did some and the kids helped." We "mostly ate muskrat and fish", though when "Dad worked out in town" we ate "steaks and chips" (Nin.Da.Waab.Jig 1982–1984g). It seems that households dependent on wage labor could experience considerable difficulty when work was not available.[18] At the other extreme, we find about twenty-two households involved in a summer commercial fishery. These were operating with crews of four to six hands recruited from family members or from other households (Jones 1988:87). The species harvested included carp, catfish, sheephead, bullhead, and various types of sunfish (Jones 1988:32). Because of its seasonal nature, fishing was supplemented with guiding duck hunters and trapping muskrat.

Farming households could enhance their self-reliance through harvesting a wide range of resources available on the reserve. These included trees (for gathering maple syrup), fish, muskrat, birds, rabbits, grouse, berries, nuts, and wood for fuel and construction. As in the more distant past, these resources also might have provided a means of generating revenue. By this time commercial fishing seemed to have been confined to a few specialized households. However, the sale of firewood to homes in Algonac, Michigan, was widely practiced, and households continued to collect the raw materials required for making crafts. Muskrats, trapped extensively by some, could still provide a source of income for those households using only a few traps or simply hunting with spears. The way these activities fit into the reproductive strategy of farm households is suggested by the following comment:

At that time ... if somebody want money they just go out there, kill three or four muskrats—five maybe, take them home. We used it for meals—for meat, fur. ... You go out there, catch five or ten muskrats, and get what you want. No way you go out there and slaughter them. They saved them for the next week, for us too. In my young days, as far I know, nobody didn't even hunt Sundays. Some used to trap Sundays, but I wouldn't go out there. That's because nobody would steal, just take care of their own traps. (Nin.Da.Waab.Jig 1982–1984f)

The reference to stealing was used to draw attention to the more laissez-faire approach to contemporary hunting. However, it can serve to return us to the question of the household's rights of access to resources. The bulk of the reserve, which was mainly marshland or forest, was not held by individuals under certificates of possession but was held in common. With the exception of regulations pertaining to leased lands (hunting clubs and a large farm), which were sources of conflict, and regulations covering the removal of timber and hay from common property (a permit was required), resources could be used freely. Despite being an "open resource" for band members, there was a degree of informal regulation by users. This seems to have been most well developed in areas where resources were used commercially, including limiting access to fishing areas cleared for nets, traplines set for muskrat, and the ponds and blinds maintained for duck hunting. Nevertheless, households retained the right to exploit a wide array of subsistence resources and to derive income from them. In doing so, informal regulations were honored.

Household Exchange

Even among households that were not specialized, variations in the composition and level of output did occur. These could result from differences in taste, skills, quality and location of land, equipment, available labor, and the impact of micro-environmental variations (flooding for example). Consequently, at any time a particular household might generate a surplus in one area while experiencing a shortage in another. This provided the basis for exchange between households. One characteristic form of exchange was barter. It was explained this way:

My Dad didn't hunt, and in order for us to get any muskrat or duck, well, my mother did a lot of canning, and she always had a garden. She had chickens, and geese, turkey, and when she heard like Wesley Jones used to have fish, well, she'd get something ready and she'd go and trade it off. They were always trading; what you didn't have you knew somebody had it, and it was like that all the time. That's how people survived. (Nin.Da.Waab.Jig 1982–1984c)

Bartering also occurred at off-reserve fairs, where crafts would be exchanged for clothing or other items needed by households.

Not surprisingly, there was a high incidence of labor exchange. This ranged from a simple exchange of labor between individuals to work bees which involved several households. The latter included bees for gathering maple syrup, wood-cutting, sewing, or quilt and basket making. As we shall see below, bees were intensely social occasions. There were other exchanges. When livestock was slaughtered, it was shared with other households because it could not always be preserved. In such cases the return was delayed until another household was in a position to reciprocate. More generally, the ethos attributed to the time was one in which it was expected that those in need would receive assistance from other households, and in which much sharing occurred as a matter of course. The extent to which this applied in practice is unknown. However, people invariably described these practices as being common.

To appreciate the nature of the local economy, it is necessary to recognize the limited dependence on externally produced goods and services. Given the limited access to income, we can assume that this was not entirely by choice. As we have seen, the range of products generated by households was very wide. The reserve's farm output included wheat, corn, oats, buckwheat, potatoes, beans, peas, tomatoes, milk, pigs, fruit from orchards, and other products. If not dried or canned, vegetables and fruit were preserved in root cellars and in straw-lined pits covered with earth, and these staples were used throughout the winter. In addition, there were many products available from the environment. These included muskrat, ducks, fish, rabbits, nuts, berries, and wood. Nevertheless, not all of the items entering the household's cycle of reproduction were made on the reserve. Commodities such as oil for lamps, tools, clothes, baking powder, lard, flour, sugar, and salt were desirable, though some substitution was possible and people could do without. One resident noted that "it wasn't really necessary to buy anything except maybe salt, sugar. Even sugar, they used to make their own out of boiling maple syrup" (Nin.Da.Waab.Jig 1982–1984d). Another added that "the only thing I remember my uncle buying was like, ah, lard maybe, not too much of that because at one time they used to have pigs and cows, and things like that so they had plenty. And flour and baking powder and salt ... sugar, maybe a little bit of oil for our kerosene lamps. Maybe a new axe or whatever the men needed. And clothing" (Nin.Da.Waab.Jig 1982–1984e).

The limited dependence on externally produced goods or services underlies the frequently heard assertion that the people of Walpole knew nothing about the Great Depression of the 1930s until it was over. This is perhaps an exaggeration, especially for those families who had come to depend on wage labor. However, households were undoubtedly able to limit or curtail their demand for purchased goods and to meet most of their needs through their own labor. As one informant put it, I had "no shoes" during the Depression, "but we never went hungry" (Nin.Da.Waab.Jig 1982–1984). However, this was not always enough, for it seems that some families had to sell their land, though not necessarily vacate it, during this period so that provisions could be bought. It should be clear that the local economy was not isolated from the effects of the Depression. On the contrary, the commitment to the labor-intensive work regime of the household and the reliance on subsistence production was linked to the lack of available employment. Evidence for this can be found in the rapid movement into wage labor that occurred during the first decade of the century. Conversely, this can also be seen in the rapid reentry into the household economy when the opportunities for employment in the region were diminished. As the exodus of the 1940s shows (see below), the stability of the household economy was intimately connected to the more general cycles of the capitalist economy.

Household and Community Relations

During the period under discussion (1920–1940), reserves were firmly under the control of the federal government, though many administrative concerns were handled by elected councils. Despite the political and administrative power of Indian Affairs, those interviewed invariably suggest that there was a considerable degree of local autonomy. In saying this, the point of reference was not the power of elected councils, but a realm of freedom experienced in everyday life. The basis for this was the household's access to the resources required for social and material reproduction as well as limited dependence on externally produced goods and services (there were no bills to pay). In addition, they controlled the work regime and forged their own relationships with other households, thereby meeting their needs for materials, labor, and sociability. With communications difficult, the locus of social life was to be found on the reserve. Moreover, given the absence of what we now call the "leisure industry," recreation was developed within the context of household and community relations. However, the term autonomy has to be used with care. Apart from the political and economic constraints already noted, the experience of domination was inscribed in the reserve's social life in other ways.

The social relations of the household were a focal point for mobilizing the labor required for cultural and material reproduction. It was a labor-intensive regime, drawing heavily on the work of all members of the household. Unavoidably, the young were incorporated into the routines of work and pleasure. It was not a matter of choice: "My grandmother always had things to do. And it was understood that you helped. You weren't told to do it. They expected you, and you knew it. So we passed our time making blankets, going to sewing bees, wood bees" (Nin.Da.Waab.Jig 1982–1984e).

Through these routines, the young acquired the skills required for the reproduction of the household economy and learned the patterns of authority of the household. The work was labor intensive, and there were times when work had to be done. Yet control of the work regime meant that adult members of households could usually determine its time, duration, and intensity. This allowed opportunity for daily contact with neighbors and for patterns of visiting which were "not pressured by time."

As we have noted, there was considerable cooperation between households during moments of collective labor (work bees). The importance of these was more than economic, for the gains derived were as much social as anything else. One such wood bee described in an interview makes this clear. A wood bee was open to friends, neighbors, and relatives, for anyone was free to take part. Somebody would simply announce that they were going to have a wood bee. This left the members of other households to decide whether or not they would participate. Perhaps as many as two dozen households would arrive on the morning of the bee. The men would go into the bush with cross-cut saws and axes, cut down trees and then cut and split them. Wagons were used to haul the wood from the bush. The women and children stayed in the house. Older women sewed blankets and made quilts, while the younger women would prepare the food. At noon the men would return for a large dinner, followed by a period of relaxation before returning to the bush. A meal would be served in the evening, and a party would follow. The largest room in the house would be cleared, guitars and violins would be brought out, and people would square dance and sing. Younger children were put to bed and looked after by older children, or they would be taken home by the older people.

Always some of the older men would be sitting around telling stories. The whole occasion would continue until perhaps two in the morning. These gatherings, then, were more than a means of completing a task. They were invariably turned into a social occasion marked by eating, dancing, and storytelling.

Households cooperated in creating a wide variety of social activities, such as tea meetings and sports events (including log sawing and nail drawing), which were a central part of social life. As one enthusiastic respondent expressed it: "All the recreation—baseball . . . we used to play a lot of that. Running-in they used to call it, old and young get out there and play. Lacrosse, ball and stick, played at all the fairs. And them tea meetings. Square dances. Dances, almost every night there'd be dances in the halls, in the private house. . . . Almost every night" (Nin.Da.Waab.Jig 1982–1984b).

A point worthy of emphasis is that social life involved the participation of all ages. The value attached to this remains, for it is reflected in contemporary concerns over the emergence of generation as a point of social separation.

We cannot ignore that there were other organizations which had an interest in influencing the social and cultural life of the reserve. In this respect, the church was critical, for its objectives included the establishment and maintenance of a new cultural order. The extent to which elements of uniquely Ojibwa or Potawatomie beliefs and values remained part of household and community life is unclear. Their presence is to be suspected, for the Native language remained in place. However, while this question must be put aside, we can note that the morality and beliefs associated with Christianity were incorporated into community life. In the minutes of the regular and general councils we find mention of a variety of concerns which reflect this. One set of resolutions sought to stop the "bad practices" of "white people . . . while resorting on the Island on Sunday," to close Indian groceries on Sunday (Nin.Da.Waab.Jig 6 July 1903), and to "stop the dances on the Island" (Nin.Da.Waab.Jig, February 21, 1910; Nin.Da. Waab.Jig, July 6, 1903).

We also find attempts to address the "problem" of those living together out of wedlock by devising ways of forcing couples to get married or wives to rejoin their husbands.[19] Other motions enjoined the churches to publicize the "problem" and enlist the support of Indian Affairs by requesting that annuities be withheld. Described as customary marriage, this "problem" has often received the attention of missionaries and the department in the course of their "civilizing mission". Of course, it must be recognized that the very presence of such resolutions indicates that there was not a total agreement among band members. However, we must also accept the fact that it was band members on the council who were proposing and supporting these resolutions. It would be naïve to think, especially at this point in time, that they were simply voicing the will of the agent or the missionaries.

Activities associated with the reserve's churches (Methodist and Church of England) were an important part of social life. People identified the 1920s and 1930s as a time when Sunday was not a day of work but one on which most would attend services. For those living some distance away, even getting to church was an intensely social event. The long walk to church on a Sunday morning was described with pleasure, for it was done with groups of families from neighboring farms. For the young, it was not simply a matter of choice, for "the older people always made sure" that they attended. However, as one respondent put it, there was nothing else to do and in "those days you didn't have babysitters, so you had to take all your children." You always "stood outside the church and gossiped and talked to other people who lived way on the other side" (Nin.Da.Waab.Jig 1982–1984c). It was a place where people could enjoy singing, listen to good speakers, meet neighbors and friends, and get news. The church was also a focal point for the organization of social events, such as picnics and tea meetings, which were an important part of community life. The events were organized and controlled by church members and were attended by members drawn from both congregations. In other words, the routines and teachings of the church had been absorbed and incorporated into the formation of household and community relations.

The social and cultural life of households had been influenced by organizations representing nonindigenous political, economic, and religious interests. However, interpretations of the outcome of this influence are not without ambiguity. On the one hand, the incorporation of particular practices reflects a process of domination and cultural loss. On the other, these same practices, when incorporated into the routines of household and community, became embedded in their own cultural life. In short, they were part of the community's traditions. We have already noted that the church became one of the focal points of community life.

Another institution incorporated into the life of the community, and reflecting the ambiguities in the processes of domination, was the annual agricultural fair. In one sense its presence reflected the interest of government and mission to establish a sedentary agrarian community modeled after settler farming. At its inception it invoked competitions designed to enhance the quality and quantity of farm produce, livestock, and domestic production generally. During the twentieth century the fair incorporated myths of Indianness into a "wild west show" and bareback horse racing, and also offered a wide range of sports and other forms of entertainment. The result was a major event attracting several thousand visitors to the island, some travelling from nearby cities such as Detroit on excursion boats. Not only did the fair provide an important source of income from the sale of crafts and foods, but it was an occasion "not to be missed". In other words, it had become their event. Organized by the people of Walpole, it provided an important source of income and was considered to be one of the social highlights of the year: "Ah, that fair was the best thing in the world. There were about eight or nine passenger boats land. . . . Two or three thousand people get off each boat and walk down to the fair grounds by the church. . . . It was a good fair. Best fair in the country!" (Nin.Da.Waab.Jig 1982–1984e).

Within the political and economic constraints of the reserve, the people of Walpole created and controlled the household and community relations of work and leisure. These provided the relational context within which the young experienced the community's patterns of authority and were exposed to skills, knowledge, meaning, and values which were incorporated into everyday life. The intensity of social interaction within household and locality meant that the nature of the social world was frequently reconfirmed. The degree of control over the experiences of the young, and therefore over the reproduction of the social relations of household and community, is clearly expressed in a response to a question concerning the lack of women's political power in the 1920s and 1930s:

Women had a lot more say because they had control of the families. They had control of the children. You shape the thoughts of your child. Now mothers don't even worry about their children. What they think, or what they do.... We were Christians, but a lot of the old teachings were still prevalent.... There were a lot of things that the young people were taught that is not being taught now. So while the women ... didn't go to vote ... they still had control over family. A lot more than they do now. (Nin.Da.Waab.Jig 1982–1984d)

There was, then, a realm of everyday life which was relatively free from the direct intervention of the Indian agent. It is this to which people are referring when they extol the virtues of community life in the past and their place in it. However, community control was by no means total, for the young were not free from external influence. In addition to the church were the schools, which had been on the reserve for over half a century. The schools, secular by this time, were not seen as a threat, though we can assume that education must have continuously posed a challenge to the authority of local language and knowledge. However, discontinuities were probably minimal, for attendance at reserve schools did not prevent anyone from being absorbed into the routines of household and community. For those who were sent to boarding schools the disjuncture was particularly acute. Several respondents who were young at the time made the point that they could not understand the stories which were told in "Indian". One of these was sent to a boarding school when she was five or six years old and then went to school in Detroit. Returning to the reserve in her mid-teens, she found that she "could never understand what kind of stories they were telling," because "they always talked in Indian." Although some of the stories were translated into English, she noted that "I felt kind of hurt; I think that's when I realized how much I missed my language" (Nin.Da. Waab.Jig, 1982–1984e). For those attending reserve schools the effects were more subtle, for the young remained entwined in the relationships of household and community.

The Decline of the Household Economy

The household economy and the community life associated with it were rapidly transformed during the 1940s. The major impetus for this was the economic expansion which occurred in the region. During the first forty years of the century there had always been some movement to and from the reserve as people sought wage employment. This, as we have noted, was particularly obvious in the first twenty years, when a mass exodus of farm laborers was quickly followed by their return. Industrial expansion in the region during the 1940s was also associated with a movement of labor out of the agrarian economy. However, in contrast to the earlier experience, this time the household economy declined and the associated way of life unraveled.

The process was simple enough. Some thought that it was "easier to work eight or nine hours a day" than maintain the labor-intensive regime of the household. Whatever reasons motivated individuals to seek paid employment, the loss to the household's labor supply meant that tasks had to be abandoned or supported by an intensification of the work regime of those who remained. Unless they entered the work force, which they did in greater numbers, women were very likely to assume the burden. However, it was too hard for women to maintain alone because "what the man did around the home, the women had to do. . . . My aunt did for awhile, but it was too hard. And, my grandmother was getting pretty well on in years, but she'd still go out there and work. But the gardens kept getting smaller and smaller. And so as a result, they didn't have enough food to last them all winter" (Nin.Da.Waab.Jig 1982–1984e). As a result, those engaged in seasonal work did not always have enough food for the winter. Consequently, they might continue to "go out trapping, or hunting muskrats. Did a lot of fishing to put food on the table. Muskrat meat we still ate. And duck, venison. But to have all the fresh vegetables and to be able to trade with your neighbors, I think that sort of just disappeared" (Nin.Da.Waab.Jig 1982–1984e).

The loss of labor also affected those households involved in commercial fishing, for they too experienced difficulty in recruiting family or nonfamily labor (see Jones 1988:89). A further casualty was the labor required to sustain work bees and the social life that was so intimately entwined with the routines of the household economy. Thus, even those who did not seek change found that it was unavoidable. They might, as some of the older people did, take solace in a narrower range of activities, but these were increasingly isolated as the relationships locating them in the household economy evaporated.

Those who remember the time express ideals about human relationships which they feel have been diluted, if not lost. For example, in contrasting the past with the present, it is observed that people do not share as much; visiting and neighborliness have fallen aside; people are out for themselves and will not work together; and distinctions between old and young have emerged which have fragmented a social life once unified on a different basis. It is not that such ideals are lost, but that the context within which they derived their significance and authority has been replaced by a reconstituted social order. Nor is it suggested that such ideals are without current significance, for they are invoked in discourse to describe the present. In this respect, the issue is not simply one of continuity or loss, for the ideals assume their meaning and authority in a restructured relational context.

There was little alternative to wage labor or to the household economy for most Walpole farmers, for the development of commodity production was limited by the political and economic circumstances of reserve life. The problems faced by agricultural producers generally are instructive. Canadian agriculture was increasingly characterized by concentration of land ownership, specialization, and capitalization of the productive process. As a corollary, many left the land out of necessity or because their aspirations could not be realized or sustained through farming (Hedley 1985, 1988). The further development of commodity production on Walpole would have required this type of outcome. We have already noted some of the constraints faced by reserve farmers who might have wished to expand. These included the limited size of existing holdings and the difficulty of accumulation of land in an essentially subsistence regime. A further complicating factor, at least since the land was surveyed, was the fragmentation of holdings resulting from inheritance. There was also less likelihood of losing the land through indebtedness, for there were no property taxes, and land could not be used to underwrite a loan from outsiders. However, the same regime that protected Indian ownership created an additional obstacle, for it prevented land from being used as collateral. As a result, given the lack of alternative sources, those households interested in commercially oriented farming lacked the capital necessary to obtain land, to meet the high costs of draining reserve lands, or to mechanize the productive process adequately. Faced with these formidable constraints, it is not surprising that the reserve's high-quality farmland was leased to farmers from the surrounding areas in the post-war years. In other words, paid employment was the only viable alternative to the labor-intensive farm household.[20]

Conclusion

During the first four decades of this century household relations were the primary social context through which labor was
mobilized in the production and reproduction of material and
cultural life. Individuals possessed exclusive rights to specific
plots of land and retained rights of access to other resources.
The latter might be formally defined through the provisions of
the Indian Act or informally regulated by the community.
Households drew upon local resources, supplemented with
occasional wage labor, to meet their own material needs,
though the effort of the household was joined with that of
others during moments of collective labor. There was little
choice, for alternatives to the household economy were limited and the government, as it had traditionally done, insisted
that its "wards" be self-supporting. Under these circumstances, the mutual self-interest of household members and
the complementary interests of different households were the
foundation for the reproduction of economic and cultural life
on the reserve. This is not to infer a homogeneity of interests
between the members of the same household or between
those of different households. Rather, it is suggested that the
mutuality and complementarity which existed was largely held
in place by the political and economic constraints of reserve
life.

The mutual interests of households, forged within these
constraints, structured not only the processes of material
reproduction but also the reproduction of community relations and local culture. People did retain a considerable
degree of local autonomy, but the form of this autonomy was
tied to the social conditions of the household economy. An
awareness of this allows us to understand the rapid transformation which occurred in the 1940s. Economic expansion in
the region allowed members of Walpole households to reas-
sess their commitment to the labor-intensive practices and
characteristic patterns of consumption making up the local
economy. Individuals were "free" to sell their labor to the high-

bandry, supplemented with hunting and fishing (Benson 1970 [1860]:32; McKee and Schlenker 1980:100). Another tribal class, including some mixed bloods and intermarried whites, gradually built towns in the region, established homesteads along the rich riverbottom lands of the Red River, and/or came to occupy positions of tribal leadership in the new Choctaw Nation (Graebner 1945:236; Debo 1934:60, 110–11). Full bloods were in the numerical majority for several decades and held the balance of political power into the 1880s, however (Baird 1972:23, 183).

Since the mid-nineteenth century Choctaws have been under economic, political, and cultural siege by white entrepreneurs and settlers interested in gaining access to the tribe's wealth, particularly timber, coal, and land. Today the tribe owns little more than sixty-five thousand acres. The multinational corporation, Weyerhaeuser Company, Inc., currently is the largest single private land-owner in the ten and one-half county Choctaw Nation region that was formerly owned by the Choctaw people.

Multinational corporations (MNCs) such as Weyerhaeuser are mega-enterprises in the world of private corporate business. MNCs enter a region to profitably extract local material wealth, take advantage of cheap labor supplies, or otherwise benefit materially from the enterprise. Using a "coordinated global strategy," MNCs amass a high degree of material control over their sphere of investment by monopolizing all aspects of a production process, including the raw materials base, corporate financing, research and development, and product marketing (Gilpin 1975:10; Sherman 1987:241–43; Evergreen State College 1975:53; see also J. Nash 1979a). Corporate activities are vertically and horizontally integrated with a centralized managerial structure, and they control access to strategically accessible resources, development capital, technology, and markets throughout the sphere of investment (Gilpin 1975:10; Bonilla and Girling 1973:50; J. Nash 1979a:188–92).

By using foreign subsidiaries both as sources of raw materials and as markets for finished products, MNCs take advantage of locally available resources, cheap labor supplies, and local consumer demand, while simultaneously enhancing corporate profits for the parent company (Evergreen State College 1975:5; see also J. Nash 1979a). Weyerhaeuser is an archetype of just such a multinational enterprise, with manufacturing plants in nearly thirty states and twelve foreign countries. It has a controlling interest in 5.8 million acres of domestic and 10.6 million acres of foreign land, mainly in Canada and the Far East (Weyerhaeuser *Annual Report* 1980, 1987). Today more than 50 percent of Weyerhaeuser's exports are to Japan, which it supplies from its Pacific coast tree farms (Weyerhaeuser *Annual Report* 1987). In 1982 the company obtained mineral exploration rights to six million acres, including more than eight hundred thousand acres in the Oklahoma region (Weyerhaeuser *Annual Report* 1982:9). Members of Weyerhaeuser's corporate board of directors sit on the boards of at least seven financial institutions, several universities, the Burlington Northern Railroad, Boeing Company, and various insurance and real estate companies. These interlocks permit the corporation to maintain strategic ties with allied industries, financial institutions, and marketing sources, thereby maximizing investment opportunities while reducing costs of production (Sherman 1987:241–42; Evergreen State College 1975:5ff, 10).

Weyerhaeuser's corporate success is directly attributable to its strategy of horizontal and vertical integration, foreign investment, capital-intensive production strategies, and high-yield forestry. Weyerhaeuser views its forestry practices as an "agricultural enterprise," relying heavily on scientific research and development to produce high-yield species. Vertical and horizontal integration has brought under Weyerhaeuser's corporate wing a wide array of enterprises, thereby maximizing production capacity, product use, and profitability in a sometimes unpredictable business. Wholly owned Weyerhaeuser subsidiaries include facilities for growing and harvesting timber; processing plants to make building materials, pulp, paper, and packaging products; the Weyerhaeuser Real Estate Company; home construction and mortgage companies; six railroads; and a twelve-story office building (Weyerhaeuser *Annual Reports* 1979–1982; Evergreen State College 197; Weyerhaeuser *Annual Report* 1980). With the largest timberland inventory of any company in the world, Weyerhaeuser is the only major timber producer that is wholly self-sufficient in timber for its various subsidiary enterprises (Weyerhaeuser *Annual Report* 1982:7). Diversification of corporate enterprises has maximized product use and enabled the corporation to compensate for market declines by accruing greater revenues from its diversified investments in soft disposables (mainly Sears-sold diapers), chemicals, nursery supplies, home construction, and most recently, oil exploration (Weyerhaeuser *Annual Report* 1980:17–19, 1982:9).

The localities where MNCs engage in productive activities or extract local resources often are noteworthy for the absence of internal mechanisms for local self-development, since local communities seldom have the technological know-how, financial assets, or inclination to develop indigenous resources on their own behalf. The relationship between the multinational corporation and the "satellite" or peripheral region is viewed by some as one in which new energy is infused into the region in the forms of jobs, cash, and economic growth (according to the World Bank and the "trickle-down theory"), and by others as one in which wealth is extracted and removed from the region to the detriment of the local population (according to dependency theory and theories of imperialism and colonialism). The crucial element in the situation of multinational corporate penetration, however, is that regardless of the benefits, the relationship between the core or metropolitan sector and the peripheral sector is inherently unequal. The core sector is the repository of technological knowledge, capital resources, and political know-how, while the periphery provides raw materials and cheap, readily available labor. The periphery lacks the means—technologically, economically, and politically—to develop its own resources, and therefore it permits—or is otherwise enticed or coerced into permitting—outsiders to develop these resources, ostensibly on its behalf (Bonilla and Girling 1973; Gilpin 1975:46–55).

Contrary to claims by the MNC that it generates new jobs, infuses the local region with increased income and consumer buying power, and absorbs unemployed workers, the facts often show that these claims are exaggerated or simply untrue. The MNC is typically far more opportunistic in its relationship to the dependent labor force, the community where it resides, and with respect to the raw materials it expropriates (Nash 1979a). As Thomas Walker pointed out in Nicaragua, "the common citizen is important not as a potential consumer but rather as a source of cheap and easily exploitable labor.... [S]ignificant benefits almost never 'trickle down' to the people, no matter how long the process goes on and no matter how much development takes place" (T. Walker 1981:3). The labor force may be drawn to the region because its own land base has been expropriated in a region where few or no alternative employment opportunities exist, as in situations of migrant labor (see Laite 1981). Or the population may serve as an available labor force by its very proximity to the industrial or extraction enterprise, as an indigenous population displaced by the intrusive developer. The Choctaws are an example of this type of dependent relationship, where a permanently based local population has become an essential component of the multinational timber-extraction enterprise.

Weyerhaeuser's activities in southeastern Oklahoma reflect patterns typical of multinational corporate development throughout the Third World (Walker 1981; Clapham 1985; Goodman and Redclift 1982; Laite 1981; Cardoso and Faletto 1979; J. Nash 1979a, 1979b; Frank 1969). Weyerhaeuser claimed that it created one thousand new jobs since it entered southeastern Oklahoma in 1969 (Weyerhaeuser 1977); however, in response to the economic downturn in the early 1980s, resulting in declines in housing starts, during 1982 it shut down a plant in Broken Bow and laid off 295 workers at its plant at Craig. During 1981 and 1982, 400 workers out of a total work force of 1,800 (nearly 25 percent) were laid off in Oklahoma alone, including 65 salaried and nearly 360 hourly workers (Hankins interview, 2 June 1982).

This current study investigates Choctaws as a dependent labor force and analyzes the economy of southeastern Oklahoma as a variant of a dependent satellite economy with striking similarities to many dependent economies throughout the Third World. Economic dependency is characterized by several crucial factors: outside control of local resources; lack of internal technological expertise; concentration of income and political control; and an easily exploitable labor force (Walker 1981:3)—in short, economic and political subordination by a dominant sector of a peripheral sector (see Clapham 1985).

The MNC promotes underdevelopment as a result of three phenomena, according to Dos Santos: "First, it subjects the labor force to highly exploitative relations which limit its purchasing power. Second, in adopting a technology of intensive capital use, it creates very few jobs in comparison with population growth, and limits the generation of new sources of income. . . . Third, the remittance abroad of profits carries away part of the economic surplus generated within the country" (1970:235). This form of dependent development, called by Dos Santos "technological-industrial dependence," is shaped by corporate reliance on a high degree of technological and capital input to produce an ever-increasing rate of return on investments, while the local area is exploited as a source of raw materials and cheap labor.

Research for this essay was conducted in the southeastern Oklahoma Choctaw region from 1980 to 1982, to investigate the political economy of the Choctaws and their relationship to what appeared to be the predominant controller of the region's most important resources, timber and timberland, by Weyerhaeuser Company, Inc. To examine how Weyerhaeuser's production strategy related to the local Choctaws it was necessary to overcome some of the shortcomings of traditional anthropological analysis, which typically investigates small-scale communities as if they existed as autonomous entities isolated from outside economic or political influences. It was essential, as Nader (1969) suggests, to "study up" as well as "down," to examine those institutions which control resources and their relationship to the local communities they affect.

This current investigation is based in large part upon in-depth interviews in fifty rural Choctaw households located in two counties, Pushmataha and McCurtain. Interviews were also conducted with Weyerhaeuser and tribal officials, union representatives, timber workers, and Bureau of Indian Affairs officials to assemble data on the workings of various institutions that impact significantly on the lives of local rural Choctaws. Relationships of Choctaws to their tribe, culturally, socially, politically, and economically, were also investigated, to learn how the tribal entity has weathered both the expropriation of the former reservation land base of 6.8 million acres and the takeover of indigenous leadership structures by a white majority political structure. This current study aims to analyze the Choctaw political economy as a dependent economy, and to show how the formerly independent Choctaw people serve the MNC as a dependent satellite work force through systems of labor organization, taxation policies, public welfare subsidies, and indigenous subsistence activities, all of which benefit the MNC at the expense of the local workers and local community.

Weyerhaeuser's Production Strategy and the Choctaw Response

Weyerhaeuser entered the Choctaw Nation timber region in 1969 when it bought the holdings of a large local timber producer, Dierks Forests, Inc., estimated to consist of about 1.8 million acres of land, in the largest private timberland transaction recorded in the history of the United States timber industry. This purchase added to Weyerhaeuser's already substantial national and world-wide land holdings and con-trolling interests in land, estimated to be more than 15 million acres. Oklahoma timberland was a strategic Weyerhaeuser purchase because its location in the heartland of the conti-nental United States made it accessible to both east- and west-coast markets. Southeastern Oklahoma was also advan-tageous because the local labor force was both comparatively inexpensive and not highly unionized, making a move by Wey-erhaeuser to the southern heartland of the United States espe-cially attractive (*Pulp and Paper* 1972:39).

Weyerhaeuser's major timberland concentration is in Push-mataha and McCurtain Counties, where it owns approximately 50 percent of the land area. This region, about fifty to seventy-five miles north and northeast of Weyerhaeuser's main wood-processing plants at Valliant and Wright City, Oklahoma, is also the home of many Choctaw families, the remnants of the first Choctaw settlers who migrated from their Mississippi homeland during the infamous Trail of Tears of 1831–1833. This followed the signing of the Treaty of Dancing Rabbit Creek, which established the Choctaw Nation in Indian Terri-tory. Choctaws, along with whites and blacks, today inhabit homesteads and settlement enclaves in the many towns and hamlets interspersed throughout Weyerhaeuser's vast land holdings. Throughout the region clearcuts are starkly evident, some as large as 350 acres, the maximum allowable cut. Stands of trees, mainly loblolly pine, are seen in various stages of reforestation.

The southeastern Oklahoma timber region is one of the poorest regions in Oklahoma. Minority unemployment in McCurtain and Pushmataha Counties is particularly high, with rates of 15 and 20 percent recorded respectively in 1980, while the state's overall unemployment rate was approxi-mately 10 percent (Oklahoma IMPACT 1981). Incomes in these two counties are also far below state averages. In 1980 nearly half of Pushmataha County residents, 45.4 percent, lived below the poverty level; while in McCurtain County 37.1 percent lived below that level.

Choctaws constitute only about 10 percent of the population of these two counties, so the region's economic distress
is not unique to that segment. However, statistics indicate that
the region's economic problems—a shortage of job opportunities, high rates of unemployment and underemployment—
are experienced by them with a greater degree of severity than
the rest of the population. Choctaw households typically earn
anywhere from $4,000 to $20,000 per year; however, annual
per capita incomes reveal actual income disparities between
Choctaws and other local residents. In a sample of fifty rural

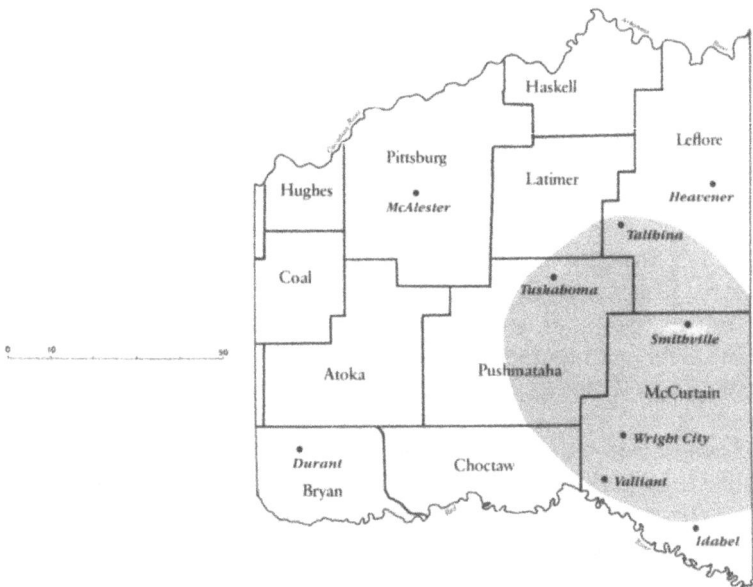

Fig. 10.1. The Choctaw Nation, including current county boundaries, towns
in the region, and in the shaded area, the major forestland concentration.
(Reproduced from *Journal of Forest and Conservation History,* October
1988; adapted from Choctaw Nation of Oklahoma, Planning Department,
Comprehensive Plan of the Choctaw Nation [Durant, Okla., 1980], and
from map 39, "Choctaw Nation: Important Places," in Morris et al., *Historical Atlas of Oklahoma,* 2d ed. [Norman: University of Oklahoma Press,
1976])

Choctaw households surveyed between 1980 and 1982, average annual per capita incomes were $1,769; while per capita average income in McCurtain County was $5,418, and in Pushmataha County, $4,386, during the same period.[1] Of fifty households surveyed, wage earners were found to work predominantly part time, due to the lack of full-time jobs available. A staggering 84 percent (32) of wage earners living permanently in the Choctaw households surveyed worked part time while only 16 percent (6) worked full time. Occupations in households surveyed were mainly as timber workers or in chicken processing plants located in nearby Arkansas towns. Of 15 workers employed in tree-related occupations, 13 worked part time, while only 2 worked full time, both Weyerhaeuser employees.

Local Choctaws who work in the woods are employed mainly as part-time timber cutters and tree planters. Timber cutters are organized into independent (nonunionized) work crews of four to seven men under the employ of a head contractor. The head contractor, or crew boss, obtains work contracts directly from Weyerhaeuser, through competitive bidding, and then hires his own crew for a particular job. Approximately 70 percent of Weyerhaeuser's timber is cut by independent crews of this kind.

Twenty to twenty-five contract labor crews operated in the timber region in 1981 and 1982, although only eight were operating profitably, while the rest were struggling just to make expenses, according to one contractor. Crews were often composed of kinsfolk. For example one crew consisted of two brothers, two half brothers, and one unrelated individual, most of whom were part Choctaw. The head contractor supplies all of the heavy equipment for his crew, while the cutters themselves supply their own chainsaws. One contractor stated that he had $240,000 invested in heavy equipment in 1982, including a skidder, used to drag logs to transport vehicles, and a logging truck, which he repairs himself, to reduce operating costs.

This same contractor explained the process by which he

and his fellow contractors were able to turn a profit in a business which is directly tied to fluctuations in Weyerhaeuser's demand for timber. This contractor said that his crew consisted of five, including himself, although optimally he would hire two additional log cutters if sufficient work were available. He paid his crew $6.00 per hour each, and they averaged a three-day work week, with occasional weeks without work due to lack of contracts, inclement weather, or other factors. His profit margin depended on tax remuneration on depreciation allowances on his heavy equipment, which in 1981 amounted to $76,000 on equipment worth about $296,000. He claimed that he trades in his heavy equipment every two years to write off the depreciation costs. In this way he pays nothing for his equipment and is able to profit substantially more from his gross earnings than he would under a different system of taxation. As this individual claimed, a successful contractor, "must be foremost a good businessman" (Kincaid interview, 6 June 1982). The timber slump of 1981–1982 reduced logging activities for this particular crew to a three-day week, although it appears that even prior to the housing crisis logging crews normally worked less than full time.

Contractors typically provide only legally obligated benefits to their workers. The contractor interviewed said that his workers are eligible for workmen's compensation, although they do not receive family health insurance benefits, nor are they paid for layoffs, holidays, or sick days. Tree planting and tree maintenance, including thinning and insect control, are also performed by part-time crews hired through private contractors. Contractors hiring tree planting crews afford their workers even less job security than do logging contractors, since planting season is only about four and one-half months long, from January through mid-May. Planters are paid at piecework rates, an average of $36.00 per thousand trees in 1982. Workers reported that they planted from 1,000 to 1,500 trees per day, with women planting fewer than men, and novice workers planting more slowly than experienced workers. Tree planting is a physically rigorous job which entails trekking through recently clearcut acreage covered with deep ruts and stumpage in which seedlings must be set. Approximately half the planters are females and older workers who take advantage of the seasonally available work. Workers are told that if trees are set too far apart or if the stand does not take, they must return to the site to replant, the cost of which is taken out of their wages.

This system of using contract labor benefits Weyerhaeuser significantly, since the corporation does not have to pay various costs of production, which are instead borne by workers and contractors. The company does not have the expense of maintaining a permanent work force which may not be profitably used throughout the year. Furthermore, there is no cost of transporting workers to widely scattered regions of the estimated 890,000 acres of active timberland in southeastern Oklahoma, nor are there costs of maintaining tree-harvesting equipment, since these expenses are borne by the contracted crews themselves. Furthermore, fringe benefits such as health insurance, vacation pay, and other employee benefits are not paid by Weyerhaeuser, but rather by the contractors or workers or not at all, further eroding the already substandard wages.

The union representing full-time Weyerhaeuser workers, Local 5–15 of the International Wood Workers of America, strongly opposes Weyerhaeuser's use of contract labor, for several reasons. In 1982 Union President Randall Rice stated that the contract labor system eroded jobs available to permanent workers and brought in outside workers, since several contracting crews had come from outside as roving contractors, taking jobs away from the local community. There was no Weyerhaeuser policy to insure that local workers would be preferentially hired to prevent such a practice. Furthermore, the union also objected to contractor's wage scales lower than union scales, substandard benefits, and lack of protection against job-related hazards for nonunionized workers. The union perceived contract labor as a threat to its own members' job security (Rice interview, 5 June 1982).

The relationship of exploitation between the Choctaw labor force and the corporation which controls the means of production locally is somewhat different from that between a company and a fully proletarianized urban industrial labor force. The Choctaws, like migrant laborers analyzed by Laite (1981) and Meillassoux (1981), move between the domestic subsistence sector and the wage laboring sector, rather than being wholly submerged in the wage sector as a landless labor force. Choctaws utilize the domestic subsistence sector prominently in their livelihood-maintaining strategies, thus performing an important service for the capitalist producers by shouldering the costs to reproduce their own labor force.

Choctaws make ends meet, given their sporadic earnings, by relying on diverse household-based subsistence activities, supplemented by public assistance benefits, tribal assistance programs, and otherwise "making do" (see Faiman-Silva 1984:318ff). These household-based subsistence activities are crucial to the survival of Choctaw families, since wages cannot meet the need for food, shelter, and other essentials. Furthermore, the community (and its workers), rather than Weyerhaeuser, bears the costs of low wages and seasonally available work because workers collect unemployment or public assistance benefits or resort to other subsistence strategies, such as gardening, hunting, odd jobs, even collecting aluminum cans, to compensate for low or erratic timber industry wages.

Land is an important element in the Choctaw subsistence strategy, although land assets have diminished severely since the period of "allotment in severalty" in the early twentieth century (Debo 1934). When available to the household, land is utilized for small-scale, home-based agricultural activities, including gardening and raising chickens and hogs. A small number of households are able to can or freeze an entire year's supply of garden produce. Most households also gather wild produce such as onions, poke salad greens, and wild berries, which are canned and/or frozen for home consumption.

Many also hunt and fish seasonally and produce homemade crafts, particularly quilts and beadwork. Nearly every Choctaw household also cuts its own wood for home heating (see Faiman-Silva 1984:303ff).

Another common strategy to alleviate the severe housing and financial shortages and to maximize available resources is simply to take up residence with kinsfolk. A younger nuclear family may remain for several years with parents, who assist in caring for grandchildren while the younger adults work at seasonal jobs. Occasionally three or more conjugal units will share a single dwelling, often no more than a crowded shack. Various other resources are also shared to broaden a household's resource base. Labor, wood cutting, rides, and child care, are commonly shared among kin, as are food and cash when needed, mainly among closely related kinsfolk.

Fig. 10.2. Weyerhaeuser clearcut showing logging roads and uncut acreage in background, Bethel, Oklahoma, 1981.

Fig. 10.3. Tree-planting crew near Smithville, Oklahoma, 1981.

Choctaw workers, like rural or migrant workers throughout the Third World, shift their efforts between the domestic subsistence sector and the wage-laboring sector as work becomes available. Since Choctaws are a permanent segment of the local population, with historical and cultural commitments to the region, however, they are in effect a captive labor force for the local private corporate producers. They are particularly vulnerable to exploitation, since many do not want to leave their homeland and are willing to work under almost any conditions regardless of the wages or working conditions. Jobs are simply too scarce to do otherwise. This sector of the Choctaw community—part-time wage laborers drawn from Choctaw households—experience the relationship of exploitation directly; however, the full impact of their condition as exploited laborers is obscured, in part because they are not directly employed by Weyerhaeuser.

Public Assistance and Other Public Sector Benefits

When possible, Choctaw households supplement their subsistence activities with public assistance benefits and other forms of assistance available especially to Native Americans. Most households qualify for food stamps. Others obtain old age and veterans' benefits. A "mutual help housing" program for Native American families has brought great relief to local households, replacing the dilapidated, unimproved shacks inhabited by nearly all Choctaws prior to the program's inception in 1968. Many young families have returned to the Choctaw Nation because they could obtain much-sought-after housing. This program, however, has encouraged families to return to the community even though few employment opportunities are available to support them. Funding for this and other entitlement programs was seriously curtailed during the Reagan administration, however. Families who own no land (it is necessary to own one acre to qualify for a mutual-help house) still live in substandard shacks, often rent-free on church grounds as compensation for serving as caretakers of church property.

The public assistance system reduces the material desperation of Choctaw workers and also reduces the sense of exploitation they might feel if they were not receiving such benefits. The capitalist producers again benefit from the public assistance system, as from the domestic subsistence activities of Choctaw workers, because these programs supplement inadequate wages and minimal benefits paid to part-time workers drawn from the domestic households.

Choctaws also benefit from other federal and state programs as a result of their unique status as Native Americans. These programs have emerged as a result of long-standing federal obligations and commitments to Native American people and, like other public-assistance programs, have been seriously curtailed since the Reagan administration. Tribal members by blood and their dependents are entitled to free health care at local health clinics and hospitals under a program taken over by the tribe in 1985. The tribe also employs community health representatives to seek out rural people needing health-related assistance and to inform them of available programs. In addition to the mutual-help housing program already mentioned, the tribe uses its own funds and various federal grant monies to provide housing assistance, including cash for utility bills for the elderly and disabled, weatherization funds to insulate homes, cash to purchase home heating fuel, and occasionally eyeglasses and dental services for the elderly.

Children of Native American descent are beneficiaries of various educational programs, from preschool headstart programs to full tuition scholarships for those who wish to attend college. These funds are available only to students willing to leave their communities, since specialized educational programs are not locally available, nor are the jobs for which youth will most likely be trained.

County Land Assessment and Taxation Policies

If the more obvious effects of corporate development lie in the exploitation of the local labor force and in the depletion of natural resources, corporate strategies to promote profit making also involve indirect methods of bookkeeping, land assessment, and capital investment, not so readily comprehensible to the observer. These strategies also deplete local resources and return vast profits to corporate producers, often unbeknownst to the local communities where production and profit making occur.

Local communities penetrated by MNCs rely upon revenues from corporate property and sales taxes, a factor which often entices the local population to welcome development schemes in their communities. Local property and sales tax systems, the heart of the local revenue base, often favor corporate landowners, undermining revenues returned to local communities. This process is particularly evident in the timber industry at the county level.

Weyerhaeuser is the single largest property tax payer in Pushmataha and McCurtain Counties, where the majority of its Oklahoma timberland is located. Evidence indicates, however, that Weyerhaeuser does not pay its fair share of the county property tax burden, because the method of appraisal assures that the tax rate is extremely low when compared with the actual market value of the land. For instance, Weyerhaeuser's timberland in both counties, amounting to about 808,600 acres, supposedly is assessed in a category similar to agricultural land, to compensate for periods of nonproductivity. But in fact, Weyerhaeuser paid a property tax rate of only $6.50 per acre in 1981 while agricultural producers in McCurtain County paid $17 to $25 per acre.[2] Weyerhaeuser acknowledged this shrewd business advantage in its own corporate literature: "This massive asset [approximately 11 billion cubic feet of timber located on nearly 6 million acres] is valued on our books at only $614 million, its historic costs of acquisition, planting and growing, which is only a fraction of current market value" (Weyerhaeuser *Annual Report,* 1982:8).

Weyerhaeuser land in both Pushmataha and McCurtain Counties is appraised by the corporate landowners themselves, under the guidance of the county assessor's office, since the rural counties cannot afford to hire their own appraisers. Weyerhaeuser has succeeded in obtaining a tax structure extremely favorable to its own circumstances in both counties. Table 10.1, summarizes Weyerhaeuser's tax contributions to Pushmataha and McCurtain Counties during the 1980–1981 fiscal year. Weyerhaeuser's tax payments to Pushmataha County in particular (which is, incidentally the poorest county in the state) show that the corporation paid only slightly more than 10 percent of the county's total property tax revenue, at a time when Weyerhaeuser owned more than 25 percent of the county's land.

Weyerhaeuser's self-assessment of its land values is even more questionable because its timberland in Oklahoma is currently in the process of being replanted with genetically

Table 10.1 Weyerhaeuser's two-county tax payments, 1980–1981

	McCurtain County	Pushmataha County
Total county acres	1,210,000.00	910,720.00
Weyerhaeuser timberland (acres)	545,842.00	262,736.00
Weyerhaeuser taxes paid*	$ 274,720.00	$ 104,698.00
Average assessed value per acre	$ 6.51	$ 6.32
Overall county tax revenue		$ 994,632.00

*Taxes reported are only on timberland. Weyerhaeuser paid additional property taxes on industrial sites in both counties.

Source: Pushmataha and McCurtain County Assessor's Office.

improved stock as a result of extensive technological advances in the cultivation of superior pine species. Corporate spokespeople have predicted that once their entire 890,000 acres of land in the state are cut and re-seeded with genetically improved pine stock, they will be able to enter into a predictable harvesting pattern over a thirty-year growing period. They expect to produce four times what they are currently harvesting from their unimproved acreage. Spokespeople also predict that this increase will grow five- or six-fold as new innovations are adopted in the future (Hankins interview, 2 June 1982).

These county taxation and land assessment practices do not adequately compensate local counties for the dramatic increases in value which Weyerhaeuser's timberland has achieved since its initial purchase. This phenomenon is bound to continue with ongoing replanting of old-growth mixed pine and hardwood forests with genetically improved species. If Weyerhaeuser's timberland were to remain at the current approximate $6.50 per acre tax rate, the land will diminish in its assessed-to-actual value ratio rather than increase in the future, as the value of the timber and of the land increases.

Federal tax laws benefit timber owners similarly, since the federal tax system compensates timber growers for the

extended period when their land is unproductive. Timber producers are also compensated for the potential risks associated
with their product, such as environmental disasters or other
natural phenomena that could inhibit long-term productivity.
Timber growers, like other corporations, are taxed on the
profits earned from their productive activities. Recent changes
in the federal tax laws have reduced the tax rate on timber to
compensate for the unique risks of this commodity (Weyerhaeuser *Annual Report* 1981:28, 39). While corporations
routinely pay an overall profits tax rate of 46 percent, profits on
timber revenues are charged at a rate of 28 percent, a rate
which was further reduced by Weyerhaeuser to 24 percent in
1981 as a result of various corporate deductions (Weyerhaeuser *Annual Report* 1981:39). Weyerhaeuser was, in fact,
able to pay no federal corporate taxes in 1981, although the
corporation's overall domestic earnings alone totalled $260.6
million (*Hartford Courant*, 17 August 1982).

The tax structure reflects the federal government's commitment to private capital development at the expense not only of
the local community's labor force but also of the material
wealth of the community at large. The system permits Weyerhaeuser to drastically undervalue its timber resources for tax
purposes, a practice which is simply one manifestation of
the systematic exploitation of satellite economies by metro-
politan-based corporations. In the long run, local populations
are deprived of revenues from their input both as a labor force
and as a supplier of basic raw materials, while the wealth
extracted from the community accrues to the corporate
owners.

Although timber remains by far Weyerhaeuser's single
greatest asset, building materials derived from the raw wood
constituted more than half of corporate gross revenues in
1981. This included sales to outside customers as well as
intra-corporate transfers of commodities. Weyerhaeuser's
timber and timberlands alone were estimated to be worth
$619.8 million in 1981 (Weyerhaeuser *Annual Report*
1981:27).

Timber is the building block of many derivative Weyerhaeuser enterprises, including plywood manufacture, pulp
and paper production, and packaging enterprises. Secondary
to the timber-based enterprises are Weyerhaeuser's more
recent investments in real estate and investment companies,
home construction, aquaculture, and soft disposable products. Product diversification has been an effective Weyerhaeuser strategy to compensate for declines in revenues from
its primary wood-based products during the late 1970s and
early 1980s slump in housing (Weyerhaeuser *Annual Report*
1980:13, 19). While sales of lumber and lumber-related products have fluctuated, diversified products have brought steadily increasing revenues to the corporation. Figures 10.4 and
10.5, below, depict the sales of various products during the
half-decade, 1976–1980, in both the traditional Weyerhaeuser wood products lines and in its diversified products.

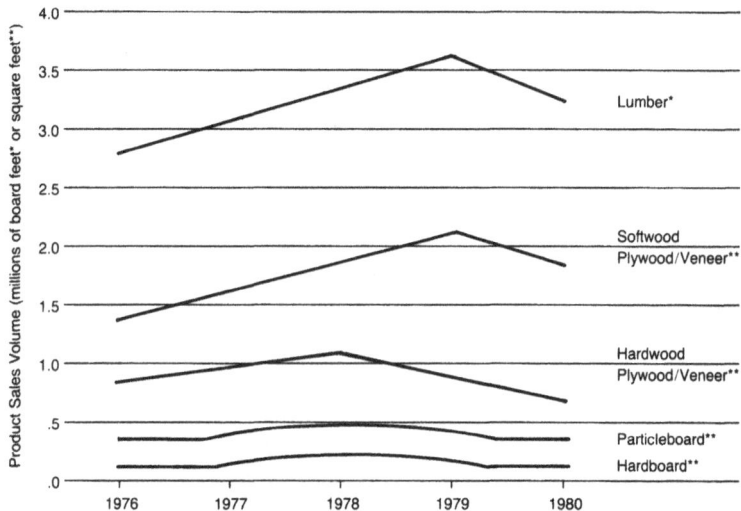

Fig. 10.4. Sales of standard Weyerhaeuser products, 1976–80. (Weyerhaeuser *Annual Report* 1980:13)

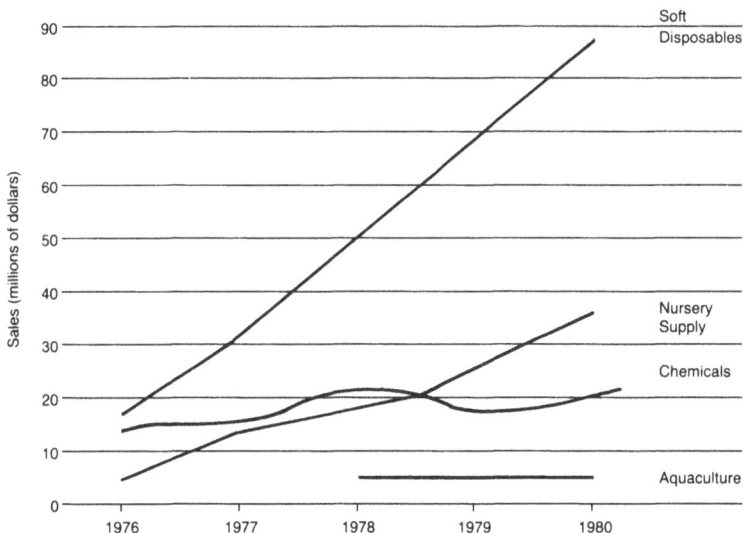

Fig. 10.5. Sales of Weyerhaeuser diversified products, 1976–80. (Weyerhaeuser *Annual Report* 1980:19)

While the sales of lumber and related products fluctuated, the diversified products brought steadily increasing returns.

The corporation has consciously taken measures to economize the labor component of its timber operations while it has focused its resources on research and development. The previous discussion examined Weyerhaeuser's use of contract labor as a cost-reducing and profit-maximizing production strategy. Weyerhaeuser has also implemented other corporate strategies to reduce costs of its unionized work force, including tough union negotiating, introducing capital-intensive equipment, and laying off workers. The labor component has remained remarkably stable throughout a period when Weyerhaeuser's potential for timber harvesting has actually increased. This fact points to the degree to which Weyerhaeuser is a capital-intensive rather than a labor-intensive industry. In concrete terms, the number of employees nationwide declined between 1979 and 1982 from a high of nearly 48,000 to 40,760 in the forest products component of Weyer-haeuser's operations (Weyerhaeuser *Annual Report* 1982: 60).

Technologically advanced equipment has also been added to plywood, containerboard, and other production mills both locally and nationally, requiring fewer, although more highly skilled, workers to perform essential production tasks. The implementation of labor-saving equipment and operations in timber harvesting and tree cultivation has been slower, and Weyerhaeuser continues to rely on contracted labor to harvest and maintain about 70 percent of its tree plantations in the Oklahoma-Arkansas region (Tharp interview, 25 January 1991).

Weyerhaeuser has coupled this orientation toward capital-rather than labor-intensive production with a view that it would no longer tolerate wage-inflation among its work force, a problem prevalent throughout the decade of the 1970s. In response to deteriorating housing starts and reduced over-all timber products demand nationwide, the corporation imple-mented various wage-freezing measures nationwide, laid off workers, and sought to negotiate scaled-down union con-tracts (*McCurtain Sunday Gazette,* 11 July 1982). Weyer-haeuser rewrote union contracts with automatic cost-of-living increases to place upon workers some of the financial burden of the declining timber products market. A contract negoti-ated in 1982 by more than two thousand members of Local 5–15 of the International Woodworkers Union in the Okla-homa-Arkansas region reflected this trend, and to avoid a costly strike the union was finally obliged to accept a contract twice rejected by its membership. This contract contained provisions for smaller annual pay raises and rejected the union's demand to represent nonunionized logging crews in contract negotiations. Contracts negotiated in 1988 again tar-geted labor to reduce the corporation's production costs. Contracts gave workers no wage increases; instead, bonuses were granted (Tharp interview, 25 January 1990).

Through these labor practices, emanating from the center of Weyerhaeuser's corporate structure (from the desk of then-President George Weyerhaeuser), Weyerhaeuser exploits its timber workers and accrues added value from the workforce that performs the backbone of the overall timber operations. Not only are workers viewed as dispensable, but also their ever-increasing productive potential, derived from technological innovations, is an essential mechanism used to reduce the negative effects of market fluctuations and to perpetuate its highly profitable multinational business enterprise. This is especially significant in light of the earlier discussion which showed that timber and timberland are in fact accruing ever-increasing wealth to the corporation in forms not reported as corporate earnings on Weyerhaeuser's balance sheet. In actuality, the capitalist tax structure permits Weyerhaeuser to write off its expenditures for capital improvements, including roads, research, and development, while the company simultaneously reduces the size of the labor force needed to create its products.

Conclusion

This survey of capitalist production in rural southeastern Oklahoma reveals the way that the capitalist sector articulates with a traditional sector, creating a relationship of exploitation on several levels. Choctaw workers are exploited in the process of production as part-time, underutilized, and underpaid timber workers. They are also exploited in the process of reproduction, as they must devise alternative means of subsistence to compensate for the inadequate wages available in the capitalist sector. Choctaw workers appear to be utilizing a strategy of maximizing their subsistence options through sharing networks, household subsistence efforts, and 'making do,' while relying upon public assistance and other public-sector benefits programs to meet their unmet economic needs. The subsistence economy, which offers the appearance of a system of Chayanovian 'household economizers' (see Chayanov 1966

[1925]; Sahlins 1972:41ff) opting for leisure time rather than material benefits, is, in fact, an example of the direct exploitation of wage laborers in an economic relationship that accrues far more benefits to the capitalist sector than to the wage-laboring sector.

As the foregoing discussion has shown, corporate profit-making strategies under capitalist relations of production use public-sector benefits programs, tax policies, and various publicly financed mechanisms to accrue added value from their wage-laborers. Weyerhaeuser's type of production strategy is not unique to the southeastern Oklahoma region, but is replicated in communities throughout the United States where underemployed and underpaid workers reside. Workers are called upon to perform unskilled or semi-skilled jobs as migrant farm laborers, in urban manufacturing and industrial jobs, and in maintenance and service occupations. This surplus labor force is typically drawn from ethnic minority populations and regions of poverty throughout the United States. Often the corporate sector takes advantage of such a work force by rejecting unionization attempts, paying only minimum or slightly above minimum wages, and failing to provide employee benefits. Since workers are readily available and jobs scarce, workers accept the substandard working conditions.

The private corporate sector is the real beneficiary of public-sector benefits programs under capitalist relations of production, as the above investigation of the Choctaw Nation has shown. Public assistance programs and tribal benefits subsidize Choctaw workers who then can remain in the region to provide their labor for Weyerhaeuser's enterprises. These programs help to support a work force at the least cost to the corporation. The corporation, then, can use employment practices which actually promote seasonal layoffs and under-employment, since workers are supported during nonproductive periods by the public sector and by their own subsistence efforts. The corporation is not held responsible for the needs of its part-time work force, but rather leaves to the state and federal governments, and to society at large, the burden of supporting workers when they are laid off or unemployed. Economic and social dilemmas faced by Choctaws represent the underlying contradictions of this situation of dependency. Although many are poor, Choctaws live in close proximity to vast wealth which is simply not accessible to them, although it once belonged to them. The entire structure of production promotes the unequal distribution of wealth, insuring that Choctaws will remain poor and exploited.

Acknowledgments

Research for this project, conducted during 1981 and 1982, was supported by the National Science Foundation under Doctoral Dissertation Research Grant No. 8022456. Any opinions, findings, and conclusions or recommendations expressed are those of the author and do not necessarily reflect the views of the National Science Foundation. I wish to express my appreciation to the NSF for making this research undertaking possible. This paper is an expanded version of a paper presented at the International Congress of Anthropological and Ethnological Sciences, Zagreb, Yugoslavia, 28 July 1988.

CHAPTER 11

How Giveaways and Pow-wows Redistribute the Means of Subsistence

John H. Moore

In the state of Oklahoma each year about three hundred Indian pow-wows and memorials of various kinds are announced by flyers, in newspapers, and at public meetings. In addition, many other small giveaways are held without public announcement, totalling altogether perhaps a thousand events.

Existing interpretations of pow-wows have tended to focus on the huge urban events, emphasizing their "pan-Indian" nature (Corrigan 1970; Young 1981). Concerning giveaways, which are sometimes conducted at pow-wows but more often are conducted separately, authors have tended to focus on the ceremony itself and the actual articles exchanged during the event—blankets, shawls, and other prestige items (K. Weist 1973; Schneider 1981; Grobsmith 1979, 1981; Kehoe 1980).

In this article I wish to emphasize small-town events and behavior away from the pow-wow ground among people whom Kehoe has recognized as a "social network." By reference to socioeconomic data, I will argue that in Oklahoma this network facilitates a system of exchange and redistribution which is crucially important for Indian people, providing needy

Native American families with the "means of subsistence." The means of subsistence I define formally as "the goods and services necessary to sustain life"—food, clothing, heating oil, and health care. I argue that pow-wows and giveaways were invented by Indian people to fill the gaps in an uncertain local economy and to compensate for government social services that often are erratic and arbitrary in their effect on Indian families.

Although giveaways and pow-wows are best known from the cultures of Plains Indians, there are similar traditional practices among many of the other native peoples of North America (Grobsmith 1979:123-24). Also, even the Plains peoples are somewhat variant among themselves in their giveaway and pow-wow behavior, as noted by the authors cited above. The practices to be described in this paper, then, are predominantly those which are common, if not universal, among Oklahoma tribes of Plains origin—Plains Apaches, Southern Arapahoes, Caddos, Southern Cheyennes, Comanches, Kiowas, Pawnees, and Wichitas, as well as the Chiwere or Dhegiha Sioux—Ioways, Kaws, Osages, Otoes, and Poncas. In addition, these practices are increasingly found among some Central Algonkian tribes in Oklahoma that have adopted certain important aspects of pow-wow culture—Delawares, Sacs, Foxes, Kickapoos, Potawatomis, and Shawnees. The particular focus of this paper will be the Southern Cheyennes and Southern Arapahoes, who are not only the most active of the pow-wow tribes of Oklahoma, but have also been the main objects of my ethnographic attention since 1969. I will emphasize here those practices which I believe are very general among southern Plains Indians. Whether this analysis is also valid for the northern groups I cannot say, since I have attended only a very few northern Plains pow-wows and have not seen the everyday practical or subsistence behavior there which might reflect symbolic pow-wow relationships.

Especially interesting for future work is the opportunity to compare Southern Cheyenne and Northern Cheyenne giveaways, since the two groups are ethnically similar and somewhat intermarried (K. Weist 1973). Grobsmith's analysis seems to indicate that the northern Plains Indian groups are different from the southerners, since she argues for a ritual rather than economic interpretation of giveaways (1981:75–76). One basic difference might be that while many northern Plains Indians live on discrete, bounded reservations in areas of low total population, Oklahoma Indians tend to constitute minority communities within areas of greater non-Indian population.

Diverse kinds of events have been called "pow-wows," and they have a multitude of functions. Best known are the large urban pow-wows which are alleged to endorse pan-Indian values (Young 1981). These large affairs provide entertainment for Indians and visitors, offer cash prizes to dancers, and present opportunities to local organizations, craftspeople, and traders for selling food and craftwork. But I will argue here that these big urban pow-wows are atypical, and in Oklahoma they are decidedly in the minority both in terms of the number of events and the number of Indian people in attendance. More typical are the rural and small-town events attended by local residents who are well acquainted with one another.

Kenneth Ashworth's research should settle the question of the relative importance of rural, family-oriented pow-wows versus the urban, commercial type. Using as his data base the pow-wows announced in the *Camp Crier*, published by the Native American Center of Oklahoma City, he counted only 41 commercial events, about 8 percent of the 541 pow-wows analyzed for his study. His sample includes two years of announced events in Oklahoma from 1978 to 1980. His map of "Primary Pow-Wow Locations and Frequencies," reproduced here as figure 11.1, shows clearly that it is rural areas, not urban ones, which are more important for pow-wow culture. Also, these rural and small-town pow-wows tend not to be "pan-Indian" in the sense of having many different tribes in attendance. Rather, the gatherings reflect the ethnicity of the sponsoring community (Ashworth 1986:92–115).

To people not familiar with Plains Indian values, several

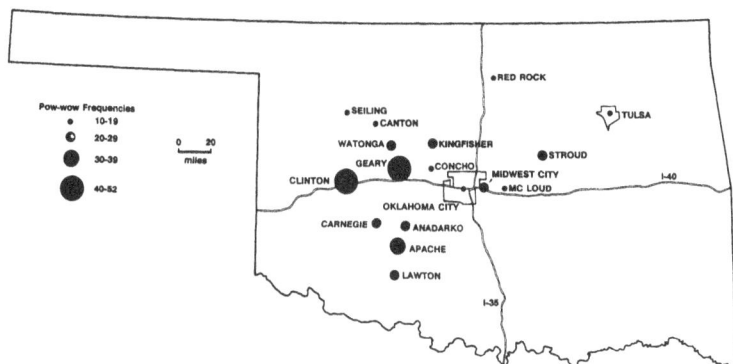

Fig. 11.1. Primary Oklahoma pow-wow locations and frequencies. (Ashworth 1986:116)

aspects of the giveaways and "specials" which are incorporated into pow-wow programs might seem unusual. Firstly, in the noncommercial pow-wows, there is no admission, and food is free. Visitors are invited to the head of the line when dinner is served, and they are given big portions of food, with many jokes about carrying a second plate or going around again. Non-Indians, accustomed to Euro-American notions of purchase and exchange, are often uncomfortable as the guests of strangers, and sometimes they seek to pay for the food, which embarrasses everyone. To compound their discomfort, such visitors are sometimes given lavish gifts during giveaways, the standard gifts being a blanket for a man and a shawl for a woman. Often I have heard visitors remark, "What's the catch?" There is no catch for visitors; they have simply been the objects of Indian hospitality.

Another mystery to visitors is that persons honored by a giveaway or special do not themselves receive gifts, but are merely observers as their sponsors give away blankets, shawls, baskets of groceries, money, clothing, dishes, furniture, and even horses and automobiles to other people in attendance at the event. But in Euro-America, it is the honoree who receives the plaque, the trophy, or the gold watch. By contrast, Plains Indian values require that the honoree gets nothing but the privilege of shaking the hands of the gift recipients, who are required by etiquette just to compliment the gift, and not say "thank you."

The Simple Giveaway

Simple giveaways, which are typical of the small Indian communities in central and western Oklahoma, are most frequently held to commemorate such occasions as (1) the death of a member of the family, after the wake and before the funeral; (2) the end of the mourning period, one year after the death of a loved one, so that the family can once again appear at public functions; (3) the return of a son from the armed services, often sponsored by the local "war mothers"; or (4) a graduation from high school or college. But in fact, any notable event can serve as the reason for a simple giveaway. If a notable event does not occur in the life of a family for a few years, then some minor event will be seized upon—a graduation from grammar school or the visit of a friend—just so the family can sponsor a giveaway and distribute the gifts which it has been receiving from other families at other giveaways.

Simple giveaways are usually held at noon or six in the evening (both are called "dinner" in local English dialect) and begin with a "feed." Members of the extended family work several days to prepare an elaborate meal of traditional foods such as boiled beef, fry bread, corn soup, and sweet rice. The time and place of the event are passed by word of mouth, and guests are expected to BYODC, "bring your own dishes and chairs." The simple giveaway is usually held in some local meeting place, such as the many "community halls" built with federal money since the 1950s, or increasingly in the tribal "multi-purpose centers," which usually incorporate a large gymnasium both for basketball and for events such as this, or local halls rented from the American Legion, Elks Club,

Moose Lodge or similar non-Indian organizations. In summer, giveaways are often held outside, at the home of the host family. At all such events, after passing through the food line guests sit and eat in chairs which they have previously arranged in a circle or in concentric circles around the hall, or around the host family's yard. When the giveaway is in the yard, the front porch of the house serves as an elevated platform for the family and master of ceremonies.

The free food itself constitutes the most direct means for providing subsistence to needy people in the community. Such people usually wait until last to eat and show by their posture and demeanor that they are in need, standing aside as the others file through the food line, eyes downcast, often with sacks or pots they have brought. These people, usually younger men and women, are colloquially said to be from families that are "hard up." At an event attended by 150 people, there might be two to five such people, representing several families.

After everyone has been served, the needy people pass through the line, receiving extra-generous portions. For them, there are no jokes about food. Sometimes they are weeping.[1] After they have passed through the line, the servers take their sacks and pots and fill them with the surplus food. There is always an abundance of food, or else the host family is embarrassed. The surplus has been prepared in the expectation that needy people will be present. In some communities, there is so much food and so many feeds that it is possible for hungry families to subsist for some time just from the food distributed at giveaways, pow-wows, and memorials. In Geary, Watonga, and Clinton, Oklahoma, for example, there is an event with dinner nearly every weekend, and sometimes two or three events.

After the dinner the host family cleans up the hall and then brings out the goods to be distributed at the giveaway. Most often the gifts are laid out on the floor in front of the chairs of the family or on the ground in front of the family. At the better-organized events there are slips of paper with the names of the intended recipients pinned to the shawls and blankets. The giveaway begins with a welcome and usually a prayer in the native language from a senior man of the family or from a well-known man who has been honored by being invited to serve as master of ceremonies (MC). He states the reason for the giveaway, and makes other appropriate remarks.

For the giveaway, the guests have physically arranged themselves into extended families (figure 11.2). It is usually incumbent on the most senior members of an extended family in the community to attend, along with a few younger relatives. Attendance at the giveaway, of itself, implies the existence of friendship and alliance between the host and guest families. Who will attend is almost perfectly predictable from the standpoint of the hosts. Problems arise when families attend who were thought to be out of town, or who were per-

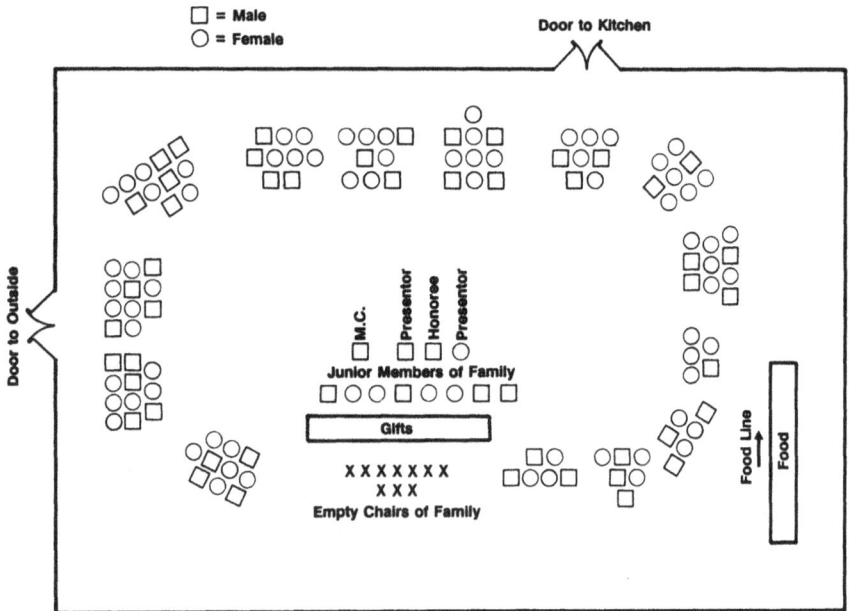

Fig. 11.2. Schematic diagram of a simple giveaway held indoors.

haps not expected because of disputes among some members of the two families. Often there is a frantic rearrangement of name slips or the finding of additional gifts while dinner is being served.

At funerals, especially, the host family makes decisions about gifts while the guests are eating. Since deaths are most often unexpected, the family may not have an adequate supply of blankets and shawls to give everyone at the funeral. Most people, then, bring both a blanket and a shawl when they come to the funeral, going home with a blanket and a shawl which someone else has brought. Most often, it is only the senior members of the extended family, usually a married couple, who receive high-status gifts like blankets and shawls, while the junior members of the family, especially children, receive small gifts of beadwork, toys, or candy which are distributed around the circle from baskets and boxes while the elders are being called out formally for the giveaway.

The giveaway begins when a man and woman from the host family step forward with a blanket and shawl, respectively, while the master of ceremonies calls out the name of a person or couple who will receive the gifts. If the giveaway is in honor of a person who is present, for example a new high school graduate, that person also stands in front, next to the people distributing the gifts.

Although the most senior and most respected guests are usually called out first, this is not always the case. Also singled out for early attention and important gifts are people who have travelled a long way to the event or people who are strangers. Especially if an honored guest at the event has brought a friend, that friend is honored lavishly, even if unacquainted with the host family. If the event is a funeral or memorial which has required an all-night meeting of the Native American Church, these members of the peyote lodge are called out early to receive gifts. Also receiving early attention are friends who have cooked and otherwise helped prepare the event but who are not members of the extended family.

Etiquette requires that hosts not give to members of their

own families, but here we have some variability among Oklahoma tribes. Comanche hosts, for example, will give to their own elderly grandparents, but Cheyennes normally will not. Such differences largely reflect significant differences in the kinship systems and kin behavior of the different tribes, and in particular differences in avoidance/respect relationships. One would not call out a relative who is avoided, since the giveaway requires that the host shake the hand of the recipient. But on the other hand, this problem can be circumvented by having the MC make the presentation. There is much variability, not only among tribes but among families, about the propriety of giving to one's own kin. But generally, my impression is that one does not give away to people who are already in the daily sharing network, however this network is defined by the tribe or family.

A simple giveaway usually lasts less than an hour, as gifts are handed forward to the presenters by junior members of the family and people are called out to receive their gifts. The recipients exhibit a great deal of modesty in their behavior. They are slow to answer the call, and some quiet discussion and shuffling of feet usually precedes the entrance of the recipients into the open area. Often the recipient holds the hand of the presenter for a while and compliments the honoree, recalls the name of some shared relative now dead, or remarks on the beauty of the gift.

Toward the end of the giveaway the hosts can tell if they have sufficient gifts for the assembled guests. If there are surplus gifts, honored guests can be called out again. If there are not enough gifts, there is a kind of pleasant embarrassment, as the MC notes the large number of people who have come unexpectedly to honor the family and the occasion. Often cash gifts are made discreetly to the last guests to be called out, folded into a handshake. If the money runs out, the last people are called out and given a handshake or a hug, while the MC comments on the embarrassment of the family. On several occasions I have noted that when an honored elder of the community comes late to the giveaway, everything stops while the elder is called out, given gifts, and complimented publicly by the MC or members of the family. The compliments are very indirect. Most often it is sufficient to note that an elder "was a close friend of my grandmother," that he or she "has lived his whole life in the community" or that she "was a founder of the war mothers." To end the giveaway the MC simply announces that the event is over and thanks everyone for attending, sometimes adding another prayer in the native language.

Two additional ethnographic facts must be noted in closing this description of a simple giveaway. First of all, people come to the giveaway expecting to receive gifts, and their presence itself implies approval of the event, friendship with the sponsoring family, and support for the honoree. Secondly, and concomitantly, one of the worst things that can happen to a family is to attend a giveaway and not receive gifts. It is a public insult and a rejection of any ongoing alliance between the hosts and the guests. This happens very seldom. Families simply do not attend giveaways where they are not wanted. However, if they want to begin a friendly relationship, they might ask indirectly if they would be welcome, and to end a friendly relationship they do not attend a giveaway and give no excuse for their absence.

Significance of Giveaways

If one only observed behavior at the giveaway itself, it might seem an empty exercise. People bring blankets and shawls to a central place where they are redistributed. Over the course of a year a family will give as many gifts as they receive. These gifts are usually not sold or even used, they just continually circulate. It would appear that everything in the course of a year comes out even, blanket for blanket and shawl for shawl. This view, however, is very superficial and does not consider the concrete economic behavior of which the giveaway is merely the social symbol.

If one explores behavior in modern Plains Indian communities on a day-to-day basis through the year, as an ethnographer, it is clear that there is a real material system for distributing the means of subsistence which underlies and parallels the symbolic system exhibited at the simple giveaway. That is, the same people that an extended family might "call out" at a giveaway are the people "called upon" for help through the year when the family is in need. These allied families are called upon only when the resources of the extended family are completely exhausted. The adult members of an extended family share among themselves casually and constantly. But when the cash is gone and the refrigerator is empty, other families must be solicited for help.

The most usual requests made by needy families which I have observed over the past twenty years are as follows: (1) food, (2) gas money for travel, (3) fuel for the home, (4) telephone calls, and (5) air fare. I am not including here the frequent requests made for goods and gifts to be distributed as part of giveaways and other ceremonies, but only those which serve to keep members of the family alive, the means of subsistence. The presentations and reciprocity of ceremonial life are very complex and beyond the range of this paper.

Solicitations of food, when they are necessary during the year, are usually made by younger members of a family, in the name of the senior members. Solicitations are directed at families known to be in no particular hardship, especially those who have just received income in some form. Typically people come to the back door or enter the front door unannounced, to call attention to their plight. The women of the family then collect what they can from the kitchen and give generously to the young people, who stand dejectedly in the kitchen or in the back yard. Less often, someone drives to the grocery store to buy food for the solicitants. Not much is said. The receivers are quiet and passive; the givers are busy and matter-of-fact.

Gas money is requested in much the same way, except it is frequently a senior person, especially the driver of the car, who comes to the front door and quietly makes the request. Most often the gas money is to take someone to the clinic or hospital or to pick up some member of the family who is stranded in another town. As at giveaways, the money is folded tightly and delivered in a handshake.

In winter, lack of fuel can pose a desperate situation for an Indian family, especially an elder living in an isolated area. Active adults, family members or not, usually make it their business in winter to visit people in vulnerable situations to make sure that they have fuel and that their stove or furnace is in working order. These visits usually make it unnecessary for someone in the needy household to solicit firewood or money for fuel oil, but solicitations are made when necessary.

Plains Indian telephone behavior may seem unusual by Anglo standards. If one visits with family heads, one commonly sees other members of the community enter the house continuously to use the phone, often for long distance calls. Whether the phone calls are reimbursed or not depends on the relative financial conditions of the family making the call and the family with the phone. The telephone of a traditional Cheyenne or Arapaho chief, in particular, is considered community property, and phone bills in the hundreds of dollars are common, endured without much complaint. Rather than say no to someone, the chief will allow the phone to be disconnected.

Air fare can become a crucial and necessary expense in at least three instances. First, it often happens that a member of the family is stranded in some distant city and in need of medical help available without cost only at an Indian hospital or clinic. Second, family members may have the promise of a job somewhere if they can show up for work. And third, if a family member dies in a distant city, it is necessary for someone to go and supervise arrangements and to collect personal property and whatever gifts might be received at the funeral.

Therefore, I am arguing here that the people called out at simple giveaways are not being honored for some abstract "status" which they enjoy in the community, but in gratitude for actual, necessary, and sometimes crucially important help in time of need. By giving gifts publicly in a ceremony, the host family is acknowledging the gifts received privately and quietly during the year. Sometimes these times of need are alluded to when the public gift is given. Here are two examples of the kinds of very indirect allusions which can be announced during a giveaway: "Sometimes people get in difficulties, and there are some who are always ready to help." "Last winter we had a situation in our family that we don't like to talk about, and we're glad to see our friends here today."

When we put giveaways into the larger context of pow-wows, as we will do in the next section, we need to note that the network of redistribution symbolized in the simple giveaway and acted out during the year is not a comprehensive network for a local community. The maximum size for a network is perhaps five extended families, by which I mean here the descendants of two or more siblings and their affines, related in some manner by kinship or marriage. Larger communities might have two or more networks, with some extended families participating in two or more networks. At any particular community giveaway or memorial service, not all the networks are represented: some families might be absent out of indifference or because of active hostility to the host family. In the next section, we will see how these familial networks are chartered as "pow-wow clubs," and how alliances, permanent or shifting, can be constructed among them.

Drums, Dancers and Sponsors

If a family wishes to make an event more significant, it invites a "drum" to provide traditional music. This addition makes the event a "pow-wow" rather than a simple giveaway. A "drum" comprises an experienced group of singers who sit around a large bass drum, or a traditional one with leather stretched over a cylinder of wood, keeping time by beating on the drum and singing appropriate traditional songs. Each singer has his own drumstick and is usually a relative of the leader. The leader is responsible for conducting practice sessions, recruiting new members, and keeping the drum's calendar. For performing at a pow-wow the drum must be paid in money and gifts, and in modern times there are enough events in Oklahoma for some groups to be fully professional, supported by their work at pow-wows.

In addition to a drum, the family must invite a "head staff" to lead the dancers who will participate. On pow-wow flyers (figures 11.3, 11.4), these staff members have titles which are most often abbreviated. A complete head staff for an average-sized pow-wow might consist of the following: HS, Head Singer; AD, Arena Director; MC, Master of Ceremonies; HMD, Head Man Dancer; HLD, Head Lady Dancer; HLBD, Head Little Boy Dancer; HLGD, Head Little Girl Dancer; and WB, Water Boy. In addition, other more specialized staff members might include such people as HMGD, Head Man Gourd Dancer or HLBD, Head Lady Buckskin Dancer.

The families who would undertake to sponsor a large pow-wow are usually members of a local pow-wow club. And here we begin to see an exhibition of the extent of sharing networks, since a local club represents the core of a local familial network. The people who pow-wow together are the same ones who can be found together during the week. In large communities with several of these clubs, they must often compete for pow-wow dates and local facilities.

The rationales for the chartering of the clubs are several. Many are gourd dance clubs, whose focal members are older men who wear distinctive sashes and carry unique fans as they dance. Among the various Plains tribes, gourd dance clubs can be more or less religious, and more or less social/ secular, and they are not entirely distinct from the veterans clubs, which require past service in the armed forces for full membership. Veterans clubs might comprise only gourd dancers, or they might also include people who do not dance at all. Among sponsoring groups, especially interesting are the war mothers clubs, which first were organized after World War I to honor sons in military service (Schweitzer 1983). Large communities sometimes have several pow-wow clubs formed

Graduation Dance

for
Gilbert Washington

Son of Darlene Washington & the late Gilbert Sr.
Grandson of Tommy & Ruby NightWalker

April 11, 1987

Barefoot Community Hall - Canton, OK
Dinner will be served 6 p.m. to 7 p.m. Dance will follow.

- Headstaff -

M.C.-	Robert Fields, Sr.	Perkins, OK
Head Drummer-	Fred Little Calf, Sr.	Clinton, OK
Head Man Dancer-	Adrian Mosqueda	Canton, OK
Head Lady Dancer-	Celeste Heap-of-Birds	Okla. City, OK
Head Teen Boy Dancer-	Mike Watan, Jr. *15 yrs.*	Weatherford, OK
Head Teen Girl Dancer-	Delana Marie Panana *13 yrs*	Arapaho, OK
Head Little Boy Dancer-	Tyree Medicine Chips *5 years*	Thomas, OK
Head Little Girl Dancer-	Renecia Rose Harris *4 years*	Seiling, OK
A.D.-	Ervin Bull	Clinton, OK

- Honorary Citizens -

Mr. & Mrs. Nelson Sage   Geary, OK

- Co-Host -

Sweetwater Family   Oklahoma & Kansas

EVERYONE WELCOMED!!!
LOTS OF RAFFLES!!!

T.V., Star Quilt, Consolation Prizes!

Fig. 11.3. Flyer for a graduation dance held in 1987.

C&A LABOR DAY POW-WOW BENEFIT DANCE

DECEMBER 13, 1986

NATIONAL GUARD ARMORY
2600 Melone Drive
El Reno, Oklahoma

SUPPER 5:00-6:00 pm
BRING YOUR DISHES & CHAIRS

MC	Hammon Motah - Carnegie, Oklahoma
HS	Joe Fish DuPont - Carnegie, Oklahoma
HMD	Francis Sweetwater - Wichita, Oklahoma
HLD	Minnie Whiteskunk - El Reno, Oklahoma
HLBD	Robin Blind - Canton, Oklahoma
HLGD	Ricque Richardson - Watonga, Oklahoma
AD	Chester Whiteman - Concho, Oklahoma
CO-HOSTS	OKLAHOMA INTER-TRIBAL VETERANS ASSOCIATION

FOR ADDITIONAL INFORMATION: A.D. TALLBIRD
                                2405 South Miles
                                El Reno, Oklahoma 73036
                                (405) 262-8619

Fig. 11.4. Flyer for a benefit dance held in 1986.

from the same large network of families, but under different
rationales and comprising people of different age or sex. For
example, the older men of a sharing network might form a
gourd clan, the younger men a veterans group, and the
women a war mothers group.

Not all the adult members of a community belong to some
pow-wow club. Some are content to participate in the social
network consisting of kinsmen and affines, without seeking to
charter it as a club or extend relationships beyond the club.
And for some families, the social network of a Native American Church or other Christian church suffices to create sharing bonds within the community as well as creating bonds
with co-religionists in other communities. The pow-wow people, essentially, are those who emphasize this institution over
others, as a means for building bridges beyond the boundaries of kin and community.

When a family giving a pow-wow gets the sponsorship of an
established pow-wow group, attendance at the event is much
higher. Attendance can be increased even more by seeking
additional cosponsoring groups or a cosponsoring nuclear or
extended family which also seeks to honor some family member or conduct a memorial giveaway. The same effect comes
from strategically inviting a head staff. In each case, accepting
the invitation implies that you will bring your extended family,
and perhaps your pow-wow club or other social group, and
that you will urge other families and groups to attend also.
Consequently, all these invitations are extremely sensitive and
delicate, since there are intimate relationships of alliance and
hostility among all the different dancers and their families, as
well as among the pow-wow groups, and one must be careful
to invite groups who are compatible with one another. In all
cases, the group or person being invited wants to know who
else has been invited. That is, the drum wants to know who the
sponsors and head staff are, the head man dancer wants to
know who the master of ceremonies will be. Usually, no one
will commit until the whole slate is drawn up, requiring lengthy
conversations among all parties. Frequently, however, a pow-

wow group will have a drum or drums they most often call upon, and the same kinds of on-going friendships prevail among certain dancers, sponsors and people invited to be the head staff.

As part of a pow-wow, a giveaway becomes more complex. Not only must the sponsoring family give to the senior people present, but also to the drum, the head staff, and the officers and members of other sponsoring organizations. But the advantage of a pow-wow over a simple giveaway is that it makes possible the distribution of gifts within a much larger network, increasing the number of people who might be called upon in time of need. That is, although the "cost" of sponsoring a pow-wow is much greater than for a simple giveaway, so are the potential benefits.

As with the simple giveaway, a pow-wow gift implies either thanks for some past favor or the obligation to help in the future, or both. Prominent men are sometimes reluctant to attend pow-wows where they have no established alliances, since it is understood that the presentation of a gift implies a serious obligation. (Perhaps that is why most gift recipients don't say "thank you.")

In Oklahoma there are perhaps a hundred or more families who are prominent participants in pow-wows all around the state—as singers, staff, sponsors, or recipients of gifts. These are the "pow-wow people." They represent all the Plains tribes in Oklahoma as well as other tribes from the central part of the state, especially Algonkians and Dhegiha Sioux, and they can be found anywhere in the state on a given weekend. The presence of a few of these families at a small pow-wow ensures its success. Most often they receive several important gifts, and they are singled out at an event for more than their equitable share of attention. But they also have enormous obligations. During a normal week at home, they are likely to be solicited by people from anywhere in pow-wow country for some favor. And having made a long trip, the solicitants sometimes expect a *big* favor—an air fare, a hundred dollars, the loan of a car.

One unique way of signalling an alliance at a pow-wow,

short of giving away, is participation in a "special." Sometimes a special is given for a person just before or after a giveaway in their honor. Sometimes a special stands alone on a pow-wow program, and often there are five or more such specials in the course of an evening. Some tension exists between the sponsors of specials and the head staff, since conducting a special causes all the dancing to stop while people march around and make speeches.

For a special, the honored person either stands next to the MC or else marches with his sponsors around the drum. Shawls and blankets are draped on his shoulders, and money is either dropped at his feet or put in a hat, if the person is marching. People in attendance show their approval by dropping money in the hat and then joining in the procession while the drummers sing an appropriate song. Some families have their own honoring songs which the singers are obliged to learn. At the end of the song, the honoree directs that the money and goods be distributed in a particular way, often singling out the drum and the head staff to receive money or goods, or perhaps a "princess" of the pow-wow or of one of the tribes, if one is present, or a soldier in uniform.

The special is a much milder way of symbolizing an alliance, and it is not taken so seriously. No list of names is called, and the spoken words are about the honoree, not about the recipients of the gifts. But still, marching in a procession behind a person carries with it some obligation to be part of a sharing network.

The social relations among the singers, staff, and pow-wow people are very complex and are beyond the scope of this paper. These same people also perform at the large commercial pow-wows and so are involved in relationships that are more explicitly pecuniary. It is significant that when a pow-wow is large enough to become commercial, it omits giveaways and specials, while adding prize money to attract straight dancers, war dancers, buckskin dancers, and fancy dancers. At that point, the pow-wow takes on an entirely different character, even though the personnel remain the same. At the really huge events, like the Red Earth Pow-Wow in Oklahoma City which had twenty-six drums in 1991, Indian families come to see their relatives dance or to be entertained, not to define and reinforce their social networks.

In this article, however, I am emphasizing the smaller pow-wows and that part of pow-wow behavior which is related to the symbolic creation or affirmation of sharing behavior. Briefly put, the essence of these small noncommercial pow-wows is that they provide the opportunity for making alliances beyond one's own pow-wow club or community network. By finding cosponsors in a neighboring community and giving away to them, one increases the network of potential helpers in case of need. By making powerful friends among the "pow-wow people," one can increase the potential for receiving large favors, even jobs. By sponsoring and participating in pow-wow "specials," people reinforce existing alliances, create weak alliances, and sometimes evaluate the possibilities for including additional people in the sharing networks.

The Political Economy of Pow-wows and Giveaways

Indian people, like most people, would be insulted by having social scientists question their motivations for participating in symbolic sharing. For them, participation in giveaways and pow-wows is motivated by "respect" for elders and guests, by love and a sense of duty to one's family and community. But as has often been noted, if people always did what they said they did, for the reasons stated at the time, there would be no need for social science. It is the social scientist's business to look past the formal and explicit structure of ceremonies for more fundamental and perhaps more important causes, in this case of pow-wow behavior.

In this section I will argue that redistribution of the means of subsistence is one of the primary functions of the events described above. I will argue this by reference to social and economic data derived from the Oklahoma counties which constitute "pow-wow country." In evaluating this thesis we must first consider why it is necessary for subsistence to be redistributed at all among American Indians. That is, why would each person in the pow-wow area not just keep their own goods and income within the extended family, instead of going to the great bother of redistributing it? There are two reasons why subsistence must be redistributed: first, because it is *scarce*, and second, because it is *erratic*.

Ashworth has already suggested the general relationship between pow-wow frequency and poverty level (Ashworth 1986:137). Looking at fifty-seven communities in pow-wow country, he correlated the number of pow-wows over a two-year period with the percent of Indian population living under the official poverty level. His results are reproduced as follows:

Pow-wow frequency *over 24-month period*	*Average percentage of* *Indian population below* *poverty level*
1–9	21.5
10–19	26.2
20–29	31.9
30–52	43.7

To supplement Ashworth's results, I have investigated the pow-wow area county-by-county for data that is more specific.[4] Beginning with all the counties in which pow-wows were reported in Ashworth's data for 1978–1980, I have had to discard some for several reasons. First of all, statistics for counties with small Indian populations are not available from the Bureau of the Census, the Oklahoma Department of Human Resources, or the Bureau of Indian Affairs, because of the privacy act. Also, some statistics are not collected by county and are not easily convertible to that basis. So the eleven counties remaining in the sample (figure 11.5) represent all the counties for which data could be obtained in some comparable form. There are special reasons for excluding Caddo, Payne, and Cleveland counties. Payne and Cleveland include the state's two major universities, with Indian student populations who organize activities which distorts any statistical treatment.

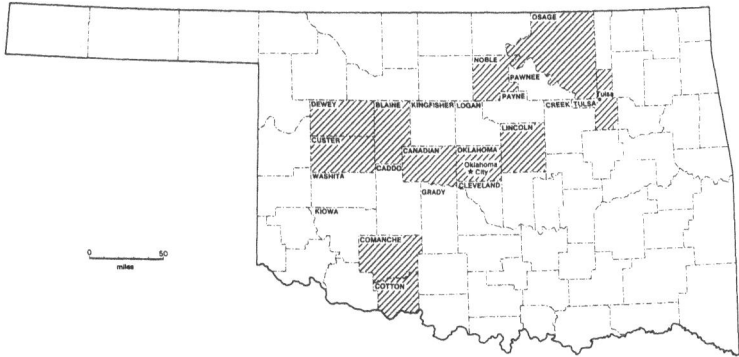

Fig. 11.5. Eleven pow-wow counties in Oklahoma.

Caddo County includes the Anadarko Area offices and facilities of the Bureau of Indian Affairs, with many fully employed Indians who are not part of the local community. This distorts both the population and the employment figures, as compared with other pow-wow counties.

The data in table 11.1 are organized by decreasing number of pow-wows per thousand Indian people in the county, the third numerical column. On this basis, I have divided the counties into three groups. If there is a correlation between number of pow-wows and level of poverty, as I predict, the measures for poverty should also be either regularly increasing from top to bottom, or regularly decreasing, to correlate with pow-wow frequency. Although this generally seems to be the case in table 11.1, there are complex relationships among the variables which deserve some comment.

First, Blaine and Dewey counties, constituting the top group, stand out both for their high frequency of pow-wows and for their high proportion of families getting food stamps, their percent of population getting Aid to Dependent Children, and high unemployment. In their participation in the work force, the next to last column, Blaine County is not exceptional and there are no data for Dewey. So the high frequency of pow-wows in these two cases correlates not with just one, but

Table 11.1. Pow-wow frequency and poverty indices for Indian people in certain Oklahoma counties, 1980

County	Tribe	Number of Pow-wows	Population	Pow-wows/ 1,000	Food Stamps (%)	ADC (%)	Part-time Work (%)	Unemployed (%)
Blaine	Cheyenne, Arapaho	96	961	99.9	23.6	17.9	26.0	36.4
Dewey	Cheyenne	17	302	56.3	41.9	14.9	—	60.4
Custer	Cheyenne	42	1,221	34.4	16.6	8.2	13.9	24.2
Lincoln	Ioway, Central Algonkian	28	907	30.9	18.7	5.3	—	20.5
Noble	Ponca, Oto	10	703	14.2	23.9	13.9	15.6	26.7
Canadian	Cheyenne	21	1,680	12.5	9.7	3.5	27.3	23.8
Comanche	Comanche	31	4,625	6.7	17.7	6.9	—	28.4
Oklahoma	Mixed	42	14,285	2.9	7.0	5.8	38.1	7.2*
Cotton	Comanche	1	490	2.0	13.1	8.8	—	14.1
Tulsa	Mixed	19	19,059	1.0	9.3	2.5	34.1	7.0*
Osage	Osage	2	4,750	0.4	6.9	2.4	26.5	26.5

*Calculated for Standard Metropolitan Statistical Area (SMSA) rather than county.

Sources: Statistics are from the following sources: 1980 Census of Population, volumes entitled "American Indians, Eskimos, and Aleuts on Identified Reservations and in the Historic Areas of Oklahoma (Excluding Urbanized Areas)," and the Oklahoma volumes of "General Social and Economic Characteristics," "General Population Characteristics," and "Detailed Population Characteristics"; Bureau of Indian Affairs documents for 1980 and 1981 from the Concho Agency and Anadarko Area entitled "Annual Report of Caseloads, Acreages Under BIA, and Surface Leasing"; and the "Annual Report, Oklahoma Department of Human Services" for fiscal 1980, July 1979 through June 1980.

with a combination of three measures of poverty; they are high in all three, but especially unemployment.

Custer, Lincoln, Noble, Canadian and Comanche counties seem to form a central group with a great deal of variability. As a group, they show that an intermediate frequency of pow-wows correlates with intermediate values for the indices of poverty as a whole. It is risky, however, to postulate any finer correlation within this central group, for at least three reasons: (1) there is interplay among the variables, for example finding employment might make one ineligible for food stamps; (2) no basis exists for determining the relative importance of the different poverty indices; and (3) the data collection periods are slightly different, ranging from late 1978 to middle 1981.

In the bottom group of counties, Oklahoma, Cotton, Tulsa and Osage, there is one clear anomaly, easily explained. Cotton County, a small area in the southwestern part of the state, participated in the oil boom at the beginning of the decade. A sparsely populated county, it produced half a million barrels of oil in 1980, providing employment for many local people. The local Indian people, experiencing high levels of employment, had no need for pow-wows.

Oklahoma County is the location of Oklahoma City and a few suburbs, and Tulsa County is almost coterminous with the city of Tulsa, giving the high figures of labor participation on the table, calculated as the number of employed Indian people over sixteen years of age, divided by the Indian population of the county. Here again, it is the combination of factors affecting poverty which correlates with the low pow-wow frequency.

Osage County is a special case, because of the county's unique status as the state's only federally acknowledged reservation,[2] and the inheritance by Osage Indians of "head rights," discrete shares of payment for subsurface minerals. Historically, Osages have been better off economically than other Oklahoma Indian groups, as evidenced by their continuing low poverty indices. In this case, however, the figures for low economic participation and low employment do not necessarily reflect poverty, but rather indicate the existence of many

Osage people who live from head-right payments and have no
need to work. Note that their other poverty indices are very
low.

The data of table 11.1, in addition to showing the level of
poverty in some of the pow-wow counties, that is, the *scarcity*
of income, also show the maldistribution of this income from
various available sources. Even though employment was
higher in 1980 than it is now, about half the Oklahoma Indian
families in the pow-wow area had no member who worked
regularly at the time of the 1980 census. The unemployment
figures on the table are for people seeking work who were
unemployed for fifteen or more weeks in calendar 1979.

Concerning employment, a special difficulty is posed for
Indian people when they do manage to find a job. Often this
means that another member of the family, a spouse, a sibling,
or a parent, loses some kind of public assistance payments. If
after a few months the job is lost, considerable paperwork is
required to re-enroll a relative in state and federal programs of
assistance. These transition periods between employment
and assistance are exceptionally troublesome to families, and
it is during these periods that the family is most likely to need
help from others in the community.

One frequent source of help for families in need is the men
and women who have recently retired to their childhood home
in a rural community or returned from a stint of work in some
distant city—Chicago or Los Angeles. Such people frequently
sponsor a pow-wow, working through their family or pow-wow
club, thereby securing a recognizable place in the community.
Men and women retired from the armed forces are especially
noticeable in this regard, as they often have some retirement
bonus to distribute to family, friends, and solicitants. In the
case of servicemen, the war mothers organizations can be
called upon as sponsors.

During the days of the military draft, the war mothers were
much more active than they are now, sponsoring events on
two prominent occasions in the career of a draftee—his shipment overseas and his discharge. The former took place after

basic and advanced training, with the family and the war mothers giving away in honor of the serviceman. At discharge, however, it is the serviceman who sponsors, singling out those who were generous to him a few years before. He is also generous privately, helping out all who ask until his money is gone. These recipients then become the people he calls on to help him make an adjustment to civilian life. Although this is perhaps the most clear-cut case of redistributive behavior, the cycle was acted out over about two years, the term of obligation under the draft. Nowadays there is necessarily a longer time from distribution to reciprocity, since the current terms of enlistment are usually from three to six years. The Persian Gulf War was handled as a special event in the pow-wow network, like a graduation, and did not seem to affect the established pattern for military service.

Although many Indian people receive lease and royalty money from ownership of trust land or from subsurface rights to land that has been sold, the form of the payments is erratic and confounds any attempt to develop a regular, dependable income. Farming and grazing leases, "surface leases," are contracted through the Bureau of Indian Affairs for a three- to five-year period and are paid annually, usually in January. As with finding a job, the receipt of a grass lease check can cause a family to lose their public assistance payments. To reestablish eligibility for some of these programs, one must demonstrate that one has no assets, and so good reasons exist for the family to quickly sponsor a pow-wow and dispose of money and property. Not surprisingly, Ashworth's data show that most benefits and memorials are held from February to May, just after the checks are received (1986:111).

In addition to the timing of the payments, the amount and distribution of lease income among individuals also creates reasons for a redistribution of resources. At allotment in severalty at the turn of the century, an Oklahoma Indian was usually allotted a parcel of land comprising 40, 80, or 160 acres. Much of the land was sold by 1950, 70 percent or more for most tribes, and the remainder fell into heirship, with each descendent most often receiving equal shares of a parent's allotment. After several generations of heirship, and because of the vicissitudes of birth, some remaining allotments still have only one owner, while others have as many as five hundred owners. In 1980 farming and grazing land produced a lease income of from $1,000 to $3,000 per allotment per year, and so an individual owner might receive an annual check for as much as $3,000, or as little as $2, depending on how many co-owners there were.

Looking at the Cheyenne and Arapaho situation, for example, in 1981 there were 732 individual leases in effect, producing an annual income of slightly over a million dollars, an average of $1,452 per lease. But this income is unevenly distributed among about five thousand heirs. Another function of the giveaways and pow-wows, then, is to provide a network for redistributing cash payments which are not only distorted calendrically, but also maldistributed among individuals.

Another kind of income distortion is provided by oil royalties, which depend on where oil was found, and how much the current production might be. In the pow-wow counties, the amount of oil pumped in 1980 ranged from 50,000 barrels, for Kiowa County, to 11 million barrels, for Osage County. In addition to royalties, there are also drilling fees and other periodic bonanzas from "adjustments" to payment schedules.

During calendar 1980, a high point of the oil boom in western Oklahoma, the Anadarko Area Office, which administers the major Plains tribes in western Oklahoma, disbursed over $8 million in oil and gas royalties to individual Indian people. Abject poverty nonetheless remained in the population, but those who had money gave it away lavishly, rewarding those who had helped them over the years and hedging against hard times to come. Embarrassed by their quick fortunes and under heavy social pressure to share with others, some Indian people began to engage in "wretched excess." A Kiowa pow-wow man publicly gave a prominent Osage man a horse with its mane and tail braided with $100 bills. A Cheyenne woman gave each of her three close woman friends a new pickup truck, the model General Motors already had dubbed the "Chevy Cheyenne." In these cases, the gifts were not merely symbolic, but constituted real, usable wealth. But these were unusual times.

During normal years things are not so flush for a typical Indian extended family. Usually, there might be a person or two in the extended family who is employed, perhaps someone else who is on public assistance, and also someone who gets occasional lease or royalty money. The point of the giveaway and pow-wow system is that it also allows a family to have "money in the bank" in the form of help given in the past to other families, symbolized by exchanges at giveaways and pow-wows. As long as possible the family will redistribute its own resources to survive, but there often comes a time when other families must be called upon to "help out." They do so willingly, not only because of friendship and respect, but also in the knowledge that sometime soon they might be in the same situation, looking for a family that has just received its lease money or some other modest bonanza. And while the timing of these bonanzas is not always predictable, it is certain that they will come. The whole giveaway complex is predicated on this expectation.

Conclusion

At the most abstract level, how one interprets giveaway behavior within the context of ethnological theory depends on the tribe under discussion; each has a somewhat different socioeconomic structure. For the Comanches, the best model might be that of a "big man" actively looking out for his community's welfare, accumulating goods, and raising his personal prestige in accordance with his success as a leader, organizer, and redistributor (Sahlins 1963). With the Cheyennes a different model is required. Although a traditional chief has high status, he has no property, taking a passive role as tribal members shower him with public and private gifts, while supplicants constantly denude him of what he has been given. The pattern seems to be some kind of "levelling," as with the potlatch of the Northwest Coast (Codere 1950). For Kiowas and Osages, ascribed status seems to be important, since personal ancestry is constantly recited at their giveaways and pow-wows (Linton 1936:113–31).

Among those Central Algonkians and Dhegiha Sioux who participate in pow-wows, the focus seems to be on the drum and on the pow-wow activities, rather than on traditional tribal roles. It is relevant that the people of these tribes are heavily intermarried with one another, so that "full-blood" Ioways or Shawnees, for example, are hard to find. That is, a community in north central Oklahoma is likely to be of mixed tribes: individuals do not owe respect to the institutions of one single tribe, but to several. With tribal institutions diluted, social attention falls on the giveaway and pow-wow, pan-Indian institutions which are universally understood and which transcend the leadership traditions of any particular tribe.

Comparing Southern Cheyenne with Northern Cheyenne giveaway practices as reported by K. Weist, there seem to be several significant differences. First of all, "tables" of goods representing horses are not ordinarily given away in Oklahoma. Also, there are no Oklahoma Cheyenne giveaways which can rival the huge presentations of goods witnessed by Weist. However, the main argument of this article, that public gifts imply private sharing arrangements, might also be valid for the Montana Cheyennes. Weist, writing in 1973, reports a very low family income level, about $3,000 per year, consisting largely of such erratic sources as "wages, welfare, and lease payments" (1973:101).

In closing, I must argue that in the cases of Oklahoma tribes, the most significant and most fundamental aspect of the giveaway and pow-wow complex is the redistributive function. It is fundamental because it keeps people alive, providing them with the means of subsistence—food, money, heat, medical care. Sociologically, the perspective of redistribution is important because it ties the formal aspect of the pow-wow, the ceremony, directly to the causal variable, the economy. In different ways, Ashworth and I have shown that poverty level is the independent variable, pow-wow frequency the dependent variable.

In the course of organizing economic redistribution, the pow-wow system allows the emergence of a new kind of community leader, the pow-wow man, with intensive and extensive networks of influence which reach across community and tribal boundaries. The need for an expansion of such networks is especially severe among the small Dhegiha and Algonkian tribes in north central Oklahoma. How these pow-wow leaders and their functions are integrated into the total social and political structure of a tribe, however, varies from group to group.

Acknowledgments

For data on pow-wows I am especially indebted to my colleague and former student Kenneth Ashworth. For their help in locating social and economic statistics I wish to thank Ruby Tiger and Chloe Buffington, of the Bureau of Indian Affairs, Michelle Summers, of the Oklahoma Geological Survey, and Kim Bernhardt, of the Oklahoma Employment Security Commission.

CHAPTER 12

Native North Americans and the National Question

George P. Castile

The "national question" came into existence with the nation state itself, as the domination and exploitation of one people by another emerged as one aspect of the division of labor in that heterogeneous kind of society (Engels 1972). The relations of the resulting "ethnic" or national groups to the state have remained an issue to the present day for both capitalist and socialist states, which remain politically perplexed by the tenacity of the identity systems of these "persistent peoples" and their refusal to become "new men" (Castile and Kushner 1981). The "Native American" peoples have presented a unique form of the national question from the first moment of their conquest and forced incorporation into European states five hundred years ago.

In the United States, from the time of our political birth in an avowedly egalitarian revolution, we have grappled with the problem of the proper relation of these aboriginal sovereign possessors of the soil to the state (Prucha 1984). However, just as blacks were not initially included in "equality," the national policy pursued by the new independent United States towards Native Americans was, for at least a hundred years, much the same as that pursued by the preceding colonial government—a *neocolonial* policy in this sense as in others. Today federal Indian policy statements speak of "government-to-government relations," but in these earliest days one can scarcely speak even of *human* relations, let alone respect for Native American governments (Reagan 1983). The "treaties" signed were ostensibly agreements between equal sovereign polities, but these "agreements" were in fact unilaterally imposed and unilaterally reinterpreted whenever convenient. The focus of these treaties was land, not the Indian peoples per se—it was *land* policy, not Indian policy. The best description of this policy era is simply one of land clearance— a period in which Native Americans had much the same status as forests, something to be cleared away so that land could be put to good use by rapidly expanding populations. The most transparent manifestation of this was the Indian Removal Act of 1830, which effectively cleared Indians from the entire eastern half of the United States (Satz 1975).

But by the late 1800s the "out of sight, out of mind" policy of sweeping Indians aside and ahead of the "frontier" necessarily faltered as the tide of settlement reached the Pacific and no further "empty" lands were available. The Indian peoples by now formed territorial enclaves surrounded by a vastly larger non-Indian population. These reserved parcels became anomalies that could no longer be politically ignored, since they had become the only remaining pockets of "unused" land for settlement. The place of these reservations and their occupants in relation to the rest of the nation has formed a "national question" ever since (Prucha 1976).

The first real "nationality" policy of the United States government, once this new situation became apparent, rapidly emerged as a program of involuntary assimilation and "civilization." Truly vanishing Americans, Indians were to cease to exist as distinctive peoples and become absorbed into the general society. At the same time, of course, their "surplus" lands would be "freed" for sale to needy citizen settlers. Regardless of the prospects for further land clearance, such a program of assimilation or cultural homogenization, a "melt-

ing pot" approach, was of course consistent with and an outgrowth of existing United States policy toward European
immigrant groups. One can argue that it is the "natural" and
inevitable policy of any and all states to seek the stability of
homogeneity and to eliminate potentially divisive minority
segmentation. Certainly, it seems historically the policy pursued by most of them, using force or persuasion, since the
rise of the nation-state (Wolf 1982).

One can even praise such policies when they are contrasted
with racist alternatives that deny some national elements integration on the grounds of inherent inferiority. Blacks, Asians,
and Indians were denied entrance to the melting pot of the
United States until the post–Civil War era on "scientific" racist
grounds (Stanton 1960; Bieder 1986). A policy of assimilation
is at least predicated on the assumption that all peoples are
capable of becoming fully functional and equal citizens of the
state. Derived from the era of the Enlightenment, this attitude
of endorsing the equality and perfectibility of all mankind is
basic to the United States Constitution—and to Marxist social
theory.

Classical Marxism, the Marxism of Marx and Engels, seems
clearly to have taken such an "assimilationist" stance on
human ethnic malleability. Both of them strongly stress the
preeminence and unity of class interest over national identity,
as in the famous passage from the "Manifesto": "National differences and antagonisms between peoples are daily more
and more vanishing. ... The supremacy of the proletariat will
cause them to vanish still faster" (Marx and Engels 1978:488).
Marx, although he wrote little specifically on the topic, seemed
generally to view the existence of national elements as an
ephemeral phenomenon of the capitalist stage of development, tending to cloud class identification for the benefit of
the ruling class, and he would presumably have endorsed the
United States assimilation policy as he did that of other
nations (Avineri 1969; Marx and Engels 1972). However,
Marxist thought on the national question, starting with the
debates between Lenin and Luxemborg, has evolved consid-

erably, and I will return to it presently (Luxemborg 1976; Lenin 1970, 1979).

With reference to the United States up to 1900, one could persuasively argue that policies directed toward Native American peoples were just what classical Marxism would suggest in an expanding capitalist society—naked exploitation of the nearly powerless minority peoples by the ruling people and ruling class. This took the form of expropriation of resources—land and all that was on it—since the Indians' labor seldom was an important factor in the larger economy. For a variety of reasons, black slavery took the place of Indian labor in the earliest days when Indian populations were still numerous enough to be potentially exploitable (G. Nash 1974). Native population thereafter rapidly fell to the point of relative economic insignificance—in 1990 less than one-half of one percent of the total by the most generous estimates.

The period of rapacious resource looting needs little sophisticated analysis, Marxist or otherwise. After 1900 the national question in relation to Native Americans becomes perplexing, and that is my focus. First emerging clearly under the administration of Franklin D. Roosevelt in the 1930s, federal policy has since then tended toward *stabilization* of the land base of what is left of the reservations, rather than further expropriation, and toward recognizing the *permanency* of the Indian peoples rather than their assimilation. It has even supported and strengthened the "governmental" authority and sovereignty of their tribal political organizations (Philip 1986). There have been periodic resurgences of the "natural" policy of assimilation—as in the 1950s drive toward "termination" of the reservation system entirely—but overall a policy of self-administration, if not self-determination, has been pursued (Burt 1982). What has emerged is a policy stance not unlike the limited "autonomy" characteristic of ethnic relations in many socialist nations (Ortiz 1984).

This political policy has been coupled with considerable effort and expenditure toward "development" of the economic status of the reservation enclaves (Reagan 1983; Swimmer

1984). Current policy, in particular, is much concerned with creating economic self-sufficiency, since Indian peoples remain among the poorest of the poor. Currently, much of federal money is expended in the administration of the reservation system and on behalf of the Native American peoples—$2.16 billion in fiscal 1988 (Friends Committee [FCNL] 1987:8). Both the political policy of self-determination and the policy of developmental investment raise problems for a political-economic model of ethnic relations based on exploitation, as suggested by classical Marxist analysis.

If one is to assume that the policy of a state necessarily serves the interest of that state and the interests of its ruling class, then the problem after 1900 increasingly becomes one of discovering the nature of the economic interest served. A "Fundamentalist" Marxist notion of exploitation through simple expropriation of resources will not now serve as it did until 1900, since most territory and virtually all useful resources had already been stripped from the reservation peoples by that point. There is one notable exception in modern times: a strong case can be made that the policy leading to the Alaska Native Claims Settlement Act of 1971 was based in a straightforward concern for access to resources (Berger 1985). However, even this latter-day resurgence of land clearance policy was clouded by the passage in December 1987 of second-thought legislation extending protection over the remaining native lands indefinitely (FCNL, 1988:5).

To save economic explanations, much has been made by some of continuing exploitation, by a cooperative effort of government authority and corporations, of the few resources remaining in Indian hands—low lease rates for grazing lands and the like (Jorgensen 1978; Talbot 1981). But in stipulating for the sake of argument that some such pattern continues, the game is simply not worth the candle. The scale and value of these remaining resources scarcely justifies the costs of maintaining the reservation system as some sort of Rube Goldberg device for control of Indian people. It is surely too costly and cumbersome a federal mechanism for the benefit of very limited advantage to minor and purely local interests. In any case, even if we were to assume that these paltry remnant resources are valuable enough to dictate national policy, how can they explain the trends since 1930? The logic of economic exploitation would seem to demand that the reservations be further reduced or dissolved, if resource distribution were the goal, as was done in the past when truly valuable resources of a national scale were at stake.

I am by no means arguing against economic analysis of ethnic relations based on resource competition or the control of labor, but I oppose the simplistic application of this analysis to inappropriate arenas. I think there is a great deal that can be explained by materialist models of "internal colonialism," both in the United States and elsewhere (Hechter 1975). For example, very persuasive arguments have been made to show that many aspects of the status of the African-American ethnic group in the United States can be directly related to the economic needs of the southern agricultural system not only in the slave period, but after the demise of the "peculiar institution" as well (Blauner 1982; Piven and Cloward 1977). An internal colonial policy of caste relations, tending toward economic deprivation of this ethnic group, served for some time in the control of labor and wages for workers in general since, among other things, blacks formed a large reserve labor army to balance against the demands of organized labor.

Some make similar appeal to Indians as "cheap labor," but often the argument is more polemical than real (Jorgensen 1978:62). Now, even more than in earlier times, Native Americans are simply not numerous enough, not even in the sparsely settled western states where they are concentrated, to be an important element in the national labor force. While there are nearly thirty million blacks, many concentrated in our major industrial cities, there are only 631,574 Indians scattered on 278 reservations and 209 Alaskan Native villages. That the depressed value of their labor might be of some minor utility to local farming elites is undeniable, but a localized reserve labor army of a few hundred is not of a scale sufficient to dictate national policy any more than is the cheapness with which their grazing land can be leased (Stern and Boggs 1971; Moore 1989). An analysis which suggests that the national policy of maintaining the reservations is a mechanism somehow comparable to the policy of tolerating the southern maintenance of racial caste simply cannot pass a utilitarian test—it makes no economic sense.

Why is there such a policy, if it seems not to serve the interests of the ruling class, so far has left the Indians themselves powerless and in poverty, and if it apparently serves no interest whatever? Let us dismiss immediately the whimsical comments of President Reagan in his summit comments at Moscow University suggesting that the reservations are maintained to "humor the Indians" (Reagan 1988). Indian policy is not made in any such response to the expressed wishes of the Indian people themselves; it is not "Indians' policy." Indian groups obviously do have policy goals and agendas and do make attempts to wrest advantage from the government. Such power brokering by other ethnic groups, however, is backed by their political "clout," but Indians have no influence in the usual sense (Bee 1982). Politically, the small scattered populations do not constitute a voting constituency of any significance nationally and tend to have negative political impact in the politics of the states where they are concentrated. Just as no one kisses babies to garner the baby vote, Indian policy is not made to court the Indian vote.

Indeed, very frequently Indian policy seems to have nothing to do with Indians at all. A case can be made that every major shift in Indian policy is ultimately rooted in larger national policy shifts made for purposes without reference to Indians. A strong movement for assimilation, begun after the Civil War, focused on the "civilizing" of blacks during Reconstruction; only later was a spin-off policy aimed at Native Americans (Mardock 1971). Franklin Roosevelt set out to alleviate the poverty of the whole nation in the Great Depression, and the Indians, willy nilly, found themselves beneficiaries of the administrative liberalism of John Collier (Kelly 1983). When the conservative Eisenhower administration set out to trim the federal bureaucracy and reduce government costs, the Bureau of Indian Affairs was slated for elimination and the reservations for termination (Fixico 1986). When Lyndon B. Johnson launched his "War on Poverty" in the 1960s, the doctrine of "maximum feasible representation of the poor" in that program spawned a new drive toward self-administration on the reservations (Castile 1989).

None of these things were conceived with the Indians in mind. Is Indian policy then simply an accident? Is that all there is, more a matter of political indifference and inertia than planned exploitation? Sadly, that is probably part of the explanation, but in their very insignificance the Native Americans do have significance. To explore that conundrum I want to turn now to look further into evolved Marxist theory, and the experience of the socialist states in their attempts to deal with their own national questions. Can this tell us anything useful for the understanding of the paradox of United States Indian policy?

Marxism and Socialism

Marx said nothing explicitly about the situation of the Native Americans under the reservation system in the United States, despite his interest in the writings of Morgan (Krader 1972). Morgan had expressed dissatisfaction with the administration of the reservations, tending toward a basically assimilationist view, but he published very little explicitly on the reservation system. There are two short articles; one, titled "The Indian Question," doubted the efficacy of the "civilizing" effort and called for the encouragement of pastoralism as the next appropriate evolutionary stage, that of "barbarism" (1876, 1878, 1959).

Official Marxism-Leninism in the Soviet Union likewise seemed largely silent about the American reservations and their peoples. There were occasional public statements of support for Indian activists such as Leonard Peltier, but the overall view seemed to reflect Marx's expectation of ultimate assimilation of all such national groups into capitalist systems (*Current Digest* 1984:19). Note, for example, the comment in the Great Soviet Encyclopedia (GSE): "A considerable number of Indians in the US are being assimilated with Americans, filling up the ranks of the American urban and rural proletariat and poor farmers" (GSE 1976:4).

Understandably, the development of Marxist-Leninist theory on the national issue has focused on the position of the nationalities under conditions of *socialism* and their role in the future of socialist states. The principal outcome of this remains the expectation of the ultimate emergence of a new international "socialist man," but in the transitional interim, during which there will be a "convergence" of peoples, a form of structural autonomy and political equality for the nationalities is anticipated (Communist Party 1987:14). This condition is usually expressed in a phrase ultimately derived from Marx "national in form, socialist in content" (Connor 1984:241).

In sum, most Marxists seem to have taken a position like that of Luxemborg's title, "There can be no Self Determination under Capitalism," suggesting that the plight of the Native Americans, like the problems of all United States national minorities, is simply a subcase of the class struggle and can only be resolved under socialism (Revolutionary Communist Party 1983; Muga 1988; Luxemborg 1976). But are there useful elements in Marxist theory for American anthropologists in our persistently nonsocialist country, for those who are not simply content to wait until, as my father used to say, "comes the revolution"? Several attempts have been made to survey the impact of Marxist theory on American anthropology in general, and all tend to the conclusion that, until very recently, it has been largely peripheral with very limited overt influence on mainstream developments (Wessman 1981; Leacock 1982; Vincent 1985; Hakken and Lessinger 1987; Bloch 1983). While the various reviewers have differing notions as to why this might be, I suspect all could agree that the question of an adverse political climate expressed by Harris's label "Un-American Anthropological Activities" explains much (Harris

1968:637). Archaeology tends to be more adventuresome in its theoretical speculations than social anthropology and is the exception to this limited impact. Recent work on the application of "critical theory" by Leone and others represents a lengthy continuity of development of explicitly Marxist theory dating to the work of V. Gordon Childe and Leslie White (Leone et al. 1987; Trigger 1985).

In recent years there have been very few explicitly Marxist-based analyses of things Indian (Talbot 1981; Ortiz 1984; K. Weiss 1984; Churchill 1983; Muga 1988). There has also emerged a somewhat larger number of Marxist-influenced "neocolonial" arguments raised by American scholars (Jorgensen 1978; Bee 1981; Snipp 1986). Far more extensive use of such concepts has been made by Latin Americanists who have been much more theoretically self-conscious about "Indigenismo" (Bollinger and Lund 1982).

Concerning the Latin American experience, let me simply note that it suggests caution in applying, in doctrinaire fashion, models appropriate to developed socialist nations, to those which are only "socializing." The Nicaraguan experience with the Miskito, for example, has suffered from a considerable failure to distinguish between reality and doctrine (Castile 1988). In the balance of this essay I will attempt to explore the utility of some Marxian-derived concepts for illuminating the "Indian question," but I have no intention of providing an analysis that seeks a "correct line" in a Marxist-Leninist or any other doctrinaire sense. Many scholars, including some modern Marxists, question whether "objectivity" is obtainable in social research. A recent commentator said of Marx that "his theory of ideology notwithstanding, Marx thought that scientific objectivity was possible and that scientific research could offset the biases associated with class positions," and in this sense I aim to be Marxian (Little 1986:3).

To begin with, and as we have seen, it is not the strictly "economistic" aspects of Marxist theory that seem useful in explaining recent Indian policy trends. Even the various "neocolonial" models are weakened by their attempts to rely on simplistic mechanisms of material exploitation (Castile 1983). I want to concentrate instead on the "political" end of political economy and do so by exploring some themes that emerged in the work of Antonio Gramsci. Although an ardent Sardinian nationalist as a youth, the mature Gramsci, like Marx, had little to say explicitly about the national question and mentions it in relation to the United States only passingly (Gramsci 1971:20). In his basic view of the nature of state power, Gramsci refined some aspects of classical Marxist theory. Here, clues to the potential significance of the economically insignificant Indians may be found.

Marx, and more especially Engels, tended to view the state as a coercive instrument, the "executive committee of the ruling class," hence their emphasis on its eventual "withering away." Gramsci, with due credit to Lenin, suggested that the power of the advanced capitalist state, indeed of any state, lies primarily in its ability to achieve cultural "hegemony." It achieves power by maintaining consensus and consent among the governed, even among the exploited classes, through a set of shared beliefs and symbols, rather than through the raw coercion of a resisting mass (Adamson 1980; Gramsci 1971). The "purpose" of federal Indian policy, its benefit to the ruling order, lies precisely in its contribution to strengthening the hegemony of the state through a manipulation of political symbols.

In an earlier paper I suggested that Indian policy had something of the same social purpose as Yanomamo wife beating (Castile 1984). According to Chagnon, "Beating a wife with a club is one way of displaying ferocity, one that does not expose the man to much danger. . . . Apparently the important thing in wife beating is that the man has displayed his presumed potential for violence and the intended message is that other men ought to treat him with circumspection, caution and even deference" (Chagnon 1983:16). Indian policy is, like the beatings received by hapless Yanomamo wives, aimed at "other men" than the Indian people themselves. The Indian, or his treatment by the state, symbolically conveys a message of state power and intentions to larger audiences.

While I have argued that the Indian peoples are not themselves a significant economic and political bloc, there are ethnonational groups in the United States which surely are. Blacks and Hispanics are the most numerous and politically potent of the many groups whose potentially centrifugal tendencies could threaten stability. Indian policy may serve principally as a mechanism to send or reinforce messages to such constituencies as these, about the status of all ethnic groups in the nation state. As purely "federal" policy, Indian policy also may serve to distinguish and define the position of the state on these ethnic questions in clear contrast to regional and local positions in the "several states." Let me offer some very tentative formulations as to how the process functions.

Congress, of course, does make policy directly aimed at African Americans and Hispanic Americans and is always under considerable political pressure to do more for the disadvantaged condition of these large and increasingly political minorities. The political problem is to deliver "enough" on the promises and pledges of equality and opportunity which are a large part of the basis of state legitimacy and cultural hegemony. An expectation of near future fulfillment of the "American dream" must be maintained if the state is to retain the acquiescence of the minority peoples who are fully aware that they benefit least in the present.

The state, of course, does actually deliver on these promises to some extent—the American dream is by no means all illusion—and even the poor are "well off" by Third World standards. But ghetto dwellers in New York do not compare their condition to the *favelas* of Rio, and there exists a continuing and visible condition of relative deprivation vis à vis the dominant class. A great deal of money is spent in the ongoing "war on poverty," but the disadvantaged condition of the ethnic populations has deep historical roots; change, even with the best of intentions, must necessarily take time. Politics is the art of the possible, and so problems are remedied, but only slowly. To immediately alleviate the plight of African and Hispanic Americans in terms of income, housing, health, and education would take a commitment of funds, not to mention a restructuring of class relations, which is simply not politically possible.

This, I think, is where the Indians come in. The Indians have several advantages as a mechanism for "demonstrations" of state intentions based on their small scale. A "gesture" toward black housing problems might cost many millions, but similar gestures toward the Indian population can be done comparatively cheaply because of the much smaller numbers. Complaining of the costs of confining the Navaho at Bosque Redondo, General Sherman is reported to have suggested that it would be cheaper to board the Navaho tribe at a New York hotel (Underhill 1953:231). This was a joke, of course, but not a joke that anyone has ever made about any other ethnic group. Their very small scale, which makes them politically insignificant, makes them useful as a vehicle for an earnest show of governmental good intentions toward all ethnics.

Perhaps more important than the low material costs is the low political investment. We have already noted the insignificance of the Indian vote. The reservations are also "administered communities," which is to say a great many of the public functions normally operated by local and state governments are administered directly by the federal government on a reservation (Castile 1974). This makes it far simpler politically for the federal government to undertake any sort of project there, whatever its nature. A federally planned program in a Chicago ghetto can only take place with the cooperation of a myriad of state and local political constituencies, but on the reservations a program can be inaugurated immediately by direct federal fiat. The usefulness of this system of direct administration may explain why it remains largely intact despite an avowed policy of turning toward self-administration since 1975 and despite a hundred previous years of the BIA "working itself out of a job."

In addition to such practical matters, to a considerable extent Indians exist politically *only* as symbols, as mental, not material, constructs. What the American people, minority or otherwise, "know" about Indians has little to do with actual life on the reservations. The isolation of most reservations means that the vast majority of the people have no first-hand experience of Indian reality. Neither official government statements nor the poetic illusions about natural ecologists in harmony with nature that are peddled by some Indian "spokesmen" are contradicted by harsh comparison with reservation actuality. The success of government promises to rebuild inner city ghettos or to "stop drugs" are known to all on a personal basis, or through constant media scrutiny, but the fact that Indians remain poor after centuries of pledges is only "discovered" infrequently, in periodic replays of the Meriam report (Meriam 1928; De Concini et al. 1989). Political statements about life on the reservations are almost like statements about the nature of life in Atlantis: you are free to construct your own reality.

Seen as a mechanism for the transmission of cultural messages, seeming paradoxes in Indian policy, which economistic approaches do not illuminate, become clearer. Sporadically since the 1930s and consistently since the late 1960s, federal policy has tended strongly to stress the preservation and protection of the quasi-sovereign status of these "dependent domestic nations." Would this seem to argue that the hegemonic message being sent here is an endorsement of some degree of ethnic national autonomy? But such a message is in complete contradiction to the fact that, historically, political autonomy of any segment of United States society has been treated as an intolerable threat to stability and hegemony. All separatist movements, from the Whiskey Rebellion and southern secession to the Mormon theocratic state and the Black Panthers, have been suppressed ruthlessly.

The resolution of this contradiction seems to be that while the current policy toward Indians—a "government to government" policy—would superficially appear to encourage such notions of ethnic autonomy, the hegemonic effect is just the opposite. The Federal policy emphasis, constantly repeated since the days of Justice Marshall, is on the *uniqueness* of the Indian legal and political status. By virtue of their status as aboriginal possessors of the soil they—and they *alone*—have this claim to the status of "domestic nations." The message in fact being sent here is that *only* Indians may aspire to this special status, and all other ethnic groups are by default ineligible and, therefore, must be discouraged from such ambitions. It is noteworthy that the recent political rhetoric of support for autonomy and self-determination for the tribes arose exactly coincident with the late 1960s quasi-separatist phase of the civil rights movement (Castile 1989). This "autonomy" theme may be the most important message sent to the ethnic audience, but there are other audiences and other messages.

Even in earlier periods when more direct economic motives were clear and paramount, Indian policy served political and symbolic purposes in the balance between regions. The northern Republican abolitionists were thwarted by the end of federal control over southern reconstruction from pursuing their attempts to assimilate blacks. They turned to Indians almost by default to "keep the faith." Hoxie, in his analysis of the appeal of Indian assimilation in the later 1800s, remarks on the political utility to its congressional supporters, suggesting that "the Indian assimilation campaign promised to be popular, safe and therapeutic" (1984:35). The major themes addressed in that policy era, "the supremacy of national institutions, cautious attempts at racial justice," suggest some continuity of symbolic utility into the present (Hoxie 1984:31).

Continuing federal-state and regional-national tensions suggest an area in which Indian policy continues to play a part and where we can reconnect our ideological analysis with the material. In the oppression of minorities it is very often regional authorities who behave most harshly, since resources of limited national impact may have considerable local significance. It is only when great discrepancies between such local and national interests arise that the central government is likely to champion seemingly altruistic causes. The civil rights movement succeeded in the South only when the Federal government withdrew its long-standing acquiescence to the oppressive system of segregation, and it did so only when national costs had exceeded local gains materially and politically (Piven and Cloward 1977). Resolution of the tension between the "state" and the states over ethnic matters has had considerable political and economic cost at times, notably in the Civil War and in the early furor of the civil rights struggle.

In recent years federal policy has conspicuously supported the rights of Indians threatened by state attempts at expropriation of political power and treaty rights. This visible support acts as a continuing pledge to other ethnic groups of federal protection against local bigotry, but the focus on the Indians as the arena of federal-state symbolic conflict, now as in the 1800s, makes it safe and less costly for all participants. Normally, the western states, with low political influence on the national scene, are the object of federal acts of good will toward Indians in the theater of the courts. Even in those states the issues, salmon fishing rights for example, are not really economically critical to anyone. In fact the federal-state political struggle, even if lost, may be to the advantage of the local politicos who are allowed by the script to publicly posture as protectors of local interests against "big government" (Castile 1985).

To some extent, by such championing of the Indians, the state places itself in the same position as the tsar held in the eyes of the Russian peasants. Peasant grievances tended to be focused on the local noble landlords, and the people looked to the central government, to the tsar, for salvation from local oppression. This particular symbolic analogy may go far to explain why the reservation system has not simply been eliminated. It has considerable positive symbolic value but, perhaps more importantly, the negative symbolic cost of nakedly eliminating the "trust" relation would cost the state considerable credibility. The loss of ethnic credibility would not perhaps be as dramatic as the slaughter of the followers of Father Gapon on Bloody Sunday, which destroyed the illusion of the tsar's benevolence, but would be similarly damaging to the federal image.

Finally, it seems I am agreeing with classical Marxists and neocolonial theorists that the Indians are indeed being exploited, for cultural hegemonic gain if not material gain. The gain to the state is indeed more than the cost. Does this shift of focus from the material offer any greater suggestion as to "what is to be done"? I think so, for having correctly identified where the importance of Indian policy to the state actually lies, we have a better clue as to where to apply the lever to effect change. Once we purge ourselves of the image of greedy capitalists (with top hats and money signs on their vests?) grasping at nonexistent resources, can we find the real villains in their more benevolent guise?

There may even be hope short of a revolution. Symbolic significance, once bestowed, can be a powerful resource exploitable by the exploited themselves, since symbols are a more protean commodity than land. Leonard Peltier, Russell Means, and other Indian activists have shown that the actors, once provided a national stage, can sometimes speak lines not written for them, to an audience that would not otherwise hear them. Perhaps, if the Native American peoples can manipulate these cultural resources correctly, they may trade them for a political stability that their material losses did not gain them.

Not only internal ethnic constituencies watch and judge the good faith of the federal government on the basis of Indian policy. In the realm of the symbolic, as in the material, we may speak usefully of a "world economy" (Wallerstein 1979). Lewis Henry Morgan noted the potentially wider audience when he said of the Native American peoples: "We are responsible for them before mankind if we do not perform our duty toward them intelligently" (1878:332). Felix Cohen said it best: "Like the miner's canary the Indian marks the shifts from fresh air to poison gas in our political atmosphere; and our treatment of Indians, even more than our treatment of other minorities, reflects the rise and fall of our democratic faith" (Cohen 1953:390).

Notes

2. The Political Economy of Lakota Consciousness

1. The Lakota orthography is adopted from Buechel (1970).

2. Indian people are also relieved of the property tax burden faced by non-Indian rural families since Indian lands have federal trust status and cannot be taxed by state or local government.

3. Historically, Lakota people have specifically appealed to the Fort Laramie Treaty of 1868, the 1877 Black Hills Agreement, and the 1889 Great Sioux Agreement.

4. In 1985 the Lakota people of Pine Ridge and Rosebud reservations were discussing amendments of their tribal constitutions which would remove most of the supervisory powers of the United States secretary of the interior over the tribal governments. Assuming this would be a much-welcomed elimination of one source of domination on the reservations, I asked a tribal officer about the proposed amendments. He was hesitant about them, and replied, "The secretary of the interior is our protector." He was referring to the constitutional role of the secretary in striking down actions of tribal governments which infringed on the rights of tribal members (tribal governments do not have supreme courts). While the issue for the tribal officer was not the role of the federal government in providing jobs and services, this case does indicate the *ambivalence* with which Lakota people view the federal government (the tribal members nevertheless ratified the amendments on both reservations). This ambivalence is also evident in the suspicion with which some Lakota view the federal "Indian self-determination" policy. One tribal councilman told me that this was more about *termination* than it was about "self-determination."

3. Learning to Labor: Native American Education in the United States, 1880–1930

1. *Learning to Labour,* Paul Willis's insightful study of working-class education in London, is the source of my title.
2. For example, Patricia Shifferd (1976) describes the employment of northern Wisconsin Chippewa in lumbering, sawmills, mines, and railroad construction during the 1880s and 1890s. John Moore (1987) has described the importance of Cheyenne seasonal labor in Oklahoma agriculture from World War I until recently.

5. Natives and the Development of Mercantile Capitalism

1. Rotstein (1967) shows how and why Indians might seek to reserve the political option of trading with both parties; unfortunately, I can say no more here.
2. The returns for 1725 are anomalous, since it is the only year in our series when HBC exports exceeded beaver exports out of Quebec; possibly Innis's Quebec figures are in error for 1725.

6. Symbiosis, Merger, and War: Contrasting Forms of Intertribal Relationship Among Historic Plains Indians

1. The relationship between ethnicity and the concept of "tribe" in Plains Indian ethnology is discussed at length elsewhere (Sharrock 1974; Albers and James 1986a; Albers and Kay 1987; Moore 1988). Although many anthropologists have discontinued using the expression "tribe," I believe that it remains an appropriate term which designates standardized ethnic names for American Indian populations. There is no suggestion here that tribal labels represent any kind of cohesive social or political body.
2. The following works (Goldman 1941; Lesser 1951; Dobyns et al. 1957; Dobyns, Ezell, and Ezell 1963; Elmendorf 1960, 1971; Suttles 1960; Hickerson 1962, 1965, 1971; Owens 1965, 1968; Walker 1967; Anastasio 1972; Burch and Correll 1972; Davis 1974; Ray 1974; McClellan 1975; Loscheider 1977; Ford 1983; Bishop 1987; Albers and Kay 1987) are just a few of many sources that deal with interethnic relationships among American Indian populations in other areas of North America.
3. Most studies of intertribal relationships among the Plains do not follow a well-formulated theoretical discourse. Aside from a few studies which use some sort of historical materialist approach (Jablow 1950; Ray 1974; Moore 1974, 1988; Klein 1977; Hanson 1987) other works (Woods 1973; Sharrock 1974; Giannettino 1977; K. Weist 1977) ground their analysis in social alli-

ance and exchange models. As applied in North America and elsewhere (Chagnon 1968; Koch 1974; Jackson 1976; Smith 1976), these models often present a static rendering of intergroup relationships because they do not confront some of the historical and material forces that give them processual dimension. When accompanied by graph theory (Hage and Harary 1983) however, some of these models offer an elegant way of conceptualizing alliance and exchange networks. Nonetheless, more needs to be done to embed alliance and exchange models in an historical frame of reference.

4. In historic times kinship was a major language of social relationship among Plains Indians. As a system of reference it was extended widely to include persons who had no biological connection to each other. It was a central metaphor in cementing partnerships with Euro-American traders whose "kinship" ties with Indians mirrored native social connections (White 1982; Anderson 1984; Albers and Kay 1987; Peers 1987:55–59).

5. There is considerable debate about the actual impact of horses and guns on native systems of production and trade. My reading of the literature supports the position of Jablow (1950) and Klein (1977) that these new forms of technology intensified the dependency of tribes on each other because in contrast to most prehistoric durable goods, the horse and gun were basic means of production. And even though they did not completely supplant native-produced technologies, they had a profound impact on indigenous production and trade.

6. There is evidence in the literature on Plains Indian partnerships with Euro-American traders that the establishment of a "kinship" tie was a mechanism to ensure not only the long-term security of exchanges between the two parties but also to encourage liberalness in reciprocity (White 1982; Peers 1987:53–56).

7. This is consistent with some of the logic behind clan relationships where members of clans in the same moiety stood in a sibling relation to each other, and it is explicated most fully in Paul Radin's (1970:153–54) work on the Winnebago; he shows that clans of the same moiety were related to each other as "friends" and that their common identification involved expectations of mutual service in ceremonial and military matters. Clans in a friend qua sibling relation also encamped with each other on the same side of a village or camp circle (Radin 1970:139–42). By contrast, members of clans in opposite moieties stood in a complementary relationship (Radin 1970:150–205). Among the Omaha, members of the same clan could not adopt each other; the pipes had to be carried to people of other clans and tribes where the parties in the adoption stood in a complementary, father-son relationship (Fletcher and La Flesche 1972:378).

8. Data on the Plains Ojibway and their Euro-American traders indicates that the specific character of a kinship tie influenced expected patterns of reciprocity (Peers 1987:53–56).

8. The Quest for Indian Development in Canada:
Contrasts and Contradictions

1. There are a number of categories of Indian people. With each category, different legal entitlements apply. Today there are treaty and non-treaty Indians with band membership and those without, "C–31" Indians—those registered as a result of the 1985 amendments to the Indian Act—and finally Indians registered under section 6(1) or 6(2) of the Indian Act.

2. Some say that "group mindedness" inhibits development. People in traditional society think that individual improvement can take place only at the expense of somebody else. Therefore, no change should occur unless others in the group are equally benefitted. But these same stagnant conditions may give rise to excessive individualism: If people think you can't change society, the best thing to do is to act as an individual and pursue selfish and short-term gains.

3. The tax department seemed to take the position that the source of the income, not the residency of the Indians, was the basis on which liability for income was to be determined (Daugherty 1978).

9. Autonomy and Constraint: The Household Economy on
a Southern Ontario Reserve

1. A registered Indian is defined on legal grounds and excludes many people of aboriginal ancestry. See Cumming and Mickenberg (1972:6) and Frideres (1988:6–17) for a discussion of this.

2. Over the years the administration of Native peoples has been conducted by different departments of the federal government. It currently rests within the Department of Indian Affairs and Northern Development. To avoid confusion, these different departments will be referred to simply as Indian Affairs.

3. See Rolf Knight (1978) for a discussion of this policy.

4. The natural resources of the reserve currently support a band-owned farm (about four thousand acres) and provide a major source of revenue from leases to hunting lodges and fishing and duck-hunting permits. A recent study of male band members between fifteen and seventy-four years of age indicated that at least 135 depend to some degree on the wildlife resources of the marsh and waterways (Laurie Montour and M. Williams 1988).

5. The Church of England missionary is credited with having established this exhibition (Canada, *Annual Report* 1887:21). This is evidence of the overlap of the interests of missions and government in creating a sedentary agrarian population. A continued interest in such events is acknowledged two decades later. At this time, the Indian Agent noted, in a rather paternalis-

tic style, that there was a "fair on the island . . . for the first time, and while it was small and somewhat crude from being a new thing to everyone connected with it, yet it was in a small way a grand success" (Canada, *Annual Report* 1899:8). Both were used to encourage the development of agrarian skills.

6. The supply of hay seems to have come from grassland areas on the reserve and is described as "practically inexhaustible." Large quantities were cut, but the agent notes, with some dissatisfaction, that it was not used to maintain stock in good condition during the winter but was "all for sale" (Canada, *Annual Report* 1897:33). Horses and cattle were largely left to forage for themselves.

7. Persons "in the business" provided seed and "helped to prepare the ground." The sale of the crop of 150 acres was assured because "purchasers have got a good deal of money invested in it already" (Canada, *Annual Report* 1901:43).

8. The number for the smallest category of farm was not given, though a very rough estimate can be made. If we use the 1890 census figure of 4.5 people per Walpole family and assume that each farm was occupied by a family, we find that 157 people occupied farms above the smallest category. Given a population of about 800, then 643 (143 families) cultivated the smaller lots or did not cultivate any land at all. If nothing else, this was indicative of the subsistence nature of most farming.

9. The nature of land-tenure arrangements to reserve land and resources at this time remains unclear. Individuals did have possession of land for cultivation, but little is known about the way these rights were bestowed, their duration, or whether or not they could be inherited, given away, or sold.

10. By the early 1880s, fishing was generating an income for households (Canada, *Annual Report* 1881:xiii), and by the mid-1880s it could be described as "fairly remunerative" (Canada, *Annual Report* 1887:18). By the end of the century, large numbers of sturgeon were being caught and sold at a good price, and there were "buyers coming every day to take the night's catch" (Canada, *Annual Report* 1901:42).

11. Furs were a source of income in the agrarian economy of the 1880s (Canada, *Annual Report* 1881:xiii). This continued to be true throughout the period under discussion.

12. In 1886, for example, it was noted that work with good wages was plentiful and that those not able to seek wage work could cut oak tops into cord wood and make axe handles (Canada, *Annual Report* 1887:19).

13. It was noted that "women do a large business amongst the tourists, selling fancy baskets and souvenirs" (Canada, *Annual Report* 1913:37). Much of this business was generated by large numbers of tourists visiting the island on excursion boats.

14. These interviews were part of a community-based research project

initiated in 1981, which involved the University of Windsor and Walpole Island First Nation. They were collected by various members of the research group, Nin.Da.Waab.Jig, including me. See Hedley (1986) for a discussion of the project.

15. The reserve was surveyed in 1908. It seems that each family was awarded two acres that, if fully developed, could be increased to forty acres (Harrington 1967:31).

16. Because reserves fell within federal jurisdiction, the rights in the estate of a spouse were not protected by dower or curtesy. The minister responsible for Indian Affairs retained the power to allow a widow to continue occupying the land owned by her deceased husband until she remarried or died (Henderson 1978:25).

17. See Henderson (1978) for a detailed discussion of land tenure on Indian reserves.

18. One of those interviewed gave hardship as the reason that he was sent to a residential school during the 1930s. As no payment was required, this offered some economic relief to the rest of the household.

19. A review of the Minutes of Regular and General Council Meetings reveals a continuing concern with "immorality." For example, we find a resolution aimed at making a woman rejoin a husband she had left many years previously (Nin.Da.Waab.Jig 6 July 1903) and another aimed at obliging people living together to get married (Nin.Da.Waab.Jig 6 June 1904). A decade later at a General Council Meeting it was resolved: "that notice be given to all parties living as man and wife without getting legally married be given 2 weeks notice to get married" (Nin.Da.Waab.Jig 6 Oct. 1913).

20. In 1974 there was a return to farming with the creation of Tahgahoning Enterprise, the band-owned farm. With a focus on corn and soya bean, the farm has expanded from two hundred acres to over four thousand acres.

10. Multinational Corporate Development in the American Hinterland: The Case of the Oklahoma Choctaws

1. County data from Employment Security Commission, 1979, reported in Oklahoma IMPACT, *Profile: Poverty in Oklahoma*, 1981, Choctaw data from author's sample.

2. Figures from County Tax Assessor, Pushmataha and McCurtain counties, Oklahoma, 1982.

11. How Giveaways and Pow-wows Redistribute the Means of Subsistence

1. I have observed this kind of formal, suppliant behavior only among Cheyennes and Arapahoes. Morris Foster and Tom Kavanagh tell me they

have not seen it among Comanches or Kiowas. It may be derived from the behavior required in the serious Cheyenne and Arapaho ceremonies—sun dance and arrow worship.

2. As I show in a forthcoming article, it is only an administrative myth that reservations were abolished in Oklahoma.

References

Abel, Annie H., ed.
1939 *Tabeau's Narrative of Loisel's Expedition to the Upper Missouri.* Norman: University of Oklahoma Press.

Adair, E. R.
1947 Anglo-French Rivalry in the Fur Trade during the Eighteenth Century. *Culture* 8:434–55.

Adamson, Walter L.
1980 *Hegemony and Revolution: A Study of Antonio Gramsci's Political and Cultural Theory.* Berkeley: University of California Press.

Albers, Patricia
1974 The Regional System of the Devil's Lake Sioux. Ph.D. diss., University of Wisconsin, Madison.
1982 Sioux Kinship in a Colonial Setting. *Dialectical Anthropology* 6: 253–69.
1985 Autonomy and Dependency in the Lives of Dakota Women: A Study in Historical Change. *Review of Political Economics* 17(3):109–34.

Albers, Patricia, and William James
1985 Historical Materialism vs. Evolutionary Ecology: A Methodological Note on Horse Distribution and American Plains Indians. *Critique of Anthropology* 6(1):87–100.
1986 On the Dialectics of Ethnicity: To Be or Not To Be Santee. *Journal of Ethnic Studies* 14:1–27.

1991 Horses Without People: A Critique of Neoclassical Ecology. In *Explorations in Political Economy: Essays in Criticism,* ed. R. K. Kanth and E. K. Hunt, 5–31. Savage, Md.: Rowman and Littlefield Publishers.

Albers, Patricia, and Jeanne Kay
1987 Sharing the Land: A Study in American Indian Territoriality. In *A Cultural Geography of North American Indians,* ed. T. E. Ross and T. G. Moore, 47–91. Boulder, Colo.: Westview Press.

Allaire, Gratien
1984 "Fur Trade Engagés, 1701–1745." In *Rendezvous.* See Buckley, 1984.

Althusser, Louis
1969 *For Marx.* New York: Vintage Books.

Anastasio, Angelo
1972 The Southern Plateau: An Ecological Analysis of Intergroup Relations. *Northwest Anthropological Research Notes* 6:109–229.

Anders, G.
1980 Indians, Energy and Economic Development. *Journal of Contemporary Business* 9:57–74.

Anderson, Gary
1984 *Kinsmen of Another Kind: Dakota-White Relations in the Upper Mississippi Valley, 1650–1862.* Lincoln: University of Nebraska Press.

Anderson, Robert
1951 A Study of Cheyenne Culture History, with Special Reference to the Northern Cheyenne. Ph.D. diss., University of Michigan.

Aristotle
1981 [c. 330 B.C.] *The Politics.* Translated and revised by Thomas Sinclair and Trevor Saunders. New York: Penguin Books.

Asante, S.
1979 Restructuring Transnational Mineral Agreements. *American Journal of International Law* 73(3):335–71.

Asch, M.
1987 Capital and Economic Development: A Critical Appraisal of the Recommendations of the Mackenzie Valley Pipeline Commission. In *Native People, Native Lands.* See B. Cox, 1987.

Ashworth, Kenneth
1986 The Contemporary Oklahoma Pow-wow. Ph.D. diss., University of Oklahoma.

Attewell, Paul A.
1984 *Radical Political Economy Since the Sixties*. New Brunswick, N.J.: Rutgers University Press.

Avineri, Shlomo
1969 *Karl Marx on Colonialism and Modernization*. Garden City, N.Y.: Doubleday.

Baer, Hans A.
1982 On the Political Economy of Health. *Medical Anthropology Newsletter* 14:1–2, 13–17.

Baer, Hans, Merrill Singer, and John H. Johnsen
1986 Toward a Critical Medical Anthropology. *Social Science and Medicine* 23:95–98.

Baird, W. David
1972 *Peter Pitchlynn: Chief of the Choctaws*. Norman: University of Oklahoma Press.

Ball, Terence; James Farr; and Russell Hanson, eds.
1989 *Political Innovation and Conceptual Change*. Cambridge: Cambridge University Press.

Ball, Timothy R.
1984 The Hudson's Bay Company Journals as a Source of Information for the Reconstruction of Climate. In *Rendezvous*. See Buckley, 1984. 43–50.

Banaji, Jairus
1980 Summary of Selected Parts of Kautsky's 'The Agrarian Question.' In *The Articulation of Modes of Production,* ed. Harold Wolpe. London: Routledge and Kegan Paul.

Bankes, N.
1983 *Resource Leasing Options and the Settlement of Aboriginal Claims*. Ottawa, Ont. Canadian Arctic Resources Committee.

Barger, Harold, and Hans H. Landsberg
1942 *American Agriculture, 1899–1939: A Study of Output, Employment and Productivity*. New York: National Bureau of Research.

Barsh, R. L.
1985 Evolving Conceptions of Group Rights in International Law. *Transnational Perspectives* 13(2):6–11.

Bartlett, Richard A.
1974 *The New Country: A Social History of the American Frontier 1776–1890*. New York: Oxford University Press.

Bee, Robert
1981 *Crosscurrents Along the Colorado: The Impact of Government Policy on the Quechan Indians.* Tucson: University of Arizona Press.
1982 *The Politics of American Indian Policy.* Cambridge, Mass.: Schenkman Publishing Company, Inc.

Benedict, Ruth
1932 Configurations of Culture in North America. *American Anthropologist* 34:1–27.

Benson, Henry
1970 [1860] *Life Among the Choctaw Indians and Sketches of the South-West.* Cincinnatti, Ohio: Johnson Reprint Co.

Berger, Thomas R.
1985 *Village Journey: The Report of the Alaska Native Review Committee.* New York: Hill and Wang.

Berreman, Gerald D.
1988 Race, Caste, and Other Invidious Distinctions in Social Stratification. In *Anthropology for the Nineties: Introductory Readings,* ed. Johnetta B. Cole, 485–521. New York: The Free Press.

Bieder, Robert E.
1986 *Science Encounters the Indian, 1820–1880.* Norman: University of Oklahoma Press.

Biolsi, Thomas
1984 Ecological and Cultural Factors in Plains Indian Warfare. In *Warfare, Culture, and Environment,* ed. R. B. Ferguson, 141–68. New York: Academic Press.
1992 *Organizing the Lakota: The Political Economy of the New Deal on Pine Ridge and Rosebud Reservations.* Tucson: University of Arizona Press.

Bishop, Charles A.
1974 *The Northern Ojibwa and the Fur Trade: A Historical and Ecological Study.* Toronto: Holt, Rinehart and Winston of Canada.
1987 Coast-Interior Exchange: The Origins of Stratification in Northwestern North America. *Arctic Anthropology* 24:72–83.

Bittle, William
1971 A Brief History of the Kiowa Apache. *Papers in Anthropology* 12:1–32.

Blauner, Robert
1982 Colonized and Immigrant Minorities. In *Majority and Minority: The*

Dynamics of Ethnicity in American Life, ed. by N. R. Yetman and C. H. Steele. Boston: Allyn and Bacon.

Bloch, Maurice
1983 *Marxism and Anthropology.* Oxford: Oxford University Press.

Boggs, James P.
1984 The Challenge of Reservation Resource Development: A Northern Cheyenne Instance. In *Native Americans and Energy Development II.* See Jorgensen, et al., 1984.

Boller, Henry A.
1972 *Among the Indians: Four Years on the Upper Missouri—1858– 1862.* Ed. M. Quaife. Lincoln: University of Nebraska Press.

Bollinger, William, and Daniel Manny Lund
1982 Minority Oppression: Toward Analyses that Clarify and Strategies that Liberate. *Latin American Perspectives* 9(2):2–28.

Bonilla, Frank, and Robert Girling, eds.
1973 *Structures of Dependency.* Palo Alto, Calif.: Stanford University Press.

Bose, Arun
1975 *Marxian and Post-Marxian Political Economy.* Baltimore, Md. Penguin Books.

Bourdieu, Pierre
1977 *Outline of a Theory of Practice.* New York: Cambridge University Press.

Bowers, Alfred
1950 *Mandan Social and Ceremonial Organization.* Chicago: University of Chicago Press.
1965 *Hidatsa Social and Ceremonial Organization.* Bureau of American Ethnology Bulletin 194. Washington, D.C.: G.P.O.

Boyd, Robert T.
1985 The Introduction of Infectious Diseases among the Indians of the Pacific Northwest, 1774–1874. Ph.D. diss., Ann Arbor: University Microfilms International.

Bradbury, John
1906 *Bradbury's Travels in the Interior of America in the Years 1809– 1811.* In *Early Western Travels,* vol. 6., ed. R. G. Thwaites. Cleveland, Ohio: Arthur H. Clark Co.

Branch, Douglas E.
1973 *The Hunting of the Buffalo.* Lincoln: University of Nebraska Press.

Brant, Charles
1949 The Cultural Position of the Kiowa Apache. *Southwestern Journal of Anthropology* 5:56–61.
1953 Kiowa Apache Culture History. *Southwestern Journal of Anthropology* 9:195–202.

Brody, H.
1975 *The People's Land: Eskimo and Whites in the Eastern Arctic.* Middlesex, England: Penguin Books.

Bruner, Edward
1961 Mandan. In *Perspectives in American Indian Culture Change*, ed. E. Spicer, 187–278. Chicago: University of Chicago Press.

Buckley, Thomas C., ed.
1984 *Rendezvous: Selected Papers of the Fourth North American Fur Trade Conference, 1981.* St. Paul, Minn.

Buechel, Eugene
1970 *A Dictionary of Lakota.* Ed. Paul Manhart. Pine Ridge, S. Dak.: Red Cloud Indian School.

Burch, Ernest S., Jr., and Thomas C. Correll
1972 Alliance and Conflict: Inter-Regional Relations in North Alaska. In *Proceedings of the American Ethnological Society, 1971*, ed. L. Guemple, 17–39.

Burkitt, Brian
1984 *Radical Political Economy: An Introduction to the Alternative Economics.* New York: New York University Press.

Burlingame, Merrill
1940 The Buffalo in Trade and Commerce. *North Dakota Historical Quarterly* 3(4).

Burt, Larry W.
1982 *Tribalism in Crisis: Federal Indian Policy, 1953–1961.* Albuquerque: University of New Mexico Press.

Campbell, Gregory R.
1989 The Changing Dimension of Native American Health: A Critical Understanding of Contemporary Health Issues. *American Indian Culture and Research Journal.* Special Edition, *Contemporary Issues in Native American Health* 13(3,4):1–20.

Canada
1869–1930 *Annual Report.* Indian Branch or the Department of Indian Affairs, Ottawa.

1890–1891 Census of Canada. In *Federal Government of Canada*. 2 vols. Ottawa.
1990 *Unfinished Business: An Agenda for All Canadians in the 1990s*. Standing Committee on Aboriginal Affairs. Ottawa, Ont.: Queen's Printer.

Cardoso, Fernando, and Enzo Faletto
1979 *Dependency and Development in Latin America*. Translated by Marjory M. Urquidi. Berkeley: University of California Press.

Carstens, Peter
1971 Coercion and Change. In *Canadian Society: Pluralism, Change and Conflict*, ed. R. J. Ossenber. Scarborough, Ont.: Prentice-Hall, Inc. of Canada.

Case, Ralph
n.d. Outline of the History of the Sioux Tribe, 1877–1934. Karl E. Mundt Papers, Microfilm Edition, Roll 104. The Karl E. Mundt Historical and Education Foundation, Dakota State College, Madison, S. Dak.

Castile, George Pierre
1974 Federal Indian Policy and the Sustained Enclave: An Anthropological Perspective. *Human Organization* 33(3):219–28.
1983 Neo-Colonial Models: 'Rotten Man' Theory and the Native Americans. Paper read at XII International Congress of Anthropological and Ethnological Sciences, Vancouver, B.C.
1984 Indians, Bears and Yanomamo Wives: Significance and Insignificance in Indian Policy. Paper read at Society for Applied Anthropology, Toronto, Ont.
1985 Indian Fighting for Fun and Profit: Sources of Indian Policy in the Pacific Northwest. Paper read at Society for Applied Anthropology, Washington, D.C.
1988 The Miskito and the Spanish. In *Central America: Historical Perspectives on the Contemporary Crisis*. ed. R. L. Woodward. Westport, Conn.: Greenwood Press.
1989 LBJ, the OEO, and the Native Americans. Paper read at Society for Applied Anthropology, Santa Fe, N. Mex.

Castile, George P., and Gilbert Kushner, eds.
1981 *Persistent People: Cultural Enclaves in Perspective*. Tucson: University of Arizona Press.

Chagnon, Napoleon A.
1968 Yanomamo Social Organization and Warfare. In *War: The Anthropology of Armed Conflict and Aggression*. ed. M. Fried, M. Harris, and R. Murphy, 109–59. Garden City, N.J.: The Natural History Press.
1983 *Yanomamo: The Fierce People*. New York: Holt, Rinehart and Winston.

Chardon, Pierre
1932 [1834] *Chardon's Journal at Fort Clark, 1834–1839*. Ed. Annie H. Abel. Department of History, State of South Dakota, Pierre.

Chartrand, J.
1987 Survival and Adaptation of the Inuit Ethnic Identity: The Importance of Inuktitut. In *Native People, Native Lands*, 241–55. See B. Cox, 1987.

Chase, Lew Allen
1922 *Rural Michigan*. New York: Macmillan Co.

Chayanov, A. V.
1966 [1925] *The Theory of Peasant Economy*. Homewood, Ill.: R. D. Irwin.

Chittenden, Hiram
1954 *The History of the Fur Trade*. 2 vols. Lincoln: University of Nebraska Press.

Chouteau, Pierre
1840 *The Letters of Chouteau and Crooks*. Miscellaneous Papers of the American Fur Company. New York: New York Historical Society.

Christie, Laird
1976 Reserve Colonialism and Sociocultural Change. Ph.D. diss., University of Toronto.

Churchill, Ward, ed.
1983 *Marxism and Native Americans*. Boston: South End Press.

Clapham, Christopher
1985 *Third World Politics, An Introduction*. Madison, Wisc.: University of Wisconsin Press.

Clark, Barry
1991 *Political Economy*. New York: Praeger Publishers.

Coale, Ansley J.
1957 How the Age Distribution of a Human Population is Determined. Cold Spring Harbor Symposia on Quantitative Biology. 22:83–89.

Codere, Helen
1950 *Fighting with Property*. New York: J. J. Augustin.

Cohen, Felix
1953 The Erosion of Indian Rights, 1950–1953: A Case Study in Bureaucracy. *Yale Law Journal* 62:348–90.

Collins, J.
1986 Smallholder Settlement of Tropical South America: The Social Causes of Ecological Destruction. *Human Organization* 45:1–10.

Comaroff, John L., and Jean Comaroff
1987 The Madman and the Migrant: Work and Labor in the Historical Consciousness of a South African People. *American Ethnologist* 14(2):191–209.
1991 *Of Revelation and Revolution: Christianity, Colonialism, and Consciousness in South Africa.* Vol. 1. Chicago: University of Chicago Press.

Communist Party of the Soviet Union, 27th Congress (CPSU)
1987 The Communist Party Program and Party Statutes." *Current Digest of the Soviet Press, Special Supplement,* December 1986.

Congressional Record
1912 Message of President Taft. 48 (August 10): 10663. Senate Document 907.

Connor, Walker
1984 *The National Question in Marxist-Leninist Theory and Strategy.* Princeton, N.J.: Princeton University Press.

Cook, Sherburne F.
1935 Diseases of the Indians of Lower California in the Eighteenth Century. *California and Western Medicine* 43:432–34.
1940 Population Trends Among the California Mission Indians. *Ibero-Americana.* Berkeley: University of California Press.
1945 Demographic Consequences of European Contact with Primitive Peoples. *Annals of the American Academy of Political and Social Sciences* 237:33–45.
1955 The Epidemic of 1830–1833 in California and Oregon. University of California Publications in American Archaeology and Ethnology 43:303–26.
1972 *Prehistoric Demography.* Reading, Mass.: Addison-Wesley Modular Publications.
1973a Interracial Warfare and Population Decline Among the New England Indians. *Ethnohistory* 20:1–24.
1973b The Significance of Disease in the Extinction of the New England Indians. *Human Biology* 45:485–508.
1976a *The Conflict Between the California Indian and White Civilization.* Berkeley: University of California Press.
1976b *The Population of the California Indians, 1769–1970.* Berkeley: University of California Press.

Cook, Sherburne, and Woodrow Borah
1969 Conquest and Population: A Demographic Approach to Mexican History. Proceedings of the American Philosophical Society 113:177–83.
1971 *Essays in Population History.* Vol. 1, *Mexico and the Caribbean.* Berkeley: University of California Press.

1974 *Essays in Population History.* Vol. 2, *Mexico and the Caribbean.* Berkeley: University of California Press.
1979 *Essays in Population History.* Vol. 3, *Mexico and California.* Berkeley: University of California Press.

Corrigan, Samuel W.
1970 The Plains Indian Powwow: Cultural Interaction in Manitoba and Saskatchewan. *Anthropologica* 12(2):253–77.

Cox, Bruce, ed.
1987 *Native People, Native Lands.* Ottawa: Carleton University Press.

Cox, Bruce
1984 Indian 'Middlemen' and the Early Fur Trade: Reconsidering the position of the Hudson's Bay Company's 'Trading Indians.' In *Rendezvous.* See Buckley, 1984.

Critchlow, Donald, and Ellis W. Hawley, eds.
1988 *Federal Social Policy.* University Park: Pennsylvania State University Press.

Culbertson, Thaddeus
1952 [1850] *Journal of an Expedition to the Upper Missouri in 1850.* Ed. J. McDermott. Bureau of American Ethnology Bulletin 147. Washington, D.C.: G.P.O.

Cumming, Peter, and Neil H. Mickenberg
1972 *Native Rights in Canada.* 2d ed. Toronto: The Indian-Eskimo Association.

Current Digest of the Soviet Press (CDSP)
1984 Soviet Scientists in Defense of Peltier, *CDSP* 36(26):19.

Dalton, George, ed.
1967 *Tribal and Peasant Economies.* New York: The Natural History Press.

Danbom, David B.
1979 *The Resisted Revolution: Urban America and the Industrialization of Agriculture, 1900–1930.* Ames: Iowa State University Press.

Daugherty, W.
1978 *Discussion Report on Indian Taxation.* Ottawa, Ont.: Department of Indian and Northern Affairs, Treaties and Historical Research Centre.

Davis, James T.
1974 *Trade Routes and Economic Exchange Among the Indians of California.* Ramona, Calif.: Ballena Press.

de Jonge, Klaas
1985 Demographic Developments and Class Contradictions in a 'Domestic' Community: The Nyakyusa (Tanzani) Before the Colonial Conquest. In *Old Modes of Production*. See van Binsbergen and Geschiere, 1985.

Debo, Angie
1961 [1934] *The Rise and Fall of the Choctaw Republic*. 2d ed. Norman: University of Oklahoma Press.

De Concini, Dennis, Chair
1989 *Report of the Special Committee on Investigations of the Select Committee on Indian Affairs, U.S. Senate*. Washington, D.C.: Government Printing Office.

Deloria, Vine, Jr.
1985 [1974] *Behind the Trail of Broken Treaties*. Austin: University of Texas Press.

Dempsey, Hugh
1972 Western Plains Trade Ceremonies. *Western Canadian Journal of Anthropology* 3:29–33.

Denevan, William M., ed.
1976 *The Native Population of the Americas in 1492*. Madison: University of Wisconsin Press.

Denig, Edwin
1929 *Indian Tribes on the Upper Missouri. Annual Report of the Bureau of American Ethnology*, Bulletin 61. Washington, D.C.
1961 *Five Indian Tribes of the Upper Missouri*. Ed. J. Ewers. Norman: University of Oklahoma Press.

Dobyns, Henry F.
1966 Estimating Aboriginal American Population: An Appraisal of Techniques with a New Hemispheric Estimate. *Current Anthropology* 7:395–416.
1976 *Native American Historical Demography: A Critical Bibliography*. Bloomington: University of Indiana Press.
1983 *Their Number Become Thinned: Native American Population Dynamics in Eastern North America*. Knoxville: University of Tennessee Press.
1984 Native American Population Collapse and Recovery. In *Scholars and the Indian Experience*, ed. William R. Swagerty, 17–35. Bloomington: Indiana University Press.

Dobyns, Henry F., Paul H. Ezell, and Greta S. Ezell
1963 Death of a Society. *Ethnohistory* 10:105–61.

Dobyns, Henry F., Paul H. Ezell, Alden W. Jones, and Greta S. Ezell
1957 Thematic Changes in Yuman Warfare. In *Cultural Stability and Cultural Change, Proceedings of the American Ethnological Society, 1957*, ed. V. Ray, 46–71.

Dodge, Richard Irving. *Our Wild Indians*. Freeport, N.Y.: Books
1970 for Libraries Press.

Dos Santos, Theotônio
1970 The Structure of Dependence. *American Economic Review* 60: 231–36.

Douglas, M.
1986 *How Institutions Think*. Syracuse, N.Y.: Syracuse University Press.

Doyal, Lesley, with Imogene Pennell
1979 *The Political Economy of Health*. Boston: South End Press.

Driben, P., and R. Trudeau
1983 *When Freedom Is Lost: The Dark Side of the Relationship Between Government and the Fort Hope Band*. Toronto, Ont.: University of Toronto Press.

Dunning, T. J.
1970 Quoted in Karl Marx, *Capital*, 1:305. New York: International Publishers.

Dupre, George, and Pierre-Philippe Rey
1980 Reflections on the Pertinence of a Theory of the History of Exchange. In *The Articulation of Modes of Production*, ed. Harold Wolpe. London: Routledge and Kegan Paul.

Early, John D., and John F. Peters
1990 *The Population Dynamics of the Mucajai Yanomama*. London: Academic Press.

Eccles, W. J.
1979 A Belated Review of Harold Adams Innis, *The Fur Trade in Canada*. *Canadian Historical Review* 60(4):419–41.

Edwards, John
1932 The Choctaw Indians in the Middle of the 19th Century, *Chronicles of Oklahoma* 10:392–425.

Egbahl, A.
1983 Ethnicite-État et Stratégie de Développement en Afrique ou le Développement-Exclusion. International Foundation for Development Alternatives. *Dossier* 36:18–29.

Eggan, Fred
1966 *The American Indian: Perspectives for the Study of Social Change.* Chicago: Aldine Press.

Ekeh, Peter P.
1974 *Social Exchange Theory.* Cambridge: Harvard University Press.

Elling, Ray
1981 Relations Between Traditional and Modern Medical Systems. *Social Science and Medicine* 15A:87–88.

Elmendorf, William W.
1960 *The Structure of Twana Culture.* Pullman: Washington State University Press.
1971 Coast Salish Status Ranking and Intergroup Ties. *Southwestern Journal of Anthropology* 27:353–80.

Elton, C. E.
1942 *Voles, Mice and Lemmings.* Oxford: Oxford University Press.
1965 Periodic Fluctuations in the Numbers of Animals: Their Causes and Effects. In *Readings in Ecology,* ed. E. J. Kormondy, 73–81. Englewood Cliffs, N.J.: Prentice-Hall, Inc.

Engels, Friedrich
1942 [1884] *The Origin of the Family, Private Property, and the State.* New York: International Publishers.
1972 [1884] *The Origin of the Family, Private Property and the State in the Light of the Researches of Lewis H. Morgan.* Introduction and notes by Eleanor Burke Leacock. New York: International Publishers.

Evergreen State College
1975 A Study of the Weyerhaeuser Company as a Multinational Corporation. Students of the "Multinational Corporation Group Contract." Olympia, Wash.

Ewers, John
1937 *Teton Dakota: Ethnology and History.* Berkeley, Calif.: U.S. Park Service.
1954 Indian Trade of the Upper Missouri Before Lewis and Clark. Missouri Historical Society Bulletin 10, no. 4:429–46.
1955 *The Horse in Blackfoot Culture.* Bureau of American Ethnology Bulletin 159. Washington D.C.: Government Printing Office.
1969 *The Horse in Blackfoot Indian Culture with Comparative Material from Other Western Tribes.* Washington, D.C.: Smithsonian Institution Press.
1975 Intertribal Warfare as the Precursor of Indian-White Warfare on the Northern Great Plains. *Western Historical Quarterly* 5:397–410.

Faiman-Silva, Sandra L.
1984 Choctaw at the Crossroads: Native Americans and the Multinationals in the Oklahoma Timber Region." Ph.D. diss., Department of Anthropology, Boston University.

Finnegan, Gregory
1980 An Assessment of *Les Engagement pour l'Ouest* in Relation to the Expansive Nature of the Fur Trade. Bachelor's thesis, Carleton University.

Fite, Gilbert C.
1981 *American Farmers: The New Minority*. Bloomington: Indiana University Press.
1989 The Transformation of South Dakota Agriculture: The Effects of Mechanization, 1939–64. *South Dakota History* 19(3):278–305.

Fixico, Donald L.
1986 *Termination and Relocation: Federal Indian Policy, 1945–1960*. Albuquerque: University of New Mexico Press.

Flannery, Regina
1953 *The Gros Ventres of Montana: Social Life*. Catholic University of America Anthropological Series, vol. 1. Washington, D.C.

Fletcher, Alice, and Francis La Flesche
1972 [1911] *The Omaha Tribe*. Lincoln: University of Nebraska Press

Ford, Richard
1983 Inter-Indian Exchange in the Southwest. In *Handbook of American Indians*. vol.10, *The Southwest*, ed. A. Ortiz, 711–22. Washington, D.C.: Smithsonian Institution.

Frank, André Gunder
1969 *Capitalism and Underdevelopment in Latin America*. New York: Monthly Review Press.

Frideres, James
1988 *Native Peoples in Canada: Contemporary Conflicts*. Scarborough, Ont.: Prentice-Hall, Canada.

Friends Committee on National Legislation (FCNL)
1987 *Indian Report* 1(Spring):27.
1988 *Indian Report* 1(Spring):29.

Fromhold, J.
1981 Inter-Tribal Influences in Plains Cree Societies. In *Networks of the Past: Regional Interaction in Archaeology*, ed. P. Francis, F. Kense, and P. Duke, 411–24. Calgary, Alb.: University of Calgary Archaeological Association.

Fudge, S.
1983 Too Weak to Win, Too Strong to Lose: Indians and Indian Policy in Canada. *B.C. Studies* 57(Spring):137–45.

Garcia, Andrew
1967 *Tough Trip Through Paradise*. Ed. Bennett Stein. New York: Ballantine.

Geschiere, Peter and Reini Raatgever
1985 Emerging Insights and Issues in French Marxist Anthropology. In *Old Modes of Production*. See van Binsbergen and Geschiere, 1985.

Giannettino, Susan
1977 The Middleman Role in the Fur Trade: Its Influence on Interethnic Relations in the Saskatchewan–Missouri Plains. *Western Canadian Journal of Anthropology* 7:22–33.

Gilpin, Robert
1975 *U.S. Power and the Multinational Corporation: The Political Economy of Foreign Direct Investment*. New York: Basic Books.

Godelier, Maurice
1972 *Rationality and Irrationality in Economics*. New York: Monthly Review Press.
1977 *Perspectives in Marxist Anthropology*. London: Cambridge University Press.

Goldfrank, Esther
1943 Historic Change and Social Character: A Study of the Teton Dakota. *American Anthropologist* 45(1).
1945 *Changing Configurations in the Social Organization of the Blackfoot Tribe in the Reserve Period*. American Ethnological Society Monograph No. 8. Seattle: University of Washington Press.

Goldman, Irving
1941 The Alkatcho Carrier: Historical Background of Crest Prerogatives. *American Anthropologist* 43:396–418.

Gonzalez, Gilbert G.
1982 *Progressive Education: A Marxist Interpretation*. Studies in Marxism, vol. 8. Minneapolis, Minn.: Marxist Educational Press.

Goodman, David, and Michael Redclift
1982 *From Peasant to Proletarian, Capitalist Development and Agrarian Transitions*. New York: St. Martin's Press.

Graebner, Norman Arthur
1945 Pioneer Indian Agriculture in Oklahoma. *Chronicles of Oklahoma* 23:232–48.

Gramsci, Antonio
1971 *Selections from the Prison Notebooks*. New York: International Publishers.
1987 *Selections from the Prison Notebooks of Antonio Gramsci*. Ed. Quintin Hoare and G. N. Smith. New York: International Publishers.

Grant, James P.
1989 *The State of the World's Children, 1989*. Oxford: Oxford University Press.

Great Soviet Encyclopedia
1976 American Indians. 3d ed., vol. 10, pp. 4–5. New York: Macmillan Co.

Gregory, C. A.
1984 The Economy and Kinship: a Critical Examination of Some of the Ideas of Marx and Levi-Strauss. In *Marxist Perspectives in Archaeology*, ed. Matthew Spriggs, 11–21. London: Cambridge University Press.

Gregory Times-Advocate
1984 *A Rosebud Review, 1913*. Gregory, S. Dak.: *Gregory Times-Advocate*.

Grinnell, George B.
1962 *The Cheyenne Indians*. 2 vols. New York: Cooper Square.

Grobsmith, Elizabeth S.
1979 The Lakhota Giveaway: A System of Social Reciprocity. *Plains Anthropologist* 24(1984):123–31.
1981 The Changing Role of the Giveaway Ceremony in Contemporary Lakota Life. *Plains Anthropologist* 26(1981):75–79.

Hage, Per, and Frank Harary
1983 *Structural Models in Anthropology*. Cambridge: Cambridge University Press.
1991 *Exchange in Oceania*. Oxford Studies in Social and Cultural Anthropology. Oxford: Clarendon Press.

Hakken, David, and Hanna Lessinger, eds.
1987 *Perspectives in U.S. Marxist Anthropology*. Boulder, Colo.: Westview Press.

Hamilton, Sahni, Barry Popkin, and Deborah Spicer
1984 *Women and Nutrition in Third World Countries*. New York: Praeger Publishers.

Hamilton, William. A Trading Expedition Among the Indians in 1858.
1900 *Montana Historical Society Contributions* (Helena), 3.

Hankins, David (Public Relations Officer, Weyerhaeuser Corporation)
1982 Interview by Sandra Faiman-Silva, 2 June, Wright City, Okla.

Hanson, Jeffery
1986 Kinship, Residence and Marriage Patterns in Hidatsa Village Composition. In *The Origins of Hidatsa Indians*, vol. 32, ed. R. Wood, 43–76. Lincoln, Nebr.: J and L Reprint Co.
1987 Hidatsa Culture Change, 1780–1845: A Cultural Ecological Approach. In *The Origins of Hidatsa Indians*, vol. 34, ed. R. Wood. Lincoln, Nebr.: J and L Reprint Co.

Harding, J.
1988 *Aboriginal Rights and Government Wrongs*. Regina, Sask.: Prairie Justice Research, University of Regina.

Harmon, Daniel
1903 *A Journal of Voyages and Travels in the Interior of North America*. New York: Meehan Publishing.

Harrington, Carolyn
1967 *An Economic Survey of the Walpole Island Indian Reserve*. Wallaceburg, Ont.: Walpole Island Indian Band Council and St. Clair Regional Development Association.

Harris, Marvin
1968 *The Rise of Anthropological Theory*. New York: Thomas Y. Crowell.

Hartford Courant, Hartford, Connecticut

Hassrick, Royal
1964 *The Sioux: Life and Customs of a Warrior Society*. Norman: University of Oklahoma Press.

Hawthorne, H. B.
1966 *A Survey of the Contemporary Indians of Canada, Part 1*. Ottawa, Ont.: Queen's Printer.

Hechter, Michael
1975 *Internal Colonialism: The Celtic Fringe in British National Development, 1536–1966*. Berkeley: University of California Press.

Hedley, M. J.
1988 The Peasant Within: Agrarian Life in New Zealand and Canada. *Canadian Review of Sociology and Anthropology* 15(1):67–83.
1986 Community Based Research: The Dilemma of Contract. *The Canadian Journal of Native Studies* 6(1):91–103.
1985 Mutual Aid Between Farm Households: New Zealand and Canada. *Sociologica Ruralis* 25:26–39.

Henderson, James M., and Anne O. Krueger
1965 *National Growth and Economic Change in the Upper Midwest.* Minneapolis: University of Minnesota Press.

Henderson, William H.
1978 *Land Tenure in Indian Reserves.* Ottawa, Ont.: Department of Indian and Northern Affairs, Research Branch, Policy, Research, and Evaluation Group.

Henriksen, Georg
1973 *Hunters of the Barrens: The Naskapi on the Edge of the White Man's World.* St. John's: Institute of Social and Economic Research, Memorial University of Newfoundland.

Henriot, P.
1977 Development Alternatives: Problems, Strategies, Values. In *The Political Economy of Development and Underdevelopment,* ed. C. Wilbur, 5–22. New York: Random House.

Henry, Alexander
1966 *Travels and Adventures in Canada and the Indian Territories: 1760–1776.* Ann Arbor, Mich.: Ann Arbor Microfilms.

Henry, Alexander, and David Thompson
1965 [1898] *New Light on the History of the Great Northwest.* Ed. E. Coues. Minneapolis Minn.: Ross and Haines.

Hickerson, Harold
1960 The Feast of the Dead among the Seventeenth Century Algonkian of the Upper Great Lakes. *American Anthropologist* 62:81–107.
1963 The Sociohistorical Significance of Two Chippewa Ceremonials. *American Anthropologist* 65:67–85.
1965 The Virginia Deer and Intertribal Buffer Zones in the Upper Mississippi Valley. In *Man, Culture and Animals: The Role of Animals in Human Ecological Adjustments,* ed. A. Leeds and A. P. Vayda, 43–65. Washington, D.C.: American Association for the Advancement of Science.
1971 *The Chippewa and Their Neighbors: A Study in Ethnohistory.* New York: Holt, Rinehart and Winston.

Hindness, B., and P. Hurst
1975 *Pre-capitalist Modes of Production.* London: Routledge and Kegan Paul.

Hobbes, Thomas
1960 [1651] *Leviathan.* Oxford: Basil Blackwell.

Hobsbawm, Eric J.
1959 *Primitive Rebels: Studies of Archaic Forms of Social Movement in the 19th and 20th Centuries*. New York: W. W. Norton and Co.

Hobson, J. A.
1938 [1902] *Imperialism*. London: George Allen and Unwin.

Hoebel, Edward A.
1960 *The Cheyennes: Indians of the Great Plains*. New York: Holt, Rinehart and Winston.

Hogan, David John
1985 *Class and Reform: School and Society in Chicago, 1880–1930*. Philadelphia: University of Pennsylvania Press.

Holder, Preston
1970 *The Hoe and the Horse on the Plains*. Lincoln: University of Nebraska Press.

Hornaday, William T.
1869 *The Extermination of the American Bison*. Washington, D.C.: Annual Report of the U.S. National Museum.

Hoselity, Bert
1972 Social Implications of Economic Growth. In *Readings in Economic Development*, 53–85. See Johnson and Kamerschen, 1972.

Howard, James
1960 The Cultural Position of the Dakota: A Reassessment. In *Essays in the Science of Culture*, ed. G. Dole and R. Carneiro, 249–68. Ann Arbor: University of Michigan Press.

Howell, Nancy
1979 *Demography of the Dobe !Kung*. New York: Academic Press.

Hoxie, Frederick E.
1979 From Prison to Homeland: The Cheyenne River Indian Reservation before World War I. *South Dakota History* 10(1):1–24.
1984 *A Final Promise: The Campaign to Assimilate the Indians, 1880–1920*. Lincoln: University of Nebraska Press.

Hudson's Bay Company
1722–1762 Fort Churchill Account Books, PA HBC B42/d/3–42, Archives.

Hugh-Jones, P., ed.
1977 *Health and Disease in Tribal Societies*. Ciba Foundation Symposium 49. London: Excerpta Medica.

Hume, David
1875 [1748] An Enquiry Concerning Human Understanding. In *Essays Moral, Political and Literary*. London: Longmans Green and Co.

Hyde, George
1937 *Red Cloud's Folk*. Norman: University of Oklahoma Press.
1951 *Pawnee Indians*. Denver: University of Denver Press.

Innis, H. A.
1929 *The Fur Trade of Canada*. Toronto, Ont.
1970 [1930] *The Fur Trade in Canada*. Rev. ed. Toronto: University of Toronto Press.

Ivanov, Robert
1985 The United States of America: Crimes Against Humanity. In *Genocide*, 37–60. Moscow: Progress Publishers.

Jablow, Joseph
1951 *The Cheyenne in Plains Indian Trade Relations, 1795–1840*. Monographs of the American Ethnological Society, No. 19. Seattle: University of Washington Press.

Jackson, Jean
1976 Vaupes Marriage: A Network System in the Northwest Amazon. In *Regional Analysis*, vol. 2, *Social Systems*, ed. Carol Smith, 65–93. New York: Academic Press.

Jacobs, Wilbur R.
1974 The Tip of the Iceberg: Pre-Columbian Indian Demography and Some Implications for Revisionism. *William and Mary Quarterly* 31: 123–32.

Jameson, Fredric
1984 Postmodernism, or the Cultural Logic of Late Capitalism. *New Left Review* 146:53–92.

Jay, Elisabeth, and Richard Jay
1986 *Critics of Capitalism: Victorian Reactions to "Political Economy."* Cambridge and New York: Cambridge University Press.

Jenness, Diamond
1932 *The Sarcee Indians of Alberta*. Bulletin No. 90 of the Publications of the National Museum of Canada, Anthropological Series 23.

Johansson, S. Ryan, and S. H. Preston
1978 Tribal Demography: The Hopiland and Navaho Populations as Seen Through Manuscripts from the 1900 U.S. Census. *Social Science History* 3(Fall):1–33.

Johnson, W., and D. Kamerschen, eds.
1972 *Readings in Economic Development*. Cincinnati, Ohio: South-Western Publishing Co.

Jones, Alan
1988 The Lake St. Clair Commercial Fishery: A Case Study of Walpole Island Indian Reserve and Independent Commodity Production. Master's thesis, University of Windsor.

Jorgensen, Joseph G.
1971 Indians and the Metropolis. In *The American Indian in Urban Society*, ed. Jack O. Waddell and O. Michael Watson, 67–113. Boston: Little Brown.
1972 *The Sundance Religion: Power for the Powerless*. Chicago: University of Chicago Press.
1978 A Century of Political Economic Effects on American Indian Society, 1880–1980. *Journal of Ethnic Studies* 6(3):1–82.
1990 *Oil Age Eskimos*. Berkeley: University of California Press.

Jorgensen, J., et al., eds.
1978 *Native Americans and Energy Development*. Cambridge, Mass.: Anthropology Resource Center.
1984 *Native Americans and Energy Development II*. Boston: Anthropology Resource Center and Seventh Generation Fund.

Jorgensen, J., S. Davis, R. Mathews.
1978 Energy, Agriculture and Social Science in the American West. In *Native Americans and Energy Development*. See Jorgensen, et al., 1978.

Judd, Carol M., and Arthus J. Ray, eds.
1980 *Old Trails and New Directions: Papers of the Third North American Fur Trade Conference*. Toronto, Ont.: University of Toronto Press.

Judy, Mark A.
1987 Powder Keg on the Upper Missouri: Sources of Blackfeet Hostility, 1730–1810. *American Indian Quarterly* 11:31–48.

Kehoe, Alice B.
1980 The Giveaway Ceremony of Blackfoot and Plains Cree. *Plains Anthropologist* 25(1987):17–26.

Keller, John F.
1983 *Power in America: The Southern Question and the Control of Labor*. Chicago: Vanguard, Press.

Keller, Robert H.
1983 *American Protestantism and United States Indian Policy, 1869–82*. Lincoln: University of Nebraska Press.

Kelly, Lawrence C.
1983 *The Assault on Assimilation: John Collier and the Origins of Indian Reform.* Albuquerque: University of New Mexico Press.

Kelman, Sander
1976 The Social Nature of the Definition Problem in Health. *International Journal of Health Services* 5:625–42.

Kenner, Charles
1969 *A History of New Mexican-Plains Indian Relations.* Norman: University of Oklahoma Press.

Kincaid, Harold (private contractor)
1982 Telephone interview by Sandra Faiman-Silva, 6 June.

Klein, Alan M.
1977 Adaptive Strategies and Process on the Plains: The 19th Century Cultural Sink. Ph.D. diss., State University of New York at Buffalo.
1980 Plains Economic Analysis: The Marxist Complement. In *Anthropology on the Great Plains,* ed. Wood and Liberty. Lincoln: University of Nebraska Press.
1983a The Plains Truth: The Impact of Colonialism on Indian Women. *Dialectical Anthropology* 9(2).
1983b The Political-Economy of Gender: A 19th Century Plains Indian Case. In *The Hidden Half: Studies of Plains Indian Women,* ed. Albers and Medicine, Washington, D.C.: University Press of America.
1989 Baseball as Underdevelopment: The Political-Economy of Sport in the Dominican Republic. *Sociology of Sport Journal* 6(2):95–112.

Koch, Klaus-Fredrich
1974 *War and Peace in Jalemo.* Cambridge: Cambridge University Press.

Knight, Rolf
1978 *Indians at Work: An Informal History of Native Indian Labor in British Columbia 1885-1930.* Vancouver, B.C.: New Star Books.

Kormondy, E. J.
1969 *Principles of Ecology.* Englewood Cliffs, N.J.: Prentice-Hall, Inc.

Krader, L.
1972 *The Ethnological Notebooks of Karl Marx.* Assen, Netherlands: Van Gorcum and Co.

Krech, Shepard
1980 Review of Ray and Freeman, 1978. *American Anthropologist* 82(3): 640–42.

Kunitz, Stephen I.
1981 Underdevelopment, Demographic Change, and Health Care on the Navajo Reservation. *Social Science and Medicine* 15A:175–92.

Kurz, Rudolph
1970 *Journal of Rudolph Frederich Kurz*, ed. J. N. B. Hewitt. Lincoln: University of Nebraska Press.

Kuznets, Simon
1972 Present Underdeveloped Countries and Part Growth Patterns. In *Readings in Economic Development*. See Johnson and Kamerschen, 1972.

Kvasnicka, Robert M., and Herman J. Viola
1979 *The Commissioners of Indian Affairs, 1824–1977*. Lincoln: University of Nebraska Press.

Laite, Julian
1981 *Industrial Development and Migrant Labour in Latin America*. Austin: University of Texas Press.

Lange, Charles
1957 Plains-Southwestern Intercultural Relations during the Historic Period. *Southwestern Journal of Anthropology* 9:212–30.

LaRocque, François
1910 *Journal of Francois Antoine LaRocque*. Ottawa Publications of the Canadian Archives, No.3. Ottawa, Ont.

Lavender, David
1969 *Bent's Fort*. Lincoln: University of Nebraska Press.

Lawson, Murray
1943 *Fur: A Study of English Mercantilism, 1700–1770*. Toronto, Ont.: University of Toronto Press.

Leacock, Eleanor
1982 Marxism and Anthropology. In *The Left Academy*, ed. B. Ollman and E. Vernoff. New York: McGraw-Hill.

Leclau, E.
1977 Feudalism and Capitalism in Latin America. In *Politics and Ideology in Marxist Theory*. London: New Left Books.

Lee, Richard B.
1990 Primitive Communism and the Origin of Social Inequality. In *The Evolution of Political Systems*, 225–46. Cambridge: Cambridge University Press.

Lenin, Vladimir I.
1960 [1917] Imperialism, the Highest Stage of Capitalism. In *Lenin: Selected Works*, 1:707–815. Moscow: Foreign Languages Publishing House.
1970 *Lenin on the National and Colonial Questions: Three Articles.* Peking: Foreign Languages Press.
1979 *The Right of Nations to Self Determination.* Moscow: Progress Publishers.

Leone, Mark P., Parker P. Potter, Jr., and Paul A. Shackel.
1987 Toward a Critical Archaeology. *Current Anthropology* 28(3):283–301.

Leons, Madeline B., and Frances Rothstein
1979 *New Directions in Political Economy: An Approach from Anthropology.* London and Westport, Conn.: Greenwood Press.

Leupp, Francis E.
1910 *The Indian and His problem.* New York: Charles Scribner's Sons.

Lewis, Meriwether, and William Clark
1969 *Original Journals of Lewis and Clark.* New York: Arno Press.

Lewis, Oscar
1942 *The Effects of White Contact upon Blackfoot Culture.* Monographs of the American Ethnological Society, No. 6. Seattle: University of Washington Press.

Limbaugh, Ronald H.
1973 *Cheyenne and Sioux: The Reminiscences of Indians and a White Soldier.* Stockton, Calif.: University of the Pacific.

Linton, Ralph
1936 *The Study of Man.* New York: D. Appleton–Century.

Lithman, Y. B.
1984 *The Community Apart: A Case Study of a Canadian Indian Reserve Community.* Winnipeg: University of Manitoba Press.

Little, Daniel
1986 *The Scientific Marx.* Minneapolis: University of Minnesota Press.

Loscheider, Mavis
1977 Use of Fire in Interethnic and Intraethnic Relations on the Northern Plains. *Western Canadian Journal of Anthropology* 7:82–96.

Lowie, Robert
1956 [1935] *The Crow Indians.* New York: Holt, Rinehart and Winston.

Luxemborg, Rosa
1976 *The National Question: Selected Writings by Rosa Luxemborg.* Ed. Horace B. Davis. New York: Monthly Review Press.

Lyng, Stephen
1990 *Holistic Health and Biomedical Medicine: A Counter System Analysis.* Albany: State University of New York Press.

McBeth, Sally
1984 The Primer and the Hoe. *Natural History* 93(8):4–12.

McClellan, Catherine
1975 *My Old People Say: An Ethnographic Survey of Southern Yukon Territory, Canada.* National Museum of Man, Publications in Ethnology 6. Ottawa.

McCullough, Martha
1990 Horse Trading Between the Southern Plains and the Eastern United States during the Eighteenth and Nineteenth Centuries. Paper Presented at Plains Conference, Oklahoma City, Oklahoma.

McCurtain Sunday Gazette, Idabel, Oklahoma, 11 July 1982.

M'Gillivray, Duncan
1929 *The Journal of Duncan M'Gillivray.* Ed. Arthur Morton, Toronto, Ont..

McKee, Jesse O., and Jon A. Schlenker
1980 *The Choctaws: Cultural Evolution of a Native American Tribe.* Jackson: University of Mississippi Press.

McWilliams, Carey
1942 *Ill Fares the Land: Migrants and Migratory Labor in the United States.* New York: Barnes and Noble.

Malone, Michael P., and Richard W. Etulain
1989 *The American West: A Twentieth-Century History.* Lincoln: University of Nebraska Press.

Malouf, Carling, and A. Arline
1945 The Effects of Spanish Slavery on the Indians of the Intermountain West. *Southwestern Journal of Anthropology* 1:378–91.

Malouf, Carling, and John Findley
1986 Euro-American Impact Before 1870. In *Handbook of North American Indians,* vol. 11; *Great Basin,* ed. W. D'Azevedo, 499–516. Washington, D.C.: Smithsonian Institution.

Mardock, Robert W.
1971 *The Reformers and the American Indian.* Columbus: University of Missouri Press.

Marquis, Thomas
1974 *Memoirs of a White Crow Indian, As Told by Thomas Leforge.* Lincoln: University of Nebraska Press.

Marx, Karl
1906 [1867] *Capital.* 3 vols. Chicago: Charles Kerr.

Marx, Karl, and Frederick Engels
1972 *On Colonialism: Articles from the New York Tribune and Other Writings.* New York: International Publishers.
1978 The Communist Manifesto. In *The Marx Engels Reader.* ed. Robert C. Tucker. New York: W. W. Norton.

Massicotte, E. Z.
1930 Répertoire des Engagements pour l'Ouest Conserves dans les Archives Judiciares des Montréal. In *Rapport de l'Archiviste de la Province de Québec, 1929–1930,* (Also *Rapports* for 1930–1931; 1931–1932; 1932–1933; 1942–1944; 1944–1945; 1945–1946; 1946–1947.) Montreal, Quebec.

Masson, L. R., ed.
1960 [1890] *Les Bourgeois de la Compagnie du Nord-Ouest.* 2 vols. (New York: by Antiquarian Press).

Maximilian, Prince of Wied
1966 *Travels in the Interior of North America.* 3 vols. In *Early Western Travels: 1748–1846,* ed. R. G. Thwaites. New York: AMS Press.

Maxwell, Joseph
1979 The Evolution of Plains Indian Kin Terminologies: A Non-Reflectionist Account. *Plains Anthropologist* 23: 13-30.

Medicine, Beatrice
1981 Native American Resistance to Integration: Contemporary Confrontations and Religious Revitalization. *Plains Anthropologist* 26:277–86.

Meillassoux, Claude
1979 Historical Modalities of the Exploitation and Overexploitation of Labour. *Critique of Anthropology* 13–14:7–17.
1981 *Maidens, Meal and Money, Capitalism and the Domestic Community.* Cambridge: Cambridge University Press.

References   321

Mekeel, H. Scudder
1943 The Economy of a Modern Teton Dakota Community. *Yale University Publications in Anthropology* 6:3–14.

Meriam, Lewis, ed.
1928 *The Problem of Indian Administration.* Baltimore, Md.: The Johns Hopkins University Press.

Miller, J.
1989 *Skyscrapers Hide the Heavens.* Toronto: University of Toronto Press.

Milloy, John S.
1973 The Plains Cree: A Preliminary Trade and Military Chronology, 1670–1870. Master's thesis, Carelton University.
1988 *The Plains Cree: Trade, Diplomacy and War, 1790 to 1870.* Winnipeg: University of Manitoba Press.

Miner, Craig H.
1976 *The Indian and the Corporation.* Columbia: University of Missouri Press.

Mintz, Sidney W.
1985 *Sweetness and Power.* New York: Penguin Books.

Mishkin, Bernard
1940 *Rank and Warfare Among the Plains Indians.* American Ethnological Society Monograph No. 3. Seattle: University of Washington Press.

Montana State Board of Health
1932 Medical Report, Dr. H. J. Warner to the Commissioner of Indian Affairs, RS 28. Montana Historical Society Archives, Helena.

Montour, Laurie, and M. Williams
1988 Walpole Island Hunting and Fishing Study. Manuscript. Wallaceburg, Ont.: Nin.Da.Waab.Jig, Walpole Island Research Centre.

Mooney, James
1896 *The Ghost Dance Religion and the Sioux Outbreak of 1890. Fourteenth Annual Report of the Bureau of Ethnology.* Washington, D.C.: Government Printing Office.

Moore, John H.
1974 Cheyenne Political History, 1829–1894. *Ethnohistory* 2:329–59.
1984 A New Orthodoxy for Navaho Studies. *Reviews in Anthropology* 11(4):282–87.
1987 The Cheyenne Indians Within the American System of Hired Labor. *Soviet Ethnography* 5:111–18.

1988 *The Cheyenne Nation: A Social and Demographic History.* Lincoln: University of Nebraska Press.
1989 The Myth of the Lazy Indian: Native American Contributions to the U.S. Economy. *Nature, Society and Thought* 2(2):195–219.

Morgan, Lewis Henry
1876 Factory System for the Indians. *The Nation* 23:58–59.
1878 The Indian Question. *The Nation* 27:332–33.
1959 *Lewis Henry Morgan: The Indian Journals, 1859–62.* Ed. Leslie White. Ann Arbor: University of Michigan Press.

Morris, William, ed.
1982 *American Heritage Dictionary.* Boston: Houghton Mifflin.

Muga, David
1988 Native Americans and the Nationalities Question: Premises for a Marxist Approach to Ethnicity and Self Determination. *Journal of Ethnic Studies* 16(1):31–51.

Myint, A.
1972 The Demand Approach to Economic Development. In *Readings in Economic Development,* ed. W. Johnson and D. Kamerschen, 218–29. Cincinnati, Ohio: South-Western Publishing Co.

Nader, Laura
1969 Up the Anthropologist—Perspectives Gained from Studying Up. In *Reinventing Anthropology,* ed. Dell Hymes, 284–311. New York: Random House, Vintage Books.

Nash, Gary
1974 *Red, White and Black: The Peoples of Early America.* Englewood Cliffs, N.J.: Prentice-Hall, Inc.

Nash, June
1979a Anthropology of the Multinational Corporations. In *New Directions in Political Economy: An Approach from Anthropology,*. ed. Madeline Barbara Léons and Frances Rothstein. Westport, Conn.: Greenwood Press.
1979b *We Eat the Mines and the Mines Eat Us, Dependency and Exploitation in Bolivian Tin Mines.* New York: Columbia University Press.

National Archives, Record Group 75, Letters Received, Washington D.C.
1903 Medical Report, Dr. E. P. Townsend to the Commissioner of Indian Affairs.
1905 Letter, G. B. Grinnell to the Commissioner of Indian Affairs.
1910 Annual Narrative and Statistical Report from Field Jurisdictions of the Bureau of Indian Affairs. Microfilm 1101–151.

1914 Trachoma Report, Dr. Dewey to the Commissioner of Indian Affairs.
1915 Annual Narrative and Statistical Report from Field Jurisdictions of the Bureau of Indian Affairs. Microfilm 1101–151.
1916 Annual Narrative and Statistical Report from Field Jurisdictions of the Bureau of Indian Affairs. Microfilm 1101–1151.
1917 Annual Narrative and Statistical Report from Field Jurisdictions of the Bureau of Indian Affairs. Microfilm 1101–151.
1919 Annual Narrative and Statistical Report from Field Jurisdictions of the Bureau of Indian Affairs. Microfilm 1101–1151.
1919 Special Memorandum, By Education-Health.
1920 Annual Narrative and Statistical Report from Field Jurisdictions of the Bureau of Indian Affairs. Microfilm 1101–1151.
1920 Report on the Tongue River Agency, Medical Supervisor to the Commissioner of Indian Affairs.
1925 Medical Report, Dr. J. R. Collard to the Commissioner of Indian Affairs.

National Archives, Record Group 75, Rosebud Agency
n.d. File 173–Dances, General Correspondence File, 1930–1940.

National Archives, Record Group 75, Superintendent.
1914 Letter to Commissioner, 11 March. File 21330–14–054, Rosebud, Central Classified Files.
1916 Letter to Commissioner, 3 April. File 38194–16–054, Rosebud, Central Classified Files.

Navarro, Vicente
1976 *Medicine under Capitalism*. New York: Prodist.
1979 *Imperialism, Health and Medicine*. Farmingdale, N.Y.: Baywood Publishing Co.

Neihardt, John
1961 *Black Elk Speaks*. Lincoln: University of Nebraska Press.

Newcomb, W. W., Jr.
1950 A Re-examination of the Causes of Plains Warfare. *American Anthropologist* 52:317–30.

Nin.Da.Waab.Jig
1903–1914 Minutes, Regular and General Council Meetings. Reference no. 2111. Wallaceburg, Ont.: Nin.Da.Waab.Jig.
1987 *Walpole Island: The Soul of Indian Territory*. Walpole Island, Wallaceburg, Ont.: Nin.Da.Waab.Jig.
1982–1984 Interviews with (a) G. Peters, (b) S. Thomas, (c) E. Sands and W. Bingham, (d) B. and D. Jacobs and M. Oliver, (e) E. Thomas, (f) R. Newakedo. Wallaceburg, Ont.: Nin.Da.Waab.Jig.

Norwood, James
1852 "Letter from James Norwood to David Mitchell, September 6, 1852," Congress, 2 Sess, S. Doc. 1, p. 359.

O'Conner, Richard
1973 *Iron Wheels and Broken Men.* New York: G. P. Putnam and Sons.

O'Laughlin, Bridget
1975 Marxist Approaches in Anthropology. *Annual Reviews in Anthropology* 4:341–70.

Oklahoma IMPACT
1981 *Profile: Poverty in Oklahoma.* Oklahoma City, Okla.: Legislative Information Action Network of the Oklahoma Conference of Churches.

Oliver, Symmes
1962 *Ecology and Cultural Continuity as Contributing Factors in the Social Organization of the Plains Indian.* University of California Publications in American Archaeology and Ethnology 48(1). Berkeley: University of California Press.

Ortiz, Roxanne Dunbar
1984 *Indians of the Americas: Human Rights and Self-Determination.* London: Zed Books.

Osburn, Alan J.
1983 Ecological Aspects of Equestrian Adaptations in Aboriginal North America. *American Anthropologist* 85:563–91.

Owen, N.
1978 Can Tribes Control Energy Development? In *Native Americans and Energy Development.* See Jorgensen, et al., 1978.

Owens, Robert
1965 The Patrilocal Band: A Linguistically and Culturally Hybrid Social Unit. *American Anthropologist* 67:675–90.
1968 Variety and Constraint in Cultural Adaptation. In *Modern Systems Research for the Behavioral Scientist.* Chicago: Aldine Press.

Oxford English Dictionary
1989 Prepared by J. A. Simpson and E. S. C. Weiner. New York: Oxford University Press.

Parkman, Francis
1911 *The Oregon Trail.* New York: Scott, Foresman and Co.

Patterson, Thomas C.
1986 The Last Sixty Years: Toward a Social History of Americanist Archeology in the United States. *American Anthropologist* 88:7–26.

Patterson, Thomas, and Christine Gailey, eds.
1987 *Power Relations and State Formation*. Washington, D.C.: American Anthropological Association.

Peers, Laura
1987 An Ethnohistory of the Western Ojibwa. Master's thesis, University of Winnipeg.

Pendley, K., and C. Kolstad
1980 American Indians and National Energy Policy. *The Journal of Energy and Development* 5:221–51.

Philip, Kenneth R.
1986 *Indian Self Rule: First Hand Accounts of Indian-White Relations from Roosevelt to Reagan*. Salt Lake City, Utah: Howe Brothers.

Phillips, Paul
1961 *The Fur Trade*. 2 vols. Norman: University of Oklahoma Press.

Piven, Frances F., and Richard A. Cloward
1977 *Poor Peoples Movements: Why They Succeed, How They Fail*. New York: Pantheon Books.

Polanyi, Karl
1968 The Economy as Instituted Process. In *Primitive, Archaic and Modern Economies*, ed. George Dalton, 139–74. Boston: Beacon Press.

Polgar, Steven
1971 Culture History and Population Dynamics. In *Culture and Population: A Collection of Current Studies*, ed. Steven Polgar, 3–8. Cambridge, Mass.: Schenkman Publishing.

Pope, Polly
1966 *Trade in the Plains: Affluence and Its Effects*. Kroeber Anthropological Papers 34:53–61.

Powers, William K.
1990 *War Dance: Plains Indian Musical Performance*. Tucson: University of Arizona Press.

Pratt, Richard Henry
1964 *Battlefield and Classroom: Four Decades with the American Indian, 1867–1904*. Ed. Robert M. Utley. New Haven: Yale University Press.

Pringle, Robert M.
1958 The Northern Cheyenne Indians in the Reservation Period. Honors thesis, Harvard University.

Prucha, Francis Paul
1976 *American Indian Policy in Crisis: Christian Reformers and the Indian, 1865–1900.* Norman: University of Oklahoma Press.
1981*Indian Policy in the United States: Historical Essays.* Lincoln: University of Nebraska Press.
1984 *The Great Father: The United States Government and the American Indians.* 2 vols. Lincoln: University of Nebraska Press.

Pulp and Paper
1972 Valiant: Where Weyerhaeuser Put It All Together. 46:39–49.

Radin, Paul
1970 [1923] *The Winnebago Tribe.* Lincoln: University of Nebraska Press.

Ramenofsky, Ann F.
1982 The Archaeology of Population Collapse: Native American Response to the Introduction of Infectious Disease. Ph.D. diss., University of Washington.
1987 *Vectors of Death: The Archaeology of European Contact.* Albuquerque: University of New Mexico Press.

Ray, Arthur
1974 *Indians in the Fur Trade: Their Role as Hunters, Trappers, and Middlemen in the Lands Southwest of Hudson Bay.* Toronto: University of Toronto Press.
1980 Indians as Consumers in the Eighteenth Century. In *Old Trails.* See Judd and Ray, 1980.

Ray, Arthur, and Donald F. Freeman
1978 *Give Us Good Measure: An Economic Analysis of Relations Between Indians and The Hudson's Bay Company Before 1763.* Toronto, Ont.: University of Toronto Press.

Reagan, Ronald
1983 *Statement by the President: Indian Policy.* Washington, D.C.: G.P.O.
1988 "Reagan Addresses Students," *The Portland Oregonian,* 1 June, p.1.

Reff, Daniel T.
1985 The Demographic and Cultural Consequences of Old World Diseases in the Greater Southwest, 1520–1660. Ph.D. diss., University of Oklahoma.
1990 *Disease, Depopulation, and Culture Change in Northwestern New Spain, 1518–1764.* Salt Lake City: University of Utah Press.

Revolutionary Communist Party (RCP)
1983 Searching for a Second Harvest. In *Marxism and Native Americans,* ed. W. Churchill. Boston: South End Press.

Rey, P. P.
1975 The Lineage Mode of Production. *Critique of Anthropology* 3:27–79.
1979 Class Contradiction in Lineage Societies. *Critique of Anthropology* 7:41–61.

Rice, Randall (President, Local 5-15, International Wood Workers of America)
1982 Telephone interview by Sandra Faiman-Silva, 5 June.

Rich, E. E.
1960 Trade Habits and Economic Motivation among the Indians of North America. *Canadian Journal of Economics and Political Science* 26(1): 36–53.

Robbins, L.
1984 Energy Developments and the Navajo Nation. In *Native Americans and Energy Development II*. See Jorgensen et al., 1984.

Roe, Frank G.
1956 *The Indian and the Horse*. Norman: University of Oklahoma Press.

Rogers, E. S., and Flora Tobondung
1975 *Parry Island Farmers: A Period of Change in the Way of Life of the Algonkians of Southern Ontario*. Mercury Series, Canadian Ethnological Services, Paper No. 31. Ottawa, Ont.: National Museum of Man.

Rölvaag, O. E.
1927 *Giants in the Earth*. New York: Harper and Row.

Romaniuk, A.
1974 Modernization and Fertility: the Case of the James Bay Indians. *Canadian Review of Sociology and Anthropology* 11:344–59.

Roseberry, William
1988 Political Economy. *Annual Review of Anthropology* 17: 161–85.

Rotstein, Abraham
1967 Fur Trade and Empire: An Institutional Analysis. Ph.D. diss., University of Toronto.

Rubenstein, Bruce Alan
1974 *Justice Denied: An Analysis of American Indian–White Relations in Michigan, 1855–1889*. Ph.D. diss., Michigan State University, East Lansing.

Sahlins, Marshall
1963 Poor Man, Rich Man, Big Man, Chief. *Comparative Studies in Society and History* 5(3):285–303.
1972 *Stone Age Economics*. Chicago: Aldine Press.

Satz, Ronald N.
1975 *American Indian Policy in the Jacksonian Era*. Lincoln: University of Nebraska Press.

Sawyer, Malcolm C.
1989 *The Challenge of Radical Political Economy: An Introduction to the Alternatives to Neo-Classical Economics*. New York: Harvester Wheatsheaf.

Schell, Herbert S.
1975 *History of South Dakota*. 3d ed. Lincoln: University of Nebraska Press.

Schilz, Thomas
1988 The Gros Ventres and the Canadian Fur Trade: 1754–1831. *American Indian Quarterly* 12:41–56.

Schmitt, Karl
1950 Wichita-Kiowa Relations and the 1874 Outbreak. *Chronicles of Oklahoma* 28:154–60.

Schneider, Mary Jane
1981 Economic Aspects of Mandan/Hidatsa Giveaways. *Plains Anthropologist* 26(1991):43–50.

Scholte, Bob
1979 From Discourse to Silence: The Structural Impasse. In *Toward a Marxist Anthropology*, ed. Stanley Diamond, 31–67. The Hague: Mouton.

Schultz, Theodore.
1972 Investment in Human Capital in Poor Countries. In *Readings in Economic Development*. See Johnson and Kamerschen, 1972.

Schultz, James Willard
1970 [1907] *My Life as an Indian*. New York: Bantam Books.

Schumpeter, Joseph
1954 *History of Economic Analysis*. Oxford: Oxford University Press.

Schwartz, Harry
1945 *Seasonal Farm Labor in the United States*. New York: Columbia University Press.

Schweitzer, Marjorie M.
1983 The War Mothers: Reflections of Space and Time. *Papers in Anthropology* 24(2):157–71.

Scott, James C.
1985 *Weapons of the Weak: Everyday Forms of Peasant Resistance.* New Haven: Yale University Press.

Seccombe, Wally
1983 Marxism and Demography. *New Left Review* 137:22–47.

Secoy, Frank
1953 *Changing Military Patterns on the Great Plains.* Monographs of the American Ethnological Society, No. 21. Seattle: University of Washington Press.

Senior, Nassau
1836 *Political Economy.* London: W. Clowes and Sons.

Sharrock, Susan
1974 Crees, Cree-Assiniboin, and Assiniboines: Interethnic Social Organization on the Far Northern Plains." *Ethnohistory* 2:95–122.
1977 Cross-Tribal, Ecological Categorization of Far Northern Plains Cree and Assiniboine by Late Eighteenth and Early Nineteenth Century Fur Traders. *Western Canadian Journal of Anthropology* 7:1–6.

Sherman, Howard J.
1987 *Foundations of Radical Political Economy.* Armonk, N.Y.: M. E. Sharpe.

Shideler, James H.
1957 *Farm Crisis, 1919–1923.* Berkeley: University of California Press.

Shifferd, Patricia
1976 A Study in Economic Change; the Chippewa of Northern Wisconsin: 1854–1900. *Western Canadian Journal of Anthropology* 6(4):16–41.

Singer, Merrill
1986 Developing a Critical Perspective in Medical Anthropology. *Medical Anthropology Quarterly* 17:128–29.
1989 The Coming of Age of Critical Medical Anthropology. *Social Science and Medicine* 28(11):1193–1203.

Smith, Adam
1979 [1776] *The Wealth of Nations.* New York: Penguin Books.

Smith, Carol
1976 Regional Economic Systems: Linking Geographical Models and Socioeconomic Problems. In *Regional Analysis,* vol. 1, *Economic Systems,* ed. Carol Smith, 9–25. New York: Academic Press.

Snipp, C. Matthew
1986 The Changing Political Economic Status of the American Indians: From Captive Nations to Internal Colonies. *American Journal of Economics and Sociology* 45(2):145–57.

Spicer, Edward H.
1962 *Cycles of Conquest.* Tucson: University of Arizona Press.

Spindler, George D., and Louise S. Spindler
1972 American Indian Personality Types and Their Sociocultural Roots. In *The Emergent Native Americans: A Reader in Culture Contact,* ed. Deward E. Walker, 502–13. Boston: Little, Brown.

Spriggs, Matthew, ed.
1984 *Marxist Perspectives in Archaeology.* Cambridge: Cambridge University Press.

Springer, James
1981 An Ethnohistoric Study of the Smoking Complex in Eastern North America. *Ethnohistory* 28:217–36.

Staniland, Martin
1985 *What is Political Economy?* New Haven, Conn.: Yale University Press.

Stannard, David E.
1989 *Before the Horror: The Population of Hawaii on the Eve of Western Contact.* Honolulu: University of Hawaii Press.

Stanton, William
1960 *The Leopard's Spots: Scientific Attitudes Toward Race in America, 1815–59.* Chicago: University of Chicago Press.

Stark, Evan
1977 The Epidemic as a Social Event. *International Journal of Health Services* 7(4):681–705.

Stern, Theodore, and James P. Boggs
1971 Whites and Indian Farmers on the Umatilla Reservation. *Northwest Anthropological Research Notes* 5(1):37–47.

Steuart, James
1767 *An Inquiry into the Principles of Political Economy.* London: A. Millar and T. Cadell.

Sunder, John
1965 *The Fur Trade of the Upper Missouri 1840–1865.* Norman: University of Oklahoma Press.

Surtees, R.
1983 *Indian Land Surrenders in Ontario 1763–1867.* Ottawa, Ont.: Indian and Northern Affairs Canada, Research Branch.

Sutherland, Ian
1977 Tuberculosis and Leprosy. In *A Geography of Human Diseases,* ed. G. Melvyn Howe, 175–96. London: Academic Press.

Suttles, Wayne
1960 Affinal Ties, Subsistence and Prestige among the Coast Salish. *American Anthropologist* 62:296–305.

Svingen, Orlan J.
1981 Reservation Self-Sufficiency: Stock Raising vs Farming on the Northern Cheyenne Indian Reservation, 1900–1914. *Montana: The Magazine of Western History* 31:14–23.
1982 The Administrative History of the Northern Cheyenne Reservation, 1877–1900. Ph.D. diss., University of Toledo.

Swimmer, Ross O., and Robert Robertson, Chairs
1984 *Report and Recommendations of the Presidential Commission on Indian Reservation Economies.* Washington, D.C.: U.S. Government Printing Office.

Szasz, Margaret Connell
1974 *Education and the American Indian: The Road to Self-Determination since 1928.* Albuquerque: University of New Mexico Press.

Talbot, Steve
1981 *Roots of Oppression.* New York: International Publishers.

Tanner, A.
1979 *Bringing Home Animals: Religious Ideology and Mode of Production of the Mistassini Cree Hunters.* St. John's: Institute of Social and Economic Research, Memorial University of Newfoundland.

Taylor, John F.
1977 Sociocultural Effects of Epidemics on the Northern Plains: 1734–1850. *Western Canadian Journal of Anthropology* 7:55–72.
1984 *Indian Band Self-Government in the 1960s: A Case Study of Walpole Island.* Ottawa, Ont.: Indian and Northern Affairs Canada, Treaties and Historical Research Centre.

Terray, Emmanuel
1972 *Marxism and Primitive Societies.* New York: Monthly Review Press.
1975 Classes and Class Consciousness in the Abron Kingdom. In *Marxist Analysis in Social Anthropology.* ed. Maurice Bloch. New York: Halsted Press.

Tharp, Darrell President, Local 5–15, International Wood Workers of America
1990 Telephone interview by Sandra Faiman-Silva, 1 January.

Thistle, Paul C.
1986 *Indian-European Trade Relations in the Lower Saskatchewan River Region to 1840.* Winnipeg: University of Manitoba Press.

Thomas, A. B.
1940 *The Plains Indians and New Mexico.* Norman: University of Oklahoma Press.

Thornton, Russell
1987 *American Indian Holocaust and Survival: A Population History Since 1492.* Norman: University of Oklahoma Press.

Thornton, Russell, and J. Marsh-Thornton
1981 Estimating Prehistoric American Indian Population Size for United States Area: Implications of the Nineteenth Century Population Decline and Nadir. *American Journal of Physical Anthropology* 55:47–55.

Titley, Brian
1986 *Narrow Vision: Duncan Campbell Scott and the Administration of Indian Affairs in Canada.* Vancouver: University of British Columbia Press.

Trennert, Robert A.
1983 From Carlisle to Phoenix: The Rise and Fall of the Indian Outing System, 1878–1930. *Pacific Historical Review* 52:267–91.
1988 *The Phoenix Indian School: Forced Assimilation in Arizona, 1891–1935.* Norman: University of Oklahoma Press.

Trigger, Bruce G.
1985 Marxism in Archaeology: Real or Spurious? *Reviews in Anthropology* 12(2):114–23.

Trimble, Michael K.
1985 Epidemiology on the Northern Plains: A Cultural Perspective. Ph.D. diss., University of Missouri.
1986 *An Ethnohistorical Interpretation of the Spread of Smallpox in the Northern Plains Utilizing Concepts of Disease Ecology.* Reprints in Anthropology, vol. 33. Lincoln, Nebr.: J and L Reprint Co.

Turshen, M.
1984 *The Political Ecology of Disease in Tanzania.* New Brunswick: Rutgers University Press.
1989 *The Politics of Public Health.* New Brunswick: Rutgers University Press.

Ubelaker, Douglas H.
1976 The Sources and Methodology for Mooney's Estimates of North American Indian Populations. In *The Native American Populations of the Americas in 1492*, ed. William H. Denevan, 243–88. Madison: University of Wisconsin Press.

Umfreville, Edward
1954 *The Present State of the Hudson's Bay Company 1790*. Ed. Stewart Wallace, Toronto, Ont.: Ryerson Press.

Underhill, Ruth M.
1953 *Red Man's America*. Chicago: University of Chicago Press.

United States Department of Commerce
1988 *County and City Data Book*. Washington, D.C.: Government Printing Office.

United States Department of the Interior, Bureau of Indian Affairs
1885 *Annual Report of the Commissioner of Indian Affairs*. Washington, D.C.: Government Printing Office.
1886 *Annual Report of the Commissioner of Indian Affairs*. Washington, D.C.: Government Printing Office.
1888 *Annual Report of the Commissioner of Indian Affairs*. Washington, D.C.: Government Printing Office.
1890 *Fifty-Ninth Annual Report of the Commissioner of Indian Affairs*. Washington, D.C.: Government Printing Office.
1895 *Annual Report of the Commissioner of Indian Affairs, 1894*. Washington, D.C.: Government Printing Office.
1897 *Annual Report of the Commissioner of Indian Affairs, 1896*. Washington, D.C.: Government Printing Office.
1919 *Fiftieth Annual Report of the Board of Indian Commissioners for the Fiscal Year ended June 30, 1919*. Washington, D.C.: U.S. Government Printing Office.
1921 *Annual Report of the Commissioner of Indian Affairs*. Washington, D.C.: Government Printing Office.
1923 *Annual Report of the Commissioner of Indian Affairs*. Washington, D.C.: Government Printing Office.
1925 *Annual Report of the Commissioner of Indian Affairs*. Washington, D.C.: Government Printing Office.
1934 Circular 2970 (3 January). Roll 14, Procedural Issuances: Orders and Circulars, 1854–1955, Microfilm Publication M1121, National Archives.

United States Senate, Subcommittee of the Committee on Indian Affairs
1932 *Survey of Conditions of the Indians in the United States*. Part 23. Montana. Washington D.C.: Government Printing Office.

Uphoff, Norman T.
1977 *The Political Economy of Development*. Berkeley: University of California Press.

Valentey, D. I., ed.
1977 *An Outline of Population Theory*. Moscow, U.S.S.R.: Progress Publishers.

van Binsbergen, Wim, and Peter Geschiere, eds.
1985 *Old Modes of Production and Capitalist Encroachment: Anthropological Explorations in Africa*. London: Routledge and Kegan Paul.

van der Klei, Jos
1985 Articulation of Modes of Production and the Beginning of Labour Migration Among the Diola of Senegal. In *Old Modes of Production*. See van Binsbergen and Geschiere, 1985.

Van Kirk, Sylvia
1980 *Many Tender Ties: Women in Fur-Trade Society, 1670–1870*. Norman: University of Oklahoma Press.

Vincent, Joan
1985 Anthropology and Marxism: Past and Present. *American Ethnologist* 12(1):137–47.

Voget, F. W.
1964 Warfare and the Integration of Crow Indian Culture. In *Explorations in Cultural Anthropology*, ed. W. H. Goodenough, 483–509. New York: McGraw-Hill.

Waldram, J.
1985 Hydroelectric Development and Dietary Delocalization in Northern Manitoba, Canada. *Human Organization* 44:41–49.

Walker, Deward E., Jr.
1967 *Mutual Cross Utilization of Economic Resources in the Plateau: An Example from Aboriginal Nez Percé Fishing Practices*. Laboratory of Anthropology, Report of Investigations, No. 41. Pullman: Washington State University.

Walker, James
1980 *Lakota Belief and Ritual*. Ed. R. DeMallie and E. Jahner. Lincoln: University of Nebraska Press.

Walker, Thomas W.
1981 *Nicaragua, The Land of Sandino*. Boulder, Colo.: Westview Press.

Wallace, Anthony
1970 *Death and Rebirth of the Seneca*. New York: Wiley and Son.

Wallerstein, Immanuel
1974 *The Modern World System: Capitalist Agriculture and the Origins of the European World Economy in the Sixteenth Century.* New York: Academic Press.
1979 *The Capitalist World Economy.* Cambridge: Cambridge University Press.

Weatherford, J. McIver
1981 *Tribes on the Hill.* New York: Rawson, Wade.

Weaver, Sally
1981 *Making Canadian Indian Policy.* Toronto: University of Toronto Press.

Wedel, Mildred
1981 *The Deer Creek Site, Oklahoma: A Wichita Village Sometimes Called Ferdinandina, An Ethnohistorian's View.* Oklahoma Historical Society Series in Anthropology No. 5. Oklahoma City: Oklahoma Historical Society

Wedel, Waldo
1941 Environment and Native Subsistence Economies in the Central Great Plains. Smithsonian Miscellaneous Collections 101.

Weiss, Lawrence David
1984 *The Development of Capitalism in the Navaho Nation: A Political-Economic History.* Minneapolis, Minn.: Marxist Educational Press.

Weist, Katherine M.
1973 Giving Away: The Ceremonial Distribution of Goods Among the Northern Cheyenne of Southeastern Montana. *Plains Anthropologist* 18(60):97–103.
1977 An Ethnohistorical Analysis of Crow Political Alliances. *Western Canadian Journal of Anthropology* 7:34–54.
1979 *Belle Highwalking: The Narrative of a Northern Cheyenne Woman.* Billings: Montana Council for Indian Education.
1983 *Beasts of Burden and Menial Slaves. The Hidden Half: Studies of Plains Indian Women.* Ed. P. Albers and B. Medicines. Latham Park, Md.: University Press of America.

Weist, Tom
1977 *A History of the Northern Cheyenne People.* Billings: Montana Council for Indian Education.

Weltfish, Gene
1965 *The Lost Universe: The Way of Life of the Pawnee.* New York: Basic Books.

Wessman, James W.
1981 *Anthropology and Marxism.* Cambridge, Mass.: Schenkman.

Weyerhaeuser Corporation
1977 Weyerhaeuser in Oklahoma." April, Tacoma, Wash.
1979–1987 *Annual Reports,* Tacoma, Wash.

Wheeler, Homer
1990 *Buffalo Days: The Personal Narrative of a Cattleman, Indian Fighter, and Army Officer.* Lincoln: University of Nebraska Press.

White, Bruce
1982 'Give Us a Little Milk': The Social and Cultural Meanings of Gift Giving in the Lake Superior Fur Trade. *Minnesota History* 48:2–12.

Whyte W., and L. Williams
1968 *Toward an Integrated Theory of Development.* New York State School of Industrial and Labor Relations. Ithaca, N.Y.: Cornell University.

Wilber, C., ed.
1977 *The Political Economy of Development and Underdevelopment.* New York: Random House.

Williams, Raymond
1977 *Marxism and Literature.* London: Oxford University Press.

Willis, Paul
1977 *Learning to Labour.* Farnborough, Eng.: Saxon House.

Wilmsen, Edwin
1989 *Land Filled with Flies.* Chicago: University of Chicago Press.

Wissler, Clark
1912 *Societies and Ceremonial Associations in the Oglala Division of the Teton-Dakota.* Anthropological Papers, vol. 12. New York: American Museum of Natural History.
1923 *Man and Culture.* New York: Thomas Y. Crowell.

Wolf, Eric R.
1982 *Europe and the People Without History.* Berkeley: University of California Press.

Wolpe, Harold, ed.
1980 *The Articulation of Modes of Production.* London: Routledge and Kegan Paul.

Wood, Raymond
1972 Contrastive Features of Native North American Trade Systems. In *For the Chief: Essays in Honor of Luther S. Cressman,* ed. F. Voget and R. Stephenson, 153–69. University of Oregon Anthropological Papers, No. 4.

1973 Northern Plains Village Cultures: Internal Stability and External Relationships. *Journal of Anthropological Research* 30:1–16.

1986 *The Origins of Hidatsa Indians: A Review of Ethnohistorical and Traditional Data.* Reprints in Anthropology, vol. 32. Lincoln, Nebr.: J and L Reprint Co.

Wood, Raymond, and Alan Downer
1977 Notes on the Crow-Hidatsa Schism. In *Trends in Middle Missouri Prehistory: A Festschrift Honoring the Contributions of Donald J. Lehmer,* ed. W. R. Wood, *Plains Anthropologist,* Memoir 13.

Young, Gloria A.
1981 *Powwow Power: Perspectives on Historic and Contemporary Intertribalism.* Ph.D. diss., Bloomington: University of Indiana.

Young, T. Kue.
1988 *Health Care and Cultural Change: The Indian Experience in the Central Subarctic.* Toronto, Ont.: University of Toronto Press.

Zakariya, H.
1976 New Directions in the Search for and Development of Petroleum Resources in the Developing Countries. *Vanderbilt Journal of Transnational Law* 9(Summer):545–77.

Contributors

Patricia Albers received her Ph.D. at the University of Wisconsin, Madison. She is professor of anthropology and associate director of the American West Center at the University of Utah. Her publications include an edited book, *The Hidden Half: Studies of Plains Indian Women,* and numerous publications on ethnicity and intergroup relations. Currently, she is writing a book on popular postcard images of American Indians.

Thomas Biolsi received his Ph.D. in anthropology from Columbia University in 1987. His revised dissertation was published as *Organizing the Lakota: The Political Economy of the New Deal on Pine Ridge and Rosebud Reservations* (University of Arizona Press, 1992). His interests are in the areas of political economy and historical anthropology generally, and the history of Indian-white relations specifically. He has conducted field research on Lakota reservations in South Dakota and archival research with BIA and other records. He is assistant professor of anthropology at Portland State University in Oregon.

Gregory R. Campbell holds a Ph.D. from the University of Oklahoma and is presently associate professor in the Anthropology Department at the University of Montana. Since 1982 he has been involved in ethnohistoric, demographic, and epidemiological research with the Northern Cheyenne. His most recent publication is a coauthored work entitled, "Prevalence of Diagnosed Diabetes and Selected Related Conditions on Six Reservations in Montana and Wyoming."

George Castile is professor of anthropology at Whitman College. His ethnographic and ethnohistorical research with Native American peoples has focused on problems of national indigenous policies in state-enclave relations in Latin America and the United States. His publications include the books *Persistent Peoples* and *The Indians of Puget Sound*, as well as numerous articles on federal-Indian relations.

Bruce Cox has taught at Carleton University in Ottawa since 1969. He has edited three volumes of anthropological writings—*Cultural Ecology* (1973), *Native People, Native Lands* (1988), and *A Different Drummer* (1989). *Drummer* was a collective project of Carleton's anthropology caucus. Cox's volume *Indians of Canada*, completed for the Mapfre America Foundation in Madrid, is to appear during 1992 as part of a series on the indigenous peoples of the Americas. A work in progress, *Trickster in Ottawa*, brings the theories of Antonio Gramsci to bear on Canadian Indian affairs policy.

Sandra Faiman-Silva is an associate professor of anthropology at Bridgewater State College, Bridgewater, Massachusetts, where she teaches courses in Latin America and Native North America, folklore, ethnicity and women's studies. She is also a community activist on Cape Cod, working with citizens' groups in the areas of racism, environmental and Native American concerns. She is currently working with members of the Mashpee Wampanoag tribe to introduce Native American curricula into local public schools. The current article is based on doctoral dissertation research conducted in the Choctaw Nation of Oklahoma.

James Frideres received his Ph.D. in 1971 from Washington State University. Since then he has taught at the University of Manitoba, the University of Hawaii, and Dalhousie University. Among his several books, which focus on ethnic relations and Native people, the most influential is *Native People in Canada: Contemporary Conflicts*. Over the past quarter-century he has carried out major research projects focusing on Native people in Canadian society, and during the past two decades he has taught on various reserves and been involved in the Native Centre at the University of Calgary. Various bands have requested his services for reviewing government policy and developing strategies for Native self-government. Currently, he is professor of sociology and associate dean of research for the faculty of social sciences at the University of Calgary.

Max Hedley received his Ph.D. from the University of Alberta. He is an associate professor of anthropology and department head in the Department of Sociology and Anthropology at the University of Windsor. His research in Canada and New Zealand has been concerned with the impact of national and global political and economic processes on the creation and transformation of agrarian households and communities. This has been recently extended to cover commodity producing households engaged in fishing and trapping. He has been associated with Walpole Island First Nation as a member of Nin.Da.Waab.Jig, a community based research group, for over ten years.

Alan Klein is professor of sociology-anthropology at Northeastern University. In addition to his long-standing interest in Native American ethnohistory, he has spent the last decade researching nationalism, resistance, and sport in a variety of settings. His books include *Sugarball: The American Game, The Dominican Dream* (Yale University Press, 1991) and *Lit-*

tle Big Men: Gender Construction and Bodybuilding Sub-culture (SUNY Press, 1992). Currently he is working on baseball, nationalism, and resistance in Mexico.

Alice Littlefield is professor of anthropology at Central Michigan University, Mt. Pleasant. Her articles on craft production in Mexico, the race concept in anthropology, and Native American education in the United States have been published in *The American Ethnologist, Current Anthropology,* and several other journals. She is co-editor, with Hill Gates, of *Marxist Approaches in Economic Anthropology.* Currently, she is working on a book about the Mt. Pleasant Indian School and researching the history of Native American labor in Michigan.

John Moore is professor of anthropology at the University of Oklahoma. He has worked with American Indian people since 1969 and is the author of over fifty articles, monographs, and books, including *The Cheyenne Nation: A Social and Demographic History* (1987). He is currently involved in the Human Genome Project, helping to decide which Native American groups will be included in a worldwide effort to construct a comprehensive chromosomal map of human genetic potential. He is also consultant to the Sand Creek Descendants Association, which seeks to determine which living people are entitled to government compensation for the 1864 massacre of several hundred Cheyennes at the Sand Creek crossing in Colorado.

Index

Sac and Fox, 241
Santa Fe, N. Mex., school, 49
Sarcee, 112–32
Saskatchewan Cluff Lake Board
   of Inquiry, 166
Schools, Canadian, 208–209
Schumpeter, Joseph, 10
Sells, Cato, 54–56, 70
Senior, Nassau, 6
Service contract, 178–79
Shannon County, S. Dak., 34
Sharrock, Susan, 114ff.
Shawnee, 241
Siblings, 290
Simple giveaway, 244–49
Slaving, 128
Smallpox, 73
Smith, Adam, 5
Social network, 240
Soldier sodalities, 120–21
Solicitations, 250–52
Southern Arapahoe, 241
Southern Cheyenne, 241
Spanish-American War, 51
Speck, Frank, 12
Steuart, James, 4
Subsistence patterns, 135
Sugar beet production, 54–55
Symbiosis, 100ff.

Taft, William Howard, 77
Tainter, C. M., 72
Taylor, John, 115

Termination, 288
Teton (Lakota), 116–32, 138,
   154
Tiyospaye, 139
Todd County, S. Dak., 28, 34, 35
Tomah, Wis., school, 49
Tongue River Reservation, 63ff.
Trachoma, 74
Trade goods, 143
Trade fairs, 126
Treaties, 38ff.; Utrecht (1713),
   90
Trickle-down economics, 218
Trimble, Michael, 115
Tuberculosis, 74ff.

Unemployment, 56
Union for Radical Political Eco-
   nomics, 10
Utilitarians, 7

Valentine, Robert, 54–55
Valliant, Okla., 221

Wacipi, 20ff.
Wage labor, 48
Walpole Island First Nation
   Reserve, 186ff.
Warner, H. J., 78
Washabaugh County, S. Dak.,
   30

Advance praise for *Free Expression Under Fire*

"Engaging, lively, and readily accessible . . . Stuart Brotman offers insightful and challenging analyses about one of the most essential rights in our nation—free expression—a right that is now very much under attack! This is an important read."
—Geoffrey R. Stone, Edward H. Levi Distinguished Professor of Law, University of Chicago

"Free expression is never a given, in America or anywhere, and it is particularly under siege at this moment. Stuart Brotman's thoughtful and illuminating book offers context and clarity as we grapple with the challenges of the moment and seek to understand them within the framework of American history and contemporary society."
—Margaret Sullivan, US columnist, *The Guardian*, and the author of *Ghosting the News: Local Journalism and the Crisis of American Democracy*

"Our universities are essential to our national future. Academic freedom is essential to our universities. *Free Expression Under Fire* is essential to understanding academic freedom—an indispensable book for this moment."
—Lawrence H. Summers, President Emeritus, Harvard University

"Stuart Brotman's invaluable book arrives at a crucial time, guiding us as we reflect on America's 250-year journey toward liberty."
—Rufus Friday, Executive Director, Center for Integrity in News Reporting

"*Free Expression Under Fire* traces how campus 'shout-downs,' social media deplatforming, and ideological signaling have tested longstanding legal and ethical defenses of expressive freedoms. Stuart Brotman effectively reframes our freedoms of expression as matters of collective cultural responsibility rather than partisan slogans."
—Nikhil Moro, Editor, *Journal of Media Law & Ethics*

"Stuart Brotman continues his fearless approach to vigorous public discourse and reporting, engaging others' ideas on controversial issues with integrity. This book stands out for its commitment to substantive dialogue as American society debates the boundaries of free expression."
—Thomas A. Mascaro, coauthor, *Assault on the Media: The Nixon Years*

"Stuart Brotman has captured the essence of today's free expression crisis, eloquently underscoring how the loss of these rights will undermine the principles that have served our country well for 250 years."
—Jane E. Kirtley, Silha Professor of Media Ethics and Law,
University of Minnesota